SOCIETY FOR NEW TESTAMENT STUDIES

MONOGRAPH SERIES

General Editor: G. N. Stanton

53

THE CONCEPT OF PURITY AT QUMRAN
AND IN THE LETTERS OF PAUL

T0382564

The concept of purity at Qumran and in the letters of Paul

MICHAEL NEWTON

Assistant Professor of Religious Studies,
Sir Wilfred Grenfell College,
Memorial University of Newfoundland

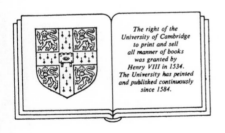

The right of the
University of Cambridge
to print and sell
all manner of books
was granted by
Henry VIII in 1534.
The University has printed
and published continuously
since 1584.

CAMBRIDGE UNIVERSITY PRESS

CAMBRIDGE
LONDON   NEW YORK   NEW ROCHELLE
MELBOURNE   SYDNEY

CAMBRIDGE UNIVERSITY PRESS
Cambridge, New York, Melbourne, Madrid, Cape Town, Singapore, São Paulo

Cambridge University Press
The Edinburgh Building, Cambridge CB2 2RU, UK

Published in the United States of America by Cambridge University Press, New York

www.cambridge.org
Information on this title: www.cambridge.org/9780521265836

First published 1985
This digitally printed first paperback version 2005

A catalogue record for this publication is available from the British Library

Library of Congress Catalogue Card Number: 84-19880

ISBN-13 978-0-521-26583-6 hardback
ISBN-10 0-521-26583-5 hardback

ISBN-13 978-0-521-02058-9 paperback
ISBN-10 0-521-02058-1 paperback

CONTENTS

ACKNOWLEDGEMENTS

I would like to express my appreciation to Dr E. P. Sanders for the inspiration, encouragement and guidance he has given me throughout this study. My thanks also go to the members of the Department of Religious Studies at McMaster University, especially to Drs Ben F. Meyer, Albert I. Baumgarten and David R. Kinsley for their many helpful suggestions.

To my wife Evelyn and our children Michèle and Rebecca I give my thanks for their patience and understanding.

ABBREVIATIONS

ArchLit	*Archiv für Liturgiewissenschaft*
ARN	Aboth de Rabbi Nathan
BA	*Biblical Archeologist*
BASOR	*Bulletin of the American Schools of Oriental Research*
BDB	F. Brown, S. R. Driver and C. A. Briggs, *A Hebrew and English Lexicon of the Old Testament* (Oxford, 1903)
BZ	*Biblische Zeitschrift*
CBQ	*Catholic Biblical Quarterly*
CD	Damascus Document
DJD	*Discoveries in the Judaean Desert*
EJ	*Encyclopedia Judaica*
EQ	*Evangelical Quarterly*
ET	English Translation
ETL	*Ephemerides Theologicae Lovanienses*
FRLANT	Forschungen zur Religion und Literatur des Alten und Neuen Testaments
HNT	Handbuch zum Neuen Testament
HTR	*Harvard Theological Review*
HUCA	*Hebrew Union College Annual*
IB	*Interpreter's Bible*
ICC	International Critical Commentary
IESS	*International Encyclopedia of the Social Sciences*
JAAR	*Journal of the American Academy of Religion*
JBL	*Journal of Biblical Literature*
JJS	*Journal of Jewish Studies*
JQR	*Jewish Quarterly Review*
JSS	*Journal of Semitic Studies*
JTS	*Journal of Theological Studies*
LXX	Septuagint
Mek.	Mekilta de-Rabbi Ishmael
MT	Masoretic Text

NEB	New English Bible
NT	New Testament
NTS	*New Testament Studies*
OT	Old Testament
1QH	Thanksgiving Hymns
1QM	War Scroll
1QpHab	Habakkuk Commentary
1QpMic	Micah Commentary
1QS	Manual of Discipline
1QSa	Rule Annexe
1QSb	Book of Blessings
11Q Temple	Temple Scroll
4QF1	Florilegium
4QPat	Patriarchal Blessings
4QpNah	Nahum Commentary
4QpPs37	Commentary on Ps. 37
4QTest	Testimonia
RB	*Revue biblique*
REJ	*Revue des études juives*
RQ	*Revue de Qumran*
RSR	*Religious Studies Review*
RSV	Revised Standard Version
Sifre Deut.	Sifre on Deuteronomy
Sifre Num.	Sifre on Numbers
Suppl.	Supplements
T.	Tosefta
TDNT	*Theological Dictionary of the New Testament*
TDOT	*Theological Dictionary of the Old Testament*
TLZ	*Theologische Literaturzeitung*
TU	*Texte und Untersuchungen*
TZ	*Theologische Zeitschrift*
USQR	*Union Seminary Quarterly Review*
Vig.Chr	*Vigiliae Christianae*
VT	*Vetus Testamentum*
WTJ	*Westminster Theological Journal*

1

INTRODUCTION

Morton Smith has pointed out that in the period of the Second Temple 'Differences as to the interpretation of the purity laws and especially as to the consequent question of table fellowship were among the principal causes of the separation of Christianity from the rest of Judaism and the early fragmentation of Christianity itself.'[1] In his introductory study of purity in Judaism Jacob Neusner adds, 'purity is an essential element in the interpretation of Israel's total religious system'.[2] The idea of purity itself has long been of interest to anthropologists, for a concern with the clean and unclean stretches far beyond the confines of the religion of Judaism.[3] It is, however, the rabbinic literature that attests to its special importance in the Jewish tradition.[4] It is only recently, though, that the role of purity within Judaism has been made the subject of specific critical studies. Jacob Neusner has surveyed the topic[5] and has since embarked on a detailed study of the legal traditions concerning purity.[6]

Neusner, however, is primarily concerned with the way in which the purity idea was employed *after* the destruction of the Temple while we, in this study, shall examine the concept of purity as it appears in two sources, the Dead Sea Scrolls and the letters of Paul,[7] which have their origin *before* AD 70. These two collections of writings reflect the belief systems of groups which removed themselves from the main stream of contemporary Judaism in that they rejected the Jerusalem Temple as the means for atonement. Both, however, continued to draw from a common stock of Jewish ideas which, as we shall show, included that of purity.

Despite this recent attention, an appreciation of the role that the concept of purity played in the religious systems of early Judaism and Christianity is not widespread; and R. J. Zwi Werblowsky's comments accurately and sadly reflect an attitude that persists: 'Notions of purity and impurity, and the existence of rites and procedures of purification, seem to produce with some scholars (mainly such as have never had a proper training in anthropology) a conditioned reflex associating these notions with magical and semi-magical realms of pollution.'[8]

One looks in vain for any attempt to give a coherent interpretation of the concern with purity in many works that purport to deal with Judaism and Christianity in the first century.[9] Either the concept of purity is completely ignored,[10] or worse, rejected as a primitive notion left over from a superstitious past to be surpassed by a higher, spiritual religion, namely Christianity.[11] This latter attitude repeats uncritically the views expressed by the nineteenth-century scholar W. Robertson Smith. In his lectures on *The Religion of the Semites*[12] he brought to his wide knowledge of ancient Judaism notions drawn from the newly-emerging discipline of anthropology.[13] What he wrote then, in the latter part of the nineteenth century, is still echoed by scholars today. The following are two examples of Robertson Smith's attitude to the concept of purity in the Jewish tradition: 'The irrationality of the laws of uncleanness from the standpoint of spiritual religion or even of the higher heathenism is so manifest that they must necessarily be looked on as having survived from an earlier form of faith and society. And this being so, I do not see how any historical student can refuse to class them with savage taboos.'[14] On the rules of corpse uncleanness he writes: 'Rules like this have nothing in common with the spirit of Hebrew religion; they can only be remains of a primitive superstition, like that of the savage who shuns the blood of uncleanness, and such like things, as a supernatural and deadly virus.'[15]

Unfortunate as it is, these attitudes can still be detected today. To many this is the last word and notions of purity remain unexamined,[16] particularly by those who have had no contact with the social sciences,[17] disciplines which themselves have developed beyond the realms set by their nineteenth-century founding fathers. In fact, what we can usefully learn from Robertson Smith today is not what he said about the religion of the Semites but rather his own world view and that of his Victorian contemporaries.[18]

When Robertson Smith wrote of the laws of uncleanness as survivals from a primitive past he was, of course, alluding to the fact, as he and many of his contemporaries saw it, that human religious consciousness developed from these 'primitive superstitions' through a higher religion, Judaism, to Christianity, where, they would maintain, one finds the epitome of spiritual religion; a religion that has nothing to do with ideas of contagion but rather with the superior values of morality. This distinction, between the idea of uncleanness and ethics, has been vigorously upheld since Robertson Smith's time.

Only recently has any attempt been made to show that it is not necessary to make this distinction. An important move in this direction is the observation by G. W. Buchanan that sin, defilement and impurity were indistinguishable in the biblical tradition. He points out that the priest on the Day of Atonement made atonement for the uncleanness (*ṭume'ah*) of the people of Israel as well as for their transgressions (*pesha'*) and all their sins (*ḥaṭa'*) (Lev. 16:16). 'Kohelet contrasted clean with unclean, the good man and the sinner' (Eccl. 9:2)[19] and Isaiah compared Israel to a menstrual garment (*beged 'idim*),[20] for all Israel has sinned and had become like one who was unclean (*ṭame'*) (Isa. 64:4-5). In Buchanan's words 'the Israelite not only used words like sin, transgression, cheating and iniquity synonymously. He also used defilement synonymously with these terms.'[21]

Indeed one frequently finds in the Bible evidence that shows that no distinction was made between immorality and pollution. We note that in Ezekiel acts traditionally considered by the purity laws to be unclean are placed alongside and are indistinguishable from acts that at first seem to have no apparent connection with the idea of purity:

> If a man is righteous and does what is lawful and right - if he does not eat upon the mountains or lift up his eyes to the idols of the house of Israel, does not defile his neighbour's wife or approach a woman in the time of her impurity, does not oppress any one, but restores to the debtor his pledge, commits no robbery, gives his bread to the hungry and covers the naked with a garment, does not lend at interest or take any increase, withholds his hand from iniquity, executes true justice between man and man, walks in my statutes, and is careful to observe my ordinances - he is righteous. (Ezek. 18:5-9)

The righteous man here neither practises idolatry, nor has contact with a menstruant nor acts oppressively towards others; for any of these acts would be unclean and an abomination (verse 12).[22] Thus, in Douglas' words: 'it remains to show that pollution has indeed much to do with morals'.[23]

The failure to appreciate the importance of the concept of purity in early Judaism and Christianity stems from this forced dichotomy between 'ritual' purity and ethics. To be sure there is a concern with purity in early Christianity, say those who maintain this distinction, but it is a concern with 'moral' purity alone and not that of 'ritual' purity.[24] One questions the rigidity of this distinction in view of the evidence that shows that ancient Judaism failed to perceive any difference between the ethical and the ritual. On the lack of distinction between uncleanness, disease and moral wrong G. F. Moore wrote: 'In Jewish laws all these fall under the comprehensive name "sin", which is at bottom a ritual, not a moral conception.'[25] Expanding these comments of Moore, F. Gavin stated that: 'by the second century B.C. the inclusion of "moral" and "religious", "ritual" and "ethical" in one sphere was both taken for granted and effectively maintained.'[26] Both Moore and Gavin wrote over fifty years ago and, in spite of Gavin's criticism of Bousset's 'fallacious' statements on the 'washings and lustrations of Pharisaism',[27] Bousset's own misunderstanding, as we have seen, has persisted.[28]

On the whole, matters concerning ritual in early Judaism and Christianity have been de-emphasized in favour of what are seen to be the inner, spiritual values of religion. But again, as Gavin indicates, 'As partners not enemies, the Jew thought of flesh and spirit: as two parts of a whole he thought of "ceremonial" or "ritual" or "legal" and "spiritual". The antonym of spiritual is neither "material" nor "legal" but *un* or *non*-spiritual.'[29] We make our approach to the study of Qumran and of Paul in the light of these words and view the concept of purity not as *either* moral *or* ritual purity but as having religious value in itself and see it used as a means of elucidating an understanding of religious belief.

Our study is prompted in particular by the work of Douglas in her *Purity and Danger* and the ongoing work of Neusner. We have already made reference to Douglas' comments regarding the misunderstanding many scholars bring to the matter of cleanness and it is with her work that we must dwell in order to appreciate the manner in which notions of purity, when they exist, permeate a society. To begin with she has made it very clear 'that anyone approaching rituals of pollution nowadays would seek to treat a people's ideas of purity as part of a larger whole'.[30] This, it will be seen, is exactly the case with our study of Paul, for his concern with the concept of purity is not peripheral[31] but reflects a far greater concern.

Douglas' work has attracted the attention of biblical scholars because of her treatment of 'the abominations of Leviticus'. In her examination of the biblical dietary rules and the questions of clean and unclean animals she rejects the views of those who would attempt to interpret these rules as aspects of primitive medicine and hygiene or would say that their aim is 'to train the Israelite in self-control'.[32] Alternatively, to say that these rules are arbitrary and irrational is, of course, to give them no interpretation at all.[33]

Taking a fresh look at Leviticus 11 and Deuteronomy 14 Douglas concludes that the creatures that are described as unclean 'are the obscure unclassifiable elements which do not fit the pattern of the cosmos'.[34] What she means by this is that, with respect to animals, the norm is set by those which both chew the cud and are cloven-hooved (Lev. 11:3; Deut. 14:6). The camel, rock badger or hare, for example, while they may appear to chew the cud,[35] are not two-toed, do not fit the norm and are therefore declared to be unclean. Fish are acceptable, that is, those which have both fins and scales and swim. Sea creatures that do not fit this pattern, such as shell fish, are considered unclean (Lev. 11:9–12; Deut. 14:9, 10).

A slightly different, but not contradictory, approach to this subject is made by Jean Sorel.[36] He observes, citing F. Jacob,[37] that the hooved or cloven-hooved animal is of necessity a herbivorous animal having no means of seizing its prey and that these plant-eating animals are exactly those that are mentioned in Genesis 1:30: 'And to every beast of the earth, and to every bird of the air, and to everything that creeps on the earth, everything that has the breath of life, I have given every green plant for food.' Animals or birds that prey on other creatures or eat carrion are not included in this creation account and therefore do not fit into the structure of what is the norm and thereby clean.

Thus one can go through the animal kingdom determining the cleanness or uncleanness of animals according to whether, in Douglas' words, they 'confuse or contradict cherished classifications'.[38] Working independently from Douglas, but like her taking a structuralist approach, Sorel came to virtually the same conclusions: 'The clean animals of the earth must conform to the plan of creation, that is to be vegetarian; they must also conform to their ideal models, that is, be without blemish'.[39] It is, therefore, through order and classification that one should approach the whole question of purity and impurity for, in Sorel's words, 'The Hebrews conceived of the order of the world as the order underlying the creation of the world. Uncleanness then is simple disorder.'[40]

Ancient Judaism, then, is one society 'where the lines of structure, cosmic or social, are clearly defined';[41] and it is within such a society that a concern with cleanness and uncleanness will occur. This structure, as illustrated by the dietary rules, is even more apparent in the wider religious system of ancient Judaism. The whole cosmos was structured according to the principle of division. Not only were the clean separated from the unclean but, according to the Genesis narrative of creation, light was divided from darkness, the waters from the firmament, day from night etc. (Gen. 1:3ff.). The Temple in Jerusalem, separated from the profane world around it, functioned as the focal point of Hebrew religion.[42] It had clearly marked lines of demarcation over which only certain individuals could pass. Furthermore it was incumbent on the priesthood, who had control of the Temple, 'to distinguish between the holy and the common, and between the unclean and the clean' (Lev. 10:10).

Thus the rules of purity reflected Israel's particular understanding of the universe in which it dwelt and covered all aspects of the people's lives. They were called upon to 'be holy, for I the Lord your God am holy' (Lev. 19:2). To be holy meant 'that individuals should conform to the class to which they belong. And holiness requires that different classes shall not be confused'.[43] It means 'keeping distinct the categories of creation. It therefore involves correct definition, discrimination and order. Under this head all the rules of sexual morality exemplify the holy. Incest and adultery (Lev. 18:6-20) are against holiness, in the simple sense of right order. Morality does not conflict with holiness.'[44]

Observance of the purity rules in everyday life, then, particularly those rituals that concern the body and deal with excreta, saliva, etc., reflect a far wider concern, namely that of the social structure itself,[45] and we shall fail to understand these rituals unless, according to Douglas, 'we are prepared to see in the body a symbol of society'.[46] In the same way, Douglas argues, and this point is important to our own study, the keeping of the dietary rules reflected those acts of sacrifice that were taking place in the Temple.[47]

It was indeed, as we have intimated, to the Temple that in the end all the concerns with purity were directed,[48] and the concept of purity, in addition, played a central role in causing the divisions among various Jewish and Jewish-Christian parties in the first century of the common era. For, in Neusner's words, 'purity . . . serves as an important mode of differentiation and definition'[49] between the religious groups of this period because 'it forms one of the common concerns of the religious life'.[50]

We feel justified, then, in using the concept of purity in pursuing our study of both the Dead Sea Scrolls and the letters of Paul in order to attain some measure of understanding of the manner in which these two bodies of literature define the religious groups that they represent. Such a study is particularly relevant in view of the wide range of influence the idea of purity appears to have held in ancient Judaism. It concerned not only land, food, sex, and human relationships in general[51] but more especially it centred on the Temple.[52] Since both Qumran and Paul identify their respective religious communities as just that, the Temple of God, we need to see how, before its destruction, they applied the purity concerns of the Jerusalem Temple to their own communities.[53]

Let us first look a little closer at the manner in which the idea of purity, according to the biblical tradition, interacted with the theology of the Temple. First and most importantly, the impure, according to the purity code, were unable to participate in the liturgy of the Temple[54] and, especially, it was the deliberate sinner who was banned from entering the sacred precincts.[55] The Temple was essentially the special dwelling place of God, and any physical or moral impurity that clung to man would tend to pollute the sanctuary and in the end lead to the divine vacating the Temple because of its uncleanness.[56] Jacob Milgrom had indicated the difference between this concept and that of the pagan who fears that the demonic will drive his god from the sanctuary and who performs magical purification rites to get rid of these demonic intruders. Israel 'has demythologised and devitalised cosmic evil'.[57] It is not evil forces beyond the control of man that can force the exit of the divine from its earthly dwelling place but man himself with the impurity caused by his own physical and moral failings. Describing what he calls 'the Priestly Picture of Dorian Gray' Milgrom writes: 'Sin may not leave a mark on the face of the sinner, but it is certain to mark the face of the sanctuary, and unless it is quickly expunged, God's presence will depart.'[58]

Much of the temple liturgy, then, was directed at cleansing the sanctuary; thus the blood of the purification offering[59] sprinkled on the *kapporet* and on the floor in front of it (Lev. 16:15f.) on the Day of Atonement purified the place where God dwelt.

The maintenance of the divine in their midst was Israel's prime objective in performing the purificatory rites of the Temple and, at the same time, keeping them ensured that the people were kept, as much as possible, in a pure state. Thus the purity rules extended back from the Temple into the homes and thence to the tables and beds of the people.[60]

We must now ask how those religious communities which separated themselves from the Jerusalem Temple continued to pursue this same idea. Both the early Christians and those at Qumran claimed to represent the Temple and believed that they enjoyed the presence of God or his Spirit. How did these two groups bring together the ideas of purity and the presence of God without relating them to the physical Temple? Jacob Neusner has answered this question as it relates to the rabbis after AD 70: 'The community of Israel now is regarded as the Temple. What kept people out of the sanctuary in olden times therefore is going even now to exclude them from the life of the community.'[61] This was made possible by the sages' extension of the priestly ideal to all Jews.[62] Before the destruction the *haverim*, at least,[63] had been teaching that one should keep the purity rules outside the Temple. Now, after AD 70, the community takes the place of the physical Temple; and it is the community which, like the Temple before it, 'generates the metaphor and lays the lines of structure defined by the clean and the unclean'.[64] God continues to dwell within the community. Torah study as well as eating requires a state of purity,[65] for it is on these occasions that God is especially present.[66]

As the *haverim*, before the events of AD 70, developed the system of purity beyond the confines of the Temple to such an extent that this system survived the destruction of the Temple itself, so the Qumran community, denouncing the Jerusalem Temple and claiming itself to constitute the true Temple, applied the rules of purity to its own self-understanding as the dwelling place of God. This much is not disputed, but a fresh examination of the Dead Sea Scrolls needs to be made in order to illustrate the manner in which purity governed other aspects of the life of the community, especially in connection with membership and internal discipline. This examination of the significance of purity at Qumran will lay the groundwork for our study of the concept of purity in another group of Jewish origin which, before AD 70, worked out a system of belief away from the Temple in Jerusalem; namely the Christian community represented by the letters of Paul.

While Gärtner,[67] Klinzing[68] and Forkman[69] make frequent passing references to purity in their studies of the role of the Temple, cult and discipline in the early Christian community, to my knowledge no study centring explicitly on purity itself in the Pauline correspondence has been made. We shall therefore take up and develop Neusner's comments regarding the idea of the Temple: namely that 'it is within this context that the role of purity in early Christianity is to be interpreted'[70] and note, at the same time, that also, in this connection, Paul speaks of the presence of God's spirit within the Church.

Thus our study will show that the idea of purity persisted in some of the earliest Christian communities. Paul, in fact, used this concept to elucidate some of the central tenets of his belief. These concerns with purity, moreover, are not merely a 'spiritualization' of the traditional Jewish view[71] under the influence of Philo and the Stoics.[72] While Paul argued that the Jewish cult was no longer valid as a means of salvation he did not completely reject the cultic concerns of the Temple[73] but used some of them to interpret his own understanding of the Christ event,[74] and in doing so he was heavily influenced by his Jewish heritage.[75]

Many of these concerns are manifested in Paul's letters by vocabulary, imagery and thought forms drawn from the vocabulary that is used to express the idea of purity in the LXX.[76] It is quite clear that Paul was familiar with and made use of a Greek Bible similar to, if not identical with the LXX,[77] for, as is well known, many of his biblical quotations accurately reproduce LXX passages.[78] Many of the concepts connected with the Temple, cult and purity used by Paul reflect, not so much the liturgical life of the Second Temple,[79] but that of temple practice as it is described in the Bible. This is, perhaps, to be expected from a Greek-speaking Jew living in the Diaspora. The Temple itself, although physically removed from his religious life, was nevertheless central to his understanding of that life. But it was not the practices of the contemporary Temple in Jerusalem that Paul used as a model for the expression of much of his new faith but rather those temple practices that he knew intimately from his extensive and accurate knowledge[80] of the contents of his Bible.[81]

Our concern then is with the concept of purity as it was applied outside the Jerusalem Temple by the Qumran community and by Paul. While our major interest is with Paul we address ourselves to the Qumran material partly because it gives us a useful parallel on which to base our subsequent study but also, and perhaps more importantly, because it is believed that a clearer understanding of the religion of the Qumran community can, in fact, be obtained by paying particular attention to the role played by the concept of purity. Our intention is to demonstrate and emphasize the overall significance that the concept of purity had for both the Qumran community and Paul. This significance, while it has not been carefully examined, is generally acknowledged as far as the Dead Sea Scrolls are concerned; but it has been overlooked, or, worse, ignored in Pauline studies.

Paul's use of the idea of purity centres, as with Qumran, upon the view that the religious community and its members represent the Temple. Our study, then, pays particular attention to cultic concepts and terminology. For it is from the Temple that many purity concerns originate. We do not restrict ourselves to this particular aspect of purity, for we find that Paul uses the concept of purity in a wider sense in connection with sexual matters, family life and in his description of the results of sinful acts. Paul's use of the concept of purity is not, then, peripheral, metaphorical or spiritualized; rather it pervades the way he conceives of himself as an apostle, his view of the Church and its members and the sort of life he expects those members to lead.

2

THE CONCEPT OF PURITY IN THE QUMRAN COMMUNITY

1. Introduction

In our study of the Dead Sea Scrolls[1] we propose to show the importance and pervasiveness of purity terminology in a pre-AD-70 Jewish group that was not associated with the Jerusalem Temple. It has previously been shown that the Qumran community thought of itself as the Temple.[2] This will be confirmed and elaborated by studying the concept of purity, which was traditionally related to the temple cult. In the Scrolls purity terminology occurs in two principal contexts: the requirements for and the consequences of admission to the community and the maintenance of status once a member was in the community. The language of purity is also used in discussions of exclusion from the community. Accordingly it is to these contexts that we turn in order to grasp the role and significance of purity in the Dead Sea Scrolls.[3]

2. Entry into the community; the 'Purity' and the 'Drink' at Qumran

And when he approaches the Council of the Community he shall not touch the Purity [*taharah*] of the Many until they have examined him about his spirit and actions, until a full year has been completed by him. (1QS 6.16, 17)

Let him not touch the Drink [*mashqeh*] of the Many until he nas completed a second year amongst the men of the Community. (1QS 6.20, 21, Rabin's translation)

Various solutions have been proposed to the problem of the meaning of the terms *taharah* and *mashqeh* (which for now we shall translate simply as 'purity' and 'drink') in the Qumran scrolls. Bearing in mind that it is in fact our task to discuss the concern with purity in the Qumran sect, one of our aims will be to discover a satisfactory understanding of these particular terms.

Two avenues of approach have been used to achieve this. One is to look at the reports of Josephus about the Essenes; the other is to use the rabbinic materials and their accounts of the pharisaic traditions regarding purity and, in particular, to look at what the rabbis say about the 'associates', the *haverim*.

Drawing on the evidence which Josephus gives and finding the rabbinic comparisons misguided, Hunzinger[4] draws close parallels between Josephus' άγνεία and the Qumran *taharah*. Drawing a similar kind of conclusion Huppenbauer[5] sees also a close connection between *taharah* and the bath through which purity is attained. Klinzing[6] works somewhat along the same lines and points out that in 1QS 5.13 the 'purity' is represented in a particular way by the water rites. Like Hunzinger he notes that there is a very close parallel between the Scroll's *taharah* and Josephus' άγνεία.

Baumgarten[7] and Rabin[8] are among those who look to the rabbinic literature for clarification of the Qumran scrolls. Both state categorically that 'purity' cannot refer to the water at all. Rabin points to 1QS 5.13: 'let him not enter the water so as to touch the Purity of the men of holiness', and remarks 'Here the water and the touching of the Purity are clearly distinguished; the ritual bath is the preliminary to touching the Purity. This can only mean that the Purity is ritually pure food.'[9] Rabin goes on to equate the so-called 'purity' with the *tohorot* of the rabbis.[10] This conclusion had already been reached by Lieberman[11] who, like Rabin, compares the concern with the purity of the Qumran sect with that shown by the *haburot* of the Pharisees and takes the Qumran *taharah* to refer, as does the rabbinic *tohorot*, to ritually clean articles, especially food.[12] Others have looked favourably upon this particular understanding of the 'purity',[13] and have taken it to refer especially to the meal which the community ate together and to which they gave special significance. A wider range of meaning is given to the term by Brownlee[14] who while excluding liquids, sees *taharah* as referring to a wide range of solid objects that belong to, or are an integral part of the community, such as 'food, vessels, (rites?) or even the bodies of the Holy Men'.

In view of the importance that appears to be assigned to matters of purity in the Qumran literature it is worthwhile to consider afresh the use of this key term *taharah* as it appears in the Scrolls. The varied approaches to an understanding of the term which have already been noted should not lead one to the conclusion that they are all mutually exclusive. There has been a tendency to define *taharah* too narrowly with apparently little appreciation of the wide range of meaning that the term actually conveys. Comparisons to the rabbinic *tohoroth*[15] are certainly useful and lead to a fuller understanding of the Qumran concern with purity, and reference may have to be made to the Josephus accounts to fill out the picture, but neither of these two sources need be the sole determining factor of our study. While we feel compelled to identify the Qumran sect with the Essenes, the account by Josephus of the Essenes is by no means complete. We therefore look to the Scrolls themselves as being the only means by which we can really come to a satisfactory conclusion regarding the theology of the sect.

Before we draw any final conclusions regarding the meaning of both the 'drink' and the 'purity' in the Scrolls we need to look in more detail at the procedure for the admission of new members to the community. This will not only illustrate the important role that the concept of purity played in the life of the sect but will help us arrive at a better understanding of the use of both *taharah* and *mashqeh*. We shall see the new member pass from being an impure outsider through an intermediate stage during which he has limited contact with the sect and its property to a time when he is considered pure in all things and can enjoy full participation in the atoning activity of the sect.

We note below that the Qumran covenanters considered themselves to be members of a temple-like community and that a major motivation for their strict adherence to the rules of purity was that they saw themselves fitted for the temple service. In view of this it is only to be expected that members of the community should have the potential ability to perform some part of the temple worship. While we shall see later how they avoided the problem of not having a membership made up entirely of the priestly class we do note here that those who wish to join[16] the community must be true Israelites 'born of Israel' (lit. 'from Israel')[17] and thus fitted by birth to take part in the temple worship.[18] Further physical requirements befitting a priestly community are set out in CD 15.15-17.[19] It may also be that the age requirements of members (1QSa 1.8ff., 2.7ff., CD 10.6f.) reflected the limitations laid down regarding the age limits for priests in the Temple (cf. Num. 4:3; 8:23). It is certainly clear that the member who becomes too 'old and tottery' and 'unable to stand still in the midst of the congregation' (1QSa 2.7) may not hold office because he is in danger of becoming impure.[20]

A prior examination is made of the new man by the *paqid*,[21] as head of the community, 'concerning his understanding and deeds'. We are not told exactly what this means but it is necessary to assume that the novice is not likely, at this stage, to come up to the standards of purity required by the community. If, however, he is to be admitted and take even a minimal part in the life of the community he is, sooner or later, going to come into contact with the full members, sit on their benches, brush inadvertently against their clothes and in general pollute the assembly. In pharisaic terms we may say that he would not be 'trustworthy' (*ne'eman*).[22] It is the preliminary examination that is described in 1QS 6.13 and subsequent examinations that would determine the man's purity and the likelihood of his being able to continue in a manner that would not bring impurity into the congregation. The two years which lapse before his full participation are to enable his complete purification. We must remember that the new member has come from outside where, according to the sect, all is impure. The long-drawn-out novitiate in one respect protects them from this outside pollution.

What does this first examination involve? The inquiry centres on the new member's 'understanding and deeds'. This phrase occurs elsewhere (1QS 5.21, 23; 6.18; CD 13.11) and in 1QS 5.21 and 6.18 it is qualified by the phrase 'in Torah'.[23] Even before the novice takes the initial step of entering the community it is likely that because of his motivation in wishing to join the community he has a basic knowledge of Torah and has been attempting to live a life in accordance with its demands as far as he was able, but not according to the sect's own understanding of it. It would not, then, seem unlikely that those who are allowed to make this approach are considered by the *paqid* as being reliable regarding the rules of purity as laid out in Torah. This reliability is revealed by the examination of the novice's understanding in Torah. Rabin[24] has suggested that *sekel* here can be taken to mean, not so much a man's intelligence, as many commentators have taken it, but a reference to the novice's 'religious knowledge'. If this be the case religious knowledge could most certainly cover the basic rules of purity.

Purity and understanding are mentioned together in 1QS 9.15 where they appear in synonymously parallel phrases: 'He [*maskil*] shall admit [*qarav*] him in accordance to the cleanness [*bor*] of his hands, and advance [*nagash*] him in accordance with his understanding [*sekel*].' Here it seems that movement through the ranks of the community depends on each member's purity and that the member's understanding is bound up with the purity of his actions.[25] This supports our own point that references to the member's understanding in 1QS 6.14 refer to his comprehension of the rules of purity, and the nature of his behaviour (his deeds) stems from this understanding.[26]

A satisfactory conclusion of this examination means that the novice is admitted into the covenant. The verb used here is *bo'* and, as has been pointed out by Lieberman,[27] it 'serves as a technical term for both the application for Haberuth and particularly for conversion'.[28] It is a form of conversion that follows this admission according to 1QS 6.15: 'he shall admit him into the covenant that he may return [*shuv*] to the truth and depart from all falsehood'. To enter the community means to enter the covenant but it may be argued that the novice is already a member of the covenant by virtue of his birth as an Israelite. The community, however, appears to differentiate between the covenant as it is generally understood and 'the covenant of the community' or, as they sometimes call it, 'the covenant of God'. To be a member of this covenant (one should hesitate to call it a *new* covenant as such)[29] means that one sees things in a completely different way and one's style of life is changed. Most importantly the 'rules of the community' are revealed. It is the sect's understanding that only to them has God given the true understanding of the covenant that he made with Moses.[30] The new member is able, once he enters the community, 'to return [*shuv*] to the law of Moses' (1QS 5.8f.) and to be instructed 'in all the rules of the community'.[31]

These 'rules of the community' are not, it seems, expected to be known or, at least, understood by those seeking to join the sect.[32] CD 15.11ff. reports of the new member who is to be kept from knowledge of the rules (*mishpaṭim*) until he is examined by the *mebaqqer* 'lest he proves simple when he examines him'. These rules are a closely-guarded secret and are to be revealed only to those proved worthy by official examination.[33] Much of what is concealed from those outside the community concerns the sect's own interpretation of scripture. The *mishpatim* referred to in 1QS 6.15 and elsewhere, and which are only revealed to members, have been described by Rabin as 'special laws which the sect has worked out in order to preserve the practice of the Law as far as the difficult present time allows'.[34] It may not be necessary to posit that these laws are extra-biblical, as Rabin is here suggesting, but rather that the 'special laws' are derived directly from the Torah but are radically interpreted and applied in full stringency. This would particularly be the case in those laws relating to the priests, the Temple and purity.

Qumran saw itself as a priestly community in its own right;[35] and while it did not see itself as a surrogate Temple and carry out sacrifices[36] it certainly conducted itself as a replacement for the defiled Temple of Jerusalem[37] and as a dwelling place for God. It becomes a 'holy house for Israel and a foundation of the holy of holies for Aaron' (1QS 8.5, 6) and 'a dwelling of the holy of holies for Aaron . . . and a house of perfection and truth for Israel'. While most translators render *qodesh qodashim* as 'most holy' they recognize that this passage sees the community comparing itself to the interior of the Temple, the Holy Place and the Holy of Holies,[38] the most sacred part of the Temple. It was here that the highest standards of purity were required[39] and it was in the Holy of Holies that the presence of God dwelt.[40]

The community, then, strives to present itself as a pure precinct within which the divine is able to dwell and expiatory acts can be performed: 'They shall atone for guilty rebellion and for sins of unfaithfulness that they may obtain lovingkindness for the Land *without* the flesh of holocausts and the fat of sacrifice. And prayer rightly offered shall be as an acceptable fragrance of righteousness, and perfection of way as a delectable free will offering' (1QS 9.4, 5).[41] In order to express this conviction the covenanters took the Temple as a model, and the biblical laws pertaining to temple purity needed to be applied wherever possible to the community and its members.[42] Thus the novice may or may not have been familiar with the temple rules of purity; but what, in any case, would have been new to him was the application of these laws to a place outside the Jerusalem Temple, to men who were not in the traditional sense considered to be priests and to acts, which, while non-sacrificial, were considered expiatory. Many aspects of the priestly role were taken over by the members of the community.[43] Those who enter the community are required to 'distinguish between the clean and the unclean and proclaim the difference between the holy and the profane' (CD 6.17) and they shall also 'keep apart from every uncleanness according to their statutes' (CD 7.3). Again we should note the use here of *mishpaṭim*, statutes, used in reference to those rules which enable purity to be maintained.

The notion of separation in the Dead Sea Scrolls

CD 6.17, in citing the words of Leviticus 10:10, is taking up the command given to Aaron and his sons; they were to drink no wine (cf. the use of *tirosh* in community meals) and decide for Israel those things which were clean and which were unclean. The task of distinguishing between the pure and impure is expressed by the use of the verb *badal* and is found frequently in the Scrolls as a word which describes the tasks of the community and its members. We have noted its direct use with the concerns of purity, but it also serves in a descriptive sense when used to denote the sect's separation from the rest of the world which in their view, as we saw above, is unclean.

The use of *badal* fits in well with the sect's priestly understanding of itself, for this word has an extensive use in the Hebrew Bible in a cultic context.[44] In Numbers 8:14; 16:9 and in Deuteronomy 10:8 it is used to describe the setting apart of the priesthood from the rest of Israel and in

Leviticus 10:10; 11:47; 20:25; and in Ezekiel 22.26; 44:23 the separation of the clean from the unclean. It is used similarly to describe the separation of Israel from the peoples in Leviticus 20:24, 26 and Ezra 6:21.[45] Thus Qumran takes up this particular biblical use of *badal* and the members of the community take over the traditional role of the priests as outlined in Leviticus 10:10: 'You are to distinguish between the holy and the common, and between the unclean and the clean.'[46] While CD 6.17 has close verbal parallels with Leviticus 10:10 it is closer still to Ezekiel 22:26 and 44:23-4 in its use of the *hiphil* of *yada'* (make known, declare). Those who are 'brought into the covenant' are to 'distinguish [*badal*] between the unclean [*tame'*] and the clean [*tahor*] and to make known [*yada'*] the difference between the holy [*qodesh*] and the profane [*hol*]' (CD 6.17, 18). While Ezekiel, describing the role of the priests in the future Temple, prophesies that 'They shall teach my people the difference between the holy [*qodesh*] and the common [*hol*] and show them how to distinguish [*yada'*] between the unclean [*tame'*] and the clean [*tahor*].' Particularly striking are the similar contexts of CD 6.14f. and Ezekiel 44:23-4.[47] In the Damascus Document the reference is to those who are in the covenant (CD 6.11) and in Ezekiel it is to the priests who are to serve in the new Temple. Both are to keep the laws of purity and teach them and both are to keep the feasts and the Sabbath. It need not come as a surprise that the writer of the Damascus Document placed 'Sabbaths' before 'feasts' when we consider the strictness of the sabbath *halakah* at Qumran[48] and the difficulty they would have experienced in the proper celebration of the feasts in the absence of the sanctuary.

The separation from the nations in Leviticus 20:24, 26 ('I am the Lord your God, who have [sic] separated you from the peoples') forms the model for the community's understanding of itself as a distinct people chosen by God. The distinction, however, at Qumran is between themselves and the rest of Israel rather than between themselves and the Gentiles.[49] An expression of this sentiment is given in 1QS 5.1: 'They [the men of the community] shall separate [*badal*][50] from the congregation of the men of falsehood.'[51] It seems that the 'men of falsehood' are other Jews who have not submitted to the authority of the Zadokite priesthood.[52] The members of the community are exhorted to separate themselves from 'all the men of falsehood' (1QS 5.10), 'those not reckoned in His Covenant' (i.e. the covenant of Qumran) (1QS 5.18), 'the habitation of ungodly men' (1QS 8.13), 'the sons of the pit' (CD 6.15) and 'all those who have not turned aside from all ungodliness' (1QS 9.20). While these groups are not really clearly defined there is no reason to suppose that they are anything other than non-sectarian Jews. The Qumran sect had no occasion to enter into a polemic with Gentiles.

We also see in 1QS 5.1 a reflection of Numbers 16. This chapter deals with the incident of Korah and the Levites and serves to explain the predominance of the family of Aaron and the subordination of the sons of Levi. In verse 9 the specific role of the Levites is pointed out: 'Is it too small a thing for you that the God of Israel has separated [*badal*] you from the congregation ['*edah*] of Israel to bring you near [*qarav*] to himself to do service ['*avad*] in the tabernacle of the Lord and to stand ['*amad*] before the congregation to minister [*sharat*] to them?' As the sons of Levi were separated from the congregation of Israel in order to be closer to God and serve him in the Temple, so is the membership of the Qumran community set apart from the rest of Israel in order to be brought near to God 'under the authority of the sons of Zadok, the priests who keep the covenant' (1QS 5.2).

We should note that Numbers 16 constitutes an attack on the Levites for their insubordination under Korah but we find no such criticism of the Levites in the Dead Sea Scrolls. In fact, CD 3.21–4.4, in its exegesis of Ezekiel 44:15, identifies three groups which go to constitute the community: 'the Priests and the Levites and the sons of Zadok', thus changing the original reading of Ezekiel by the addition of a *waw* before the terms 'Levites' and 'sons of Zadok'. Betz has noted this phenomenon in his study of the application of Ezekiel 44 in the Scrolls. He remarks: 'Cette explication contredit l'intention d'Ezéchiel qui, précisément dans le chapitre cité, n'accorde aux lévites qu'un service auxiliaire dans le temple et les sépare nettement des prêtres (XLIV 10 ss.).'[53]

Thus the Scrolls gave to the Levites a significant role within the community denied to them in Ezekiel's vision of the new Temple.[54] The community sought to organize itself like Israel in a way which it believed was God's intention. Within this structure both priests and Levites as well as the laity are represented and all are considered to be separated from the rest of Israel. But as we see from CD 3.21 to 4.4 the community also sees itself as being exclusively priestly. It is made up as follows: 'The Priests are the converts of Israel who departed from the land of Judah and [the Levites are] those who joined them. The Sons of Zadok are the elect of Israel.' In reality we must assume, for all practical purposes, that the community was made up of laymen as well as priests; that the priests given ultimate authority were those descendants of Zadok, that the Levites were given an important role, most likely in the teaching and interpretation of scripture[55] and that the Israelites and proselytes,[56] the laymen, were given, at the time of the writing of CD 3.21ff., a priestly status also and were seen, with the whole community, as a separate people, 'a kingdom of priests and a holy nation' (Exod. 19:6).[57]

A further use of *badal* is in the disciplinary statements of the community. Many of the punishments for sins committed within the community involve 'separation from the purity'. We shall take up later the significance of understanding the sinner as impure, but we shall note here the use of *badal* in the sense of 'to exclude'. The member who offends against the rules of the community becomes, in the eyes of the sect, unclean and has to be separated from the 'purity of the congregation' (1QS 6.25; 7.5, complete exclusion 7.3, 5, 16; 8.24). In those places (1QS 7.1, 5) where no mention is made of the 'purity' *badal* is still used and in 1QS 7.1 in particular it is used to denote the complete dismissal from the community. There is a good foundation for this usage in the Bible. We have a notable parallel with Ezra 10:8 (cf. Neh. 13:3) 'banned from the congregation of the exiles'. *Badal* is used here to describe the banning of those Israelites who had brought impurity upon the congregation by marrying, and refusing to give up, foreign wives. Also in Deuteronomy 29:21 *badal* is used for the 'singling out' (RSV) of the one who worshipped idols, an impure act in itself, and who has brought impurity upon himself and Israel.

The cultic verb *badal* is used then, rather than, say, *parad*[58] for such dismissals; for they are carried out for the sake of the purity of the community. By virtue of his sin a man is unclean and the community must maintain its separation from impurity: thus he is excluded.

In CD 6.15 the verb *nazar* occurs in parallel to *badal*: 'and they shall separate [*badal*] from the sons of the Pit, and they shall keep away [*nazar*] from the unclean riches of wickedness'. Now *nazar* is clearly a word with cultic overtones[59] (cf. Nazirite) and its use here supports our cultic understanding of *badal*. The word appears elsewhere in CD 7.1 where it is used in part of the instructions for those who are brought into the covenant: 'They shall keep away [*lehazir*] from fornication.' As fornication is a form of impurity it is fitting that this particular verb is used here. The other occurrence is in CD 8.8 (19.20). It appears in a list of sins committed by the apostates of the community. 'They have not kept separate from the peoples' in contradiction to the injunction of Leviticus 20:26. *Nazar* is used here in place of *badal*, which appears in the verse in Leviticus.

Badal and occasionally *nazar* are used by the community to show its concern in maintaining its purity. The words express the conviction that they were a priestly community and as such had to be protected from any intrusion of uncleanness either from without, in the form of unconverted Israelites, or from within, in the form of the sinful member who either

temporarily or permanently is tainted with impurity and has to separate
himself from the membership. Thus the community could maintain a
temple-like purity and require its members to 'keep apart from every
uncleanness according to their statutes'.

Mishpaṭim

We need now to investigate further what exactly was meant by *mishpaṭim*.
We have already indicated that 'statutes' have, in some measure, a connection with the concern with purity, and will show now that the *mishpaṭim*
were closely linked to the rules and regulations regarding the purity of the
Temple. Later rabbinic Judaism was to see, after the destruction of the
Temple, an application of the temple purity rules to everyday life[60] and
the laws which were intended for priests extended to all Israelites.[61] It
seems that Qumran was directly coming to terms with this concept of the
replacement, temporarily or otherwise, of the Jerusalem Temple. One of
the major criticisms that they made of the present Temple was that it was
polluted.[62] A concern with purity, then, was a factor in their alienation
from Jerusalem and it was in their life in the community that they attempted to maintain a temple-like purity in all their activities.

Thus the novice was introduced to the *mishpaṭim* and was prepared, if
the decision of the community allowed him to enter, for the strict purity
regulations in force among its members (1QS 6.16ff.). He may not have
any contact with the so-called 'purity'; but the community was confident,
having deliberated his case and knowing that he had received instruction
in these regulations (*mishpaṭim*) of the community, that he would respect
their purity and would not make any moves that would jeopardize it. To
help prevent this happening his property was not allowed to come into
contact with the property of the rest of the community.[63]

At the end of his first year in the Council of the Community his understanding and observance of the Law (Torah) was examined by the congregation. He had obviously, during his first year with the community, been
taught some of the sect's own interpretation of Torah and he was now
expected to come up to some of its rigorous requirements. These are
defined in the sect's *mishpaṭim* with which the initiate has now become
familiarized. If he comes up to the standards required and the priests and
the rest of the membership consider him worthy he is allowed to pass to
the next stage of membership. Now his own property which up to now has
been kept in isolation is handed over. It is still kept apart from the property of the community but it is held in his name. The community now

considers the novice trustworthy regarding solid things and he may 'touch the purity of the Many' (1QS 6.16).

Naga'

We meet here the verb *naga'*, 'to touch'. There is here an interesting parallel with what Josephus has to say about the Essenes. Hunzinger[64] has pointed out that the phrases in 1QS 6.16f. (*yiga' betaharat harabim*) and 1QS 6.20 (*yiga' bemashqeh harabim*) are very similar to Josephus' phrase in *Bell.* II.139 (τῆς κοινῆς ἄψασθαι) which he uses when he is describing the Essene novice's passage toward full membership in the sect. Hunzinger argues from this that Josephus presents us with a reasonably accurate picture of the life of the Qumran community in this respect. The similarity is indeed 'striking'[65] but by no means conclusive to Hunzinger's argument by which he attempts to show that our best understanding of the Qumran *taharah* can be derived from Josephus.

Naga' is widely used in the Hebrew Bible in the general sense of 'to touch' and also 'to be struck' or 'smitten', as it is also used in Qumran (cf. 1QSa 2.3ff.), but it has many specific applications in connection with unclean things in particular. These include corpses (Num. 31:19), animal carcasses (Lev. 11:36) and unclean persons (Lev. 15:10, 19ff.). The verb is also used in connection with those things which have to be protected from impurity; the altar (Exod. 29:37) and its utensils (Exod. 30:29) and holy things (Num. 4:15). In all these cases the LXX translates the *qal* of *naga'* with ἄπτεσθαι.[66]

Neither the use of *naga'* by Qumran nor of ἄπτεσθαι by Josephus in the light of this usage is unusual. Qumran was not unique in its use of this verb in connection with its own 'holy things'; and Josephus, or his Greek-speaking assistants,[67] had the background of the Greek Bible to enable the choice of this particular word. We need not, then, see Josephus' account of the Essenes at this point to be an accurate account of the Qumran practice. The similarity is striking, but the connection is with a common source, namely the Hebrew Bible and its Greek versions. What we have in the Qumran use of *naga'* is a further application of a term, which has cultic use in the Bible, to those things, *taharah* and *mashqeh*, which have to be protected from impurity.

Wernberg-Møller has suggested that the use of *naga'* with *taharah* may mean that the latter is 'something palpable'.[68] While we would agree that the 'purity' does refer to solids it should be noted at the same time that there are two exceptions in the Bible where the verb *naga'* refers to liquids. Numbers 19:21 reads 'and the one who touches the water of impurity will be impure until evening' (my translation). Here *naga'* is certainly used in a cultic context with the mention of 'the waters of impurity', which figure also in the Scrolls.[69] In Haggai 2:12 the prophet asks of the priests if, when 'bread, or pottage, or wine, or oil, or any kind of food' is touched by the clothing in which one carries holy flesh, it also becomes holy. Here *naga'* is used with reference to solid things as is normal, but also included are wine and oil. All these items are food and again the context is cultic. *Naga'* can be used, then, with both liquids and solids but most usually with solids. When it is used with liquids in the Bible it is invariably with reference to the purity that pertains to the activity of the Temple. In the Scrolls it is used mainly in connection with solids, e.g. *taharah*, but also finds expression in the prohibition against touching the 'drink' which is best understood as especially the liquids which accompanied the sacred meal.

Thus it is not until a further examination before the community that the novice is considered worthy to touch the 'drink of the Many'. He is, at the end of his second year, finally acceptable to the community in matters of purity and in his understanding and practice of Torah. He can offer himself in his counsel and judgement to the community. The new member is considered at this stage to be an equal among his brethren concerning Torah, justice and purity. Only now is his property pure and only now are his mental abilities (his counsel) and his judgements acceptable (1QS 6.22, 23).

Ṭaharah

Let us now examine the occurrences of *taharah* within the Scrolls. The word appears in the Damascus Document only in CD 9.21-23 which deals with the member who sins against Torah before witnesses or offends against the rules of property (*hon*). The man who is found guilty on the evidence of trustworthy witnesses is excluded from the 'purity' (CD 9.21).

This reference to the cultic discipline of the community is also found in the Manual of Discipline. Very similar phraseology to that of CD 9.21, 23 is found in 1QS 6.25; 7.3, 16; 8.24, with the exception that instead of simply the 'purity' we have the 'purity of the Many'. We may, however, conclude that with the identical context in both documents, i.e. discipline within the community, and the virtually identical use of the verb *badal*, the 'purity' of the Damascus Document and the 'purity of the Many' of the Manual of Discipline are one and the same thing.

There is one instance in the Manual of Discipline where *taharah* stands alone and does not seem to have the same meaning as in those passages just mentioned. 1QS 4.2-6 appears as a self-description of the sect, a list of virtues by which the community is recognized, and it is at 1QS 4.5 that we meet the phrase *wetaharat kavod meta'ev kol gilule niddah*, which can be translated 'and of glorious purity abhorring all idols of impurity'. This merely describes one of the qualities of the sect. From the point of view of the sect its purity would be self-evident and by nature it would display a loathing towards idols which in the biblical tradition and in first and second century Judaism were considered to be the epitome of uncleanness.[70] Thus *taharah* here is descriptive and has little direct connection with the predominant use of the noun elsewhere in the Scrolls.

That *taharah* refers not just to a descriptive quality but is also substantive is shown in 1QS 7.25. This passage deals with the relationship a member may have with one who has been expelled from the community: 'If one of the men of the community has contact [*'arav*][71] with him in his purity [*taharah*] or in his property [*hon*] which at the same time has contact with [*'arav*] the property of the many then his punishment shall be the same, he shall be expelled.' We note first that the use of 'purity' here is unique in that it refers not to the usual 'purity of the Many' but to the 'purity' that belongs to an individual, 'his purity'. This would exclude from our interpretation of 'purity' the meaning of 'community meal' *per se*[72] but it could still quite possibly refer to food (cf. Vermes). As for *hon*, this would refer not to money specifically but in a more general sense to wealth or capital.[73] This understanding of *hon* is more in keeping with the use of that particular word in the Hebrew Bible.[74]

This passage along with 1QS 8.21–4 and 9.8–9 shows that members have some control over their own possessions. They are not to have any contact with those who were once members but now have been expelled for their transgressions or who are members of a lower rank.[75] These prohibitions are closely connected with the concern for purity within the community. The novice and the expelled member are considered to be unclean as is all that they possess.[76] For the full member of the community to bring his possessions into contact with those either temporarily or permanently outside is to endanger the purity of the community. For while the member has control of his property it, along with his own being, is a constituent part of the community: and any impurity that the property or the person contacts will be passed on to the community as a whole.[77] Thus these precautions are taken in these passages in order to protect the community from contamination.

The fact that these three passages (1QS 7.24–5; 8.21–4; 9.8–9) indicate that the members have some control of their own property leads us to the conclusion, in spite of Josephus' reports to the contrary, that there was no community of goods at Qumran.[78] Rather, as Black points out, the sect formed 'a community whose property is administered and regulated *according to the Torah*, as interpreted by the priests.'[79] This meant, according to Black, that while the average member still had his own possessions, community of goods 'was limited only to the full priestly members of the sect'.[80] This is in accord with the stipulations in Torah which state that priests and Levites should hold no property but be in receipt of tithes for their service in the sanctuary.[81] Thus at Qumran there was a common fund, 'the property of the Many', to which members contributed from their own income, tithes and fines for misdemeanours.[82] From this fund the expenses of the community were met, among which would have been the payments to the Priests and Levites.

The word *hon* appears in Proverbs 3:9 and its use there may provide a clue to our understanding of the Qumran usage and to the meaning of *taharah* itself. Proverbs 3:9 reads 'Honour the Lord with your substance [*hon*] and with the first fruits of all your produce.' The use of *kavod* (honour, glorify) with the 'first fruits' suggests worship. The context does not allow us to conclude that there is here a reference to *sacrificial* worship, but rather worship in the form of the keeping of the commandments (Prov. 3:1), 'trust in the Lord' (verse 5) and acknowledgement of him in everything one does (verse 6). Sacrificial worship had no place in the life of the Qumran community, but rather praise and perfection of way substituted for the Temple rites and only those members who were in a pure state could participate. The property (*hon*) of the full member had to be maintained in a state of purity because it too formed part of the holy community, the sacred precincts, wherein the community performed its sacred acts. Just as everything that entered the Jerusalem Temple had to be free from impurity so it was the case with all the objects involved in the life of the community.

The harshest punishment that the community can give is perhaps complete exclusion, but exclusion from the 'purity of the Many' for certain periods of time is more common. 'Purity of the Many' is the phrase most frequently used both in the rules of discipline and in the procedures dealing with the admission of new members. The 'Many' is usually taken to refer to the community[83] or more specifically the fully-qualified members. The exceptions to the use of 'the Many' are in 1QS 5.13 and 8.17. In 1QS 5.13 we have the phrase *betaharat 'anshe haqodesh* in a section dealing with the prerequisites for a ritual bath which is taken prior to a new member's taking a greater part in the life of the community. Virtually the same phrase occurs in 1QS 8.17: *betaharat 'anshe haqodesh*, in reference to disciplinary action. Like the term *harabim*, *'anshe haqodesh* obviously designated the full members (cf. 1QS 9.8), so we can safely say that *harabim* and *'anshe haqodesh* refer to the same group.

Of the six occurrences of *taharah* in the absolute perhaps the most interesting, and one which points to the importance of purity in the Qumran sect, is in 1QS 6.22. Here the final acceptance of the novice into full membership is described: 'He shall be inscribed according to the order of his rank among his brethren for Torah, justice [*mishpat*], purity [*toharah*] and for contact with his property [*ule'arev 'et hono*].'[84] Having come to the end of his two year novitiate the prospective member is examined and, if the lot falls in his favour he is considered to have fully accepted the responsibility of keeping Torah, is able to sit in judgement along with his brethren, is considered trustworthy in matters of purity and, because of this, his property, which up until now has been put in trust, can be used within the community. He is now able to take a full part in the atoning activity of the sect. 'Purity' here means knowledge of the purity rules peculiar to the sect which, in particular at Qumran, are connected with the use and consumption of food.[85]

Thus purity was a major focus within the community and the regulations regarding membership, the ongoing life within the community and the disciplining of members revolve around this concern. The community as a group considered itself to be pure and all those outside to be impure. They viewed those who controlled the Temple in Jerusalem as particularly unclean and accused them of 'lying with a woman who sees her bloody discharge' (CD 5.7). The community is called upon to 'keep apart from every uncleanness according to the statutes relating to each one, and no man shall defile his holy spirit since God has set them apart' (CD 7.4).[86] As for those who are 'not reckoned in God's covenant', 'all their deeds are defilement before him' (CD 2.1).

Both novices and, to a certain extent, some penitents were considered impure. It was seen as the task of the community to protect this purity from those outside who would bring with them some impurity, particularly their possessions which are singled out for special mention. The Scrolls state explicitly that those whom the purity rules of the Bible considered impure (e.g. lepers, those suffering from a flux etc.) were automatically excluded (CD 15.15f.; cf. 1QSa 2.3ff.), but we also see that even those who wished to join the group were at first excluded from full participation for reasons of purity. The passing of time, careful examination, repentance and ritual bathing brought the novice to a level of purity that enabled him to partake in some activities of the community. He was able to touch the 'purity of the Many' and have contact with the 'property of the Many'.

The procedures for entry into the community, then, centre around a concern with purity. For a period of more than two years the prospective member passes through various stages of purity: from the relative unclean-ness of an outsider to a point where his whole being, including his personal property, is considered to be a part of the community (1QS 1.11, 12). The novice may have contact with the 'purity' after one year while his own belongings have to be handed over to be held in trust so as not to come into contact with the property of the rest of the community. Meanwhile he is able to enjoy the communal life without constantly conveying im-purity. He is obviously not considered to be completely reliable as far as purity is concerned, for he cannot touch the liquids and take a full part in the common meal; but solid objects are not considered to be susceptible to the degree of impurity that still clings to him.

The process of purification through which he passes lasts over two years. It is not achieved by washings themselves, although these have a part. It is preceded by repentance (1QS 3.1; 5.13, 14). Washings follow; but what appears to be important in the purificatory process is instruction in the sect's own laws, the study of Torah and an examination in the understand-ing of these laws and their observation. The entrant's 'knowledge in the truth of God's precepts is purified [*barar*]' (1QS 1.12). He is admitted 'in accordance with the cleanness of his hands' and 'in accordance with his understanding' (1QS 9.15). While the teaching of the Law is concealed from the 'men of falsehood', 'true knowledge and righteous judgement' is imparted to those who have chosen the way. Thus the purification takes place. The acquisition of a full understanding of the sect's interpretation of the Law enables the new member to advance towards full membership. He has been purified of the imperfections he brought with him from out-side. But even the final decision on whether a man may progress through the ranks is not entirely up to the community and its officials alone. The phrase 'and if it be his destiny' occurs in both the advancement to the 'purity' and to the 'drink'. In spite of the man's repentance, his ritual bathing, his own understanding and the judgement of the community, room is left for God's providence which has to be discerned by the mem-bership before 'he shall be inscribed among his brethren in the order of his rank for the Law, and for justice and for the purity' (1QS 6.22).

From this perspective we may now draw some conclusions regarding the terms 'purity' and 'drink'. We cannot avoid accepting the usual view that the 'drink' refers to the liquids that were involved in the communal meals. The biblical basis of the idea that liquids are prime conveyors of impurity is Leviticus 11:38, which produces a tradition which was to be elaborated by the rabbis.[87] There is no reason to suspect that the Qumran sect did not also attach importance to liquids as both conveyors of impurity and as being susceptible to impurity. We therefore conclude that exclusion from the 'drink of the Many' meant exclusion from sharing the 'new wine' (1QS 6.5, 1QSa 2.17f.) at a community meal which the probationer, in his own impurity, would contaminate. His final acceptance as a full member meant that he could share fully in the meals. He was now considered clean in all respects and could enjoy complete table fellowship, a sign itself of full participation in the life of the community.

What, then, was signified by the 'purity'? We have noted that in 1QS 6.13ff. no mention was made of a ritual bath but that it does appear that prior ablutions were required before one could in fact touch the 'purity' (1QS 5.13).[88] We may assume that the ritual bath was used by those entering the community prior to being allowed to touch the 'purity' and that the bath and the 'purity' are not identical.

The 'purity' refers to those things which belong to the community, both individually and communally. In a general sense it includes all those solid objects susceptible to impurity together with the actual atoning life of the community. This includes a knowledge and understanding of the sect's interpretation of the purity rules; but, more specifically, it can refer to food and is frequently used in this way when a distinction is made between food and property (cf. 1QS 7.24-5). The 'purity' and the 'drink' are terms, then, that cover all the pure things that belonged to the community and which were involved in its expiatory life as a substitute for the Temple in Jerusalem. For, like the Jerusalem Temple, all objects and participants were required to be in a state of purity so as to enable the divine presence to dwell in their midst.

3. Life within the community: the maintenance of purity at Qumran

Purificatory washings at Qumran

Much interest was generated as a result of the finds at Khirbet Qumran by, among other things, references in the Scrolls to frequent washings and the discovery by archeologists of large cisterns many of which had steps leading down into them. It was hastily assumed that here was a religious group that practised baptism[89] and because of its desert location had a close connection with John the Baptist.[90] While the thesis regarding John the Baptist now receives less support it is still frequently maintained that there was at Qumran a form of initiatory baptism.

Although the water cisterns have been shown to be unexceptional[91] it cannot be denied that we find, from a reading of the Scrolls, that activities involving the use of water played a not unimportant part in the life of the community. It is necessary therefore to determine what the function of the water rites was by examining the references to the ablutions in the Scrolls.

The claims that a comparison can be made between the Qumran community and Jewish proselyte baptism and, in turn, Christian baptism are based on the assumption that the sect practised an initiation rite that involved the use of water.[92] While we need not deny that the novice, in the process of becoming a full member of the community, took part in some form of ritual involving bathing, it is not necessarily proven that that rite was a unique act and was given special significance over and above the other baths that took place regularly in the community.

This position is, however, maintained by Betz. He argues that there took place, in addition to the regular ablutions, a type of proselyte baptism whereby the novice was initiated into the sect. This he sees reflected in the section 1QS 2.11ff. The actual 'baptism', in his view, is performed as part of the annual covenant renewal ceremony.[93] The novice, according to Betz, after this first immersion cannot for a further two years share in the daily washing that takes place before the community meal (1QS 6.20; Betz obviously equates the 'drink' with the meal). Betz compares the time between what he sees as the initiatory bath at Qumran and the occasion two years later when he believes the member first takes part in the daily washing before meals with the waiting period of seven days before the newly baptized proselyte can take a full part in the religious community and eat the Passover meal (M. Pes. 8.8 and par.). The seven days in the Mishnah are required by the type of impurity that the proselyte brings with him. He is compared, by the Hillelites, to one who has contracted corpse uncleanness and must thus wait seven days before being immersed and made clean. To compare this traditional seven-day period to the two years that the novice must wait at Qumran before enjoying full communion with his colleagues is stretching things a little too far. To be sure, the waiting period of the Qumran probationer has to do with his relative state of impurity but this time is taken up in preparing him for the strict rules of purity that are upheld by the community. It is a matter of making the probationer completely reliable in terms of purity and not of merely allowing the passage of time to bring about the necessary level of purity. The two years are required at Qumran for instruction and examination and not for the lessening of the power of impurity. The seven-day period proposed for the convert in Mishnah Pesahim 8.8 stems from the biblical requirement of Numbers 19:11-13 which deals with the process of becoming pure after one has been made unclean by some kind of contact with a corpse. The two years at Qumran are not based on a biblical injunction for the acquiring of cleanness but are part of the programme of preparation whereby the probationer moves up the scale of purity relative to the full members of the community.

Furthermore we question Betz's use and understanding of the Mishnah. There is certainly no guarantee that the situation depicted in Mishnah Pesaḥim 8.8 reflects Jewish practice at the time at which the Qumran community was flourishing, and in any case Betz refers only to one side of a formalized Hillelite-Shammaite dispute. In fact it appears that on at least one occasion the Shammaite opinion was the one followed, namely, the convert was allowed to partake of the Passover meal on the day of his circumcision and baptism.[94] In any case, at Qumran we are not dealing with Gentiles but with Israelites who wish to join the community, and as Israelites they are bound by the laws of purity. It would seem only natural then, that a community concerned with maintaining a high level of purity would require as a first act of a new member joining it that he be cleansed of impurities which he has brought with him from the outside world. Furthermore, it would be inaccurate to maintain, as does Betz, that the initiatory baths of the Qumran novice had nothing to do with acquiring purity.[95]

Betz's error seems to arise from the fact that he, along with a few other scholars, prefers to see at Qumran an acknowledgement of two types of uncleanness. Betz makes a distinction between external and ritual impurity ('aüsserem Schmutz') and the impurity of the soul which, in the case of the novice, is caused by the sins and failings of his life outside the community. The latter impurity Betz connects with the initiatory washings which he purports to see in 1QS 3.4-9 and the former with the daily washings of the sect. Again we must emphasize that the Dead Sea Scrolls give no evidence for such a dichotomy between ritual and moral impurity. Both moral wrongdoing and levitical impurity cause defilement which can only be removed by washing preceded by repentance on the part of the polluted person.[96]

Rather than taking the whole section 1QS 2.19ff. as an indication that the Qumran sect practised a form of initiatory baptism that bore a resemblance to the proselyte baptism of mainstream Judaism, as known from later rabbinic sources,[97] this portion of the Manual of Discipline is to be seen as parenetic and not descriptive or even prescriptive. Its intention is to point to the necessity of repentance for those wishing to join the community and to teach the uselessness of any kind of washing unless it is preceded by a submission to God's precepts. This is also the opinion of

Gnilka, who indicates why this passage is unlikely to refer to an initiation rite as put forward by Betz:

> Die Paränese kann sich unmöglich auf eine Proselytentaufe beziehen, denn ein Initationsritus ist nicht nur ein sakraler, sondern auch ein juristischer, nur in Gegenwart von Zeugen gültiger Akt, wahrend die hier beschriebenen Waschungen gerade die Möglichkeit bieten, selbständig, privat geübt zu werden, und eben vor den Waschungen ausserhalb der Gemeinde wird gewarnt.[98]

What this passage implicitly tells us is that purity was taken seriously at Qumran and that the community saw close ties between the cleansing force of the 'spirit of holiness' and that of water. A man's sins are washed by the spirit of holiness and his flesh made clean when 'sprinkled with the purifying water and sanctified by the cleansing water' and he is 'made clean by the humble submission of his soul to all the precepts of God' (1QS 3.8).

While we would question Pryke's emphasis on the sect's preparation for the holy war at the expense of other aspects of their life, namely that which stemmed from their concern with purity and their self-understanding as a temple-like community preparing for the setting up of an eschatological Temple, his comments are appropriate at this stage: 'The washings of the sectarians, probably taken before every meal, were only a part of the ordered life of meticulous purity . . . they were not initiation ceremonies, admitting the candidate into the order, and possess such a tenuous connection with Christian baptism, that it is best forgotten.'[99]

While we find no trace of baptismal initiation we have seen that the novice after one year of supervision is admitted to the 'purity of the Many'. We would prefer to take this phrase to refer to the pure objects that belong to the community,[100] but *taharah*, as we have already seen, has been taken by some to refer to the ritual baths. This is usually done by making reference to Josephus' 'purer kind of holy water'[101] but 1QS 5.13 proves this not to be the case; for in this passage the ablutions are clearly separate and preparatory to the 'purity'. If, however, the whole question of the water rites is seen from the point of view of the centrality of the concern with purity within the community then a certain amount of clarity can be brought to the problem.

The prospective member of the community was always an Israelite ('everyone born of Israel') so that we have no question of a Gentile joining and the need for a 'proselyte baptism' as such (if such a thing existed at that time in Judaism).[102] The new member, however, did come from the outside world and brought with him the impurities of that world as well as the uncleanness brought about by sin, 'for all who transgress his word are unclean' (1QS 5.14). He was therefore in need of cleansing before he could enter this priestly community which was attempting to maintain a temple-like purity. So, like the Israelite who enters the Temple in Jerusalem, bathing is required of those who enter the Qumran community. At Qumran this is not all, for the cleansing that is carried out by water is of no avail without prior repentance: 'for they shall not be cleansed unless they turn from their wickedness' (1QS 5.14).

If some initiatory rite is to be accepted here perhaps it should be when the new member joins the community; that is, when he is 'admitted into the covenant'. It is at this point that the novice undertakes a solemn oath, before witnesses, 'to return with all his heart and soul to every commandment of the law of Moses' (1QS 5.7-10).[103] After this ceremony the new member is prepared to pass through the different levels of purity of the sect. He goes through an undetermined probationary period and then, if considered by the council of the congregation to be fit, he waits another year until he reaches the level of purity which allows him to make contact with the 'purity of the Many'.

While column six, which describes the passage of the new member through the levels of purity, makes no specific mention of immersion at this time, 1QS 5.13 would suggest that a cleansing is necessary before one may touch the 'purity' and in fact one would expect that each stage through which a novice passed on his way to full membership required similar bathing. A degree of importance would be attached to the immersion taken prior to touching the 'purity of the Many'. It would not be itself an initiation bath, since the novice is already a member by virtue of having joined the covenant. Yet because it enables him to take a fuller part from now on in the life of the community it carries with it a certain degree of importance. Rowley notes in this respect:

> that for the new member his first admission to the ablutions of the sect in the water reserved for members would have a special character. It would still not be comparable with what we mean by baptism, which is an unrepeatable rite of admission, but it would have a special character as the first of a series of ablutions, to which he was admitted only after solemn enquiry and examination. Moreover, there is not the slightest evidence that it differed in form from the ablutions that would follow.[104]

The red heifer

The ablutions to which Rowley refers would appear to be similar to the washings in 'the waters of impurity, for the removal of sin' (Num. 19:9) which were prepared from the ashes of the red heifer (Num. 19:1-10), and taken from time to time within the community to maintain the purity of the membership. There is, however, no need to suggest, as Bowman has, that the water used for the baths at Qumran was actually prepared from the ashes of the red heifer according to the rite prescribed in Numbers 19:1-10.[105] True, the preparation of the ashes from the burning of a ritually-slaughtered young cow was not tied to the sanctuary at Jerusalem but took place outside the 'camp' (Num. 19:3); but we need not identify, with Bowman, the *me niddah* of 1QS 3.9 with that 'purifying water' of Numbers 19:20, 21; 31:23 which was specially prepared from the ashes of the red heifer and which was to be sprinkled on those who had contracted corpse uncleanness. Even though 'they were engaged in upholding proper standards of Levitical purity and showing that the Jerusalem varieties were invalid',[106] there is no evidence to show that the water prepared from the ashes of the red heifer was considered necessary by the Qumran community. It is not clear, even in the biblical tradition, that these waters were always required in cases of serious uncleanness such as that caused by contact with a dead body (Lev. 22:4-6; cf. Num. 6:9-12).[107]

There seems to be no strong precedence for the Qumran community to require the waters from the red heifer sacrifice,[108] even though they were concerned to maintain priestly standards of purity. They used ordinary water and while they had specifications for it, it must not be dirty nor too shallow (CD 10.10-13);[109] in the end it was not the water that was important but the prior attitude of the man being cleansed (1QS 3.4-6; 5.13-14).

Regarding the use of the term *me niddah* and the use of *niddah* elsewhere in the Scrolls we would maintain[110] that *niddah*, which usually refers to sexual impurity, was used at Qumran to underline their belief in the seriousness of all forms of impurity. These they did not distinguish as either ritual or moral but saw impurity as deriving ultimately from some form or other of immorality.

The word *niddah*, which in its original and most usual sense refers to menstrual impurity,[111] brings together in its varied usage both ritual and moral impurity. This is because sexual impurity itself has both moral and ritual connotations. It is through sexual impurity that the community sees the Jerusalem Temple to be profaned: 'they profane the Temple because they do not observe the distinction [between clean and unclean] in accordance with the law, but lie with a woman who sees her bloody discharge' (CD 5.6, 7). 'And he [the wicked priest] lived in the ways of abomination amidst every unclean defilement [*niddah*]' (1QpHab 8.13).[112]

Throughout the Scrolls *niddah* is used in connection with impurity in general. The term describes the impurity of idols (1QS 4.5) and sexual immorality (1QS 4.10; cf. Lev. 20:21). In the *Hodayot niddah* is used to describe the basic sinfulness of mankind (1QH 1.22; 12.25; cf. 1QH 17.19; Ezra 9:11; Zech. 13:1) which only God can purify (1QH 11.11).[113] The deeds of those who reject the covenant are described as defilement (*niddah*) before God (1QS 5.19; cf. Ezek. 36:17) and the sins of men are described in the same vein in 1QS 11.14; CD 2.1; 3.17. The only reference to impurity resulting from contact with a menstruant is in CD 12.2.

Me niddah, literally 'waters of impurity', are waters for removing impurity, and the waters of the baths at Qumran were used for just such a purpose. They were not prepared from the ashes of the red heifer but were clean and deep enough to enable the impure to be immersed. The term *niddah* is used in this connection with an awareness of its association with the rite of the red heifer, but at Qumran this same term typifies and exemplifies in its varied usage the community's attitude to the sources of impurity.

The function of the ablutions

It is generally considered that washing with water at Qumran took place particularly before participation in the community meal, although this is nowhere explicitly stated in the texts. That such a washing took place would, however, be expected considering the concern with matters of purity that is manifested in the Scrolls. There is evidence to support the thesis that even before the destruction of the Temple groups of Jewish men met regularly to enjoy fellowship and eat their meals in strict levitical purity.[114] These fellowship groups (*havurot*) attempted to eat their food according to the same requirements of purity that were demanded of the priests in the Temple when they ate the Temple offerings.[115] Given the existence of this sort of tradition, we can expect to find at Qumran, with that group's concern with purity, its attitude to the Temple and its own self-understanding *vis-à-vis* the future Temple, a similar approach to the participation in meals. The nature of the meal and the role that it played will be discussed below but for now let it suffice to say that the meal was eaten in a state of purity and that for those qualified to eat the meal some form of washing was first required. One of the functions of the bathings at Qumran may have been, in fact, to prepare for the meal.[116]

It has been suggested that the frequent washings practised at Qumran were in place of the sacrifices of the Temple: 'Their insistence on their own strict concept of ritual purity (and their separatist tendencies) thus conflicted with their belief in the necessities of sacrifices. This conflict was resolved by the doctrine that the rites and purifications could serve as a substitute for the sacrificial service.'[117] They believed that the services of the Temple in Jerusalem were invalidated by the impurity of the priests there, so, concludes K. G. Kuhn, 'the Old Testament concept of sacrifice is applied to the baths'.[118] This is, however, overstating the case. There is an element of truth in saying that 'the baths . . . took on a new meaning, mediating salvation from God' but this is not, as Kuhn says, 'over and above their old meaning (to secure cultic purity)'.[119] This so-called 'cultic' purity remained an important element in the life of Qumran as it did with the rest of Judaism and the attainment of this purity was a major concern of the members of the sect. Salvation was indeed mediated by the baths, but not in the way Kuhn intimates.[120] The baths meant that the members were ensured of purity and, as the members formed the community, this meant that the community itself was pure and as such a fit dwelling place for God.

By creating an environment that was pure the baths enabled the divine to be present within the community and at the same time kept the community in a condition of constant preparedness for the re-establishment of the Temple under their auspices at the end of the present age.[121] There is no need to see the baths and the meal as a substitute for sacrifice and the direct means of salvation. The community, under its present circumstances, substituted 'prayer' and 'perfection of way' for Temple sacrifice (1QS 9.4, 5).[122] The offering of prayer required purity of the worshipper ('No man entering the house of worship shall come unclean and in need of washing' CD 11.21f.), and as moral wrong-doing resulted in impurity, 'perfection of way' (*tamin derek*)[123] within the community presupposes a pure environment and this was provided partly by the baths.

The baths were but one element in the creation of a Temple community which offered a holy precinct for the offering of praise undefiled by evil. The model was that of the Jerusalem Temple which was intended to be kept undefiled and where the priests who participated in the sacrifices kept themselves pure by bathing.[124] But the Jerusalem Temple, as a means of mediating salvation, had been invalidated by the pollution of these same priests. The priests of Qumran had now taken over the role of their Jerusalem counterparts and as a sign that they were living in the last days they prepared themselves by total immersion and not just by washing the feet and hands.[125]

The baths, then, provided the means of preparing the community for its present atoning role and for such a time when the sacrifices could be performed again in the new Temple. This hope is expressed in the War Scroll, where it is said that the priests 'shall attend at holocausts and sacrifices to prepare sweet smelling incense for the good pleasure of God, to atone for all his congregation, and to satisfy themselves perpetually before him at the table of glory' (1QM 2.5, 6).[126]

In conclusion, then, the ritual bathing that took place at Qumran was concerned entirely with preserving the purity of the community. Meals were eaten in complete purity and the purity required for the Temple in Jerusalem was taken as the model for the level of purity that was to be maintained within the community. The first bath for cleansing in which the new member partook, and we cannot be completely sure when it took place, is not to be compared to initiatory immersion provided for Gentile converts to Judaism nor, for that matter, to the baptism of John or of the Christian community. It is, rather, one of the steps[127] that purified the member in order to bring him closer to full life with the community of the 'Holy Ones' who kept a strict regime of purity in their attempt to create a suitable dwelling place for the divine.

Purity and the community meal

We have dealt briefly already with the community meal and have suggested that, although the texts do not speak of it, washing was required before participation could take place in such meals. Our concern here is with purity, so that we do not need to enter fully into the discussion of the nature of the meal which is mentioned in 1QS 6.4f. and 1QSa 2.17f.[128] We would merely note our preference for the view of van der Ploeg,[129] who sees no evidence for making the claim that the Qumran meal was considered by the community to be a sacred event in itself.[130] We maintain here that the meals eaten by the full members of Qumran were in fact ordinary meals eaten in a state of purity and that the community's understanding of itself as priestly and as living in a time of preparation for the setting up of a new Temple[131] governed the manner in which these meals were viewed.

The meals were to be taken in common (1QS 6.2), that is, food was not to be shared with outsiders or with members under the ban (1QS 5.16), and like many other activities within the community strict standards of purity were applied to the meal and to those sharing in it. Although they were not considered to be 'cultic' in the sense of 'mediating salvation', as Kuhn would have it,[132] they were no less expiatory than the praise and perfection of way and indeed the whole of life as it was lived in the community. Furthermore, the way in which they were eaten sought to re-create the conditions under which the priests ate the offerings in the Temple.

Only full members of the community who were in good standing (cf.

1QS 6.23ff.) could participate. What this meant was that those who had passed through the different levels of purity within the community and had reached the stage where they could 'touch the drink of the Many' (1QS 6.20f.), could join with the others and eat the meal. Should such a full member become unclean he would be excluded from the 'purity' and thus from the meal (1QS 6.25; 7.16, 19, 23). The demand for purity of those attending the eschatological meal which is described in 1QSa is emphasized by the fact that those who would have been unfit for ministering at the Temple are barred from joining in the meal (1QSa 2.3ff.).

The meal which is mentioned in 1QS 6.3f. reveals the prominent position of the priest within the community. It is he who is to lead in the blessing of the food and drink. In the description of the eschatological banquet in 1QSa it is the priestly messiah who leads the community in the meal and again it is the priestly figure who makes the blessing before the lay messiah of Israel (1QSa 2.11f.). Thus the meal reflects the hierarchical structure of the community in which the priests, the sons of Aaron, take precedence over the lay members.

Josephus' account of the meals of the Essenes[133] on which many commentators have leant heavily in their attempts to show the cultic and sacral function of the meals, states that the membership changed their clothing in preparation for the meal.[134] This can be compared to the procedure described in Ezekiel 44:15-19, where the special clothing of the priests who minister in the Temple is described. While we have no evidence in the Dead Sea Scrolls regarding the clothing of those partaking of the meal we do note the temple-like character that is attached to the meal.

The members drink not wine but unfermented grape juice (cf. Ezek. 44:21). This can be seen as both an attempt to follow the strictures put upon the Aaronic priesthood regarding the consumption of intoxicants while they serve in the sanctuary (Lev. 10:9) and as further evidence of the community's concern to maintain purity by having grape juice and not wine.[135]

We are not told what kind of food was consumed during the meals at Qumran, but the bones of domestic animals have been found in the area around the Qumran site. These bones appear to have originally been deposited in jars before being discarded. This has prompted some to suggest, concerning the bones, that 'ils sont certainement les reliefs des repas sacrés que prenait la communauté',[136] and that the bones were carefully preserved in such a way because of the sacred nature of the meal. Van der Ploeg in his 'very important'[137] study of the meals of the Essenes offers the ingenious suggestion that the bones, the leftovers from the ordinary meals of the community, were left buried in jars in order to protect others who may dig in the soil from their impurity. If the Qumran community considered that animal bones were conveyers of impurity (cf. Lev. 11:39; M. Hullin 9.5; 11Q Temple 51), then earthenware jars would prevent this impurity from being passed on to anyone digging in the ground where they were buried.[138]

It was van der Ploeg's article that sounded the note of caution regarding the attitude of scholars in their understanding of the meals of the Qumran community. Van der Ploeg questioned the sacredness of the meals and more especially the claim that they bore some resemblance to the Christian sacrament of the eucharist.[139] The only meals spoken of in the Scrolls are described as communal (1QS 6.2; 1QSa 2.17) and, as van der Ploeg points out, 'it would have been very strange indeed if all these had been sacred'.[140]

The special character of the meals is to be defined not by their sacredness but by the concern that they be conducted according to the highest standards of purity. Here comparisons with the pharisaic *ḥavurot* are instructive. Like those in the *ḥavurot* the meals at Qumran were taken in the highest degree of purity. They also bore a resemblance to the manner in which the priests ate the offerings in the Temple.[141] They were eaten according to the standards of purity required when food was taken in the sanctuary and like those meals which the priests ate we can be sure that the community believed that they were conducted in the presence of God.[142]

Purity and the presence of God in the community

The idea that the community had to be pure in order to enjoy God's presence was a concept that was taken over from the religion of the Temple. The Temple had always been considered the special dwelling place of God (cf. 1 Kings 8:10–13),[143] and God's continued presence there depended, to a certain extent, on the continual service of the priests who performed their duties in perfect purity (Lev. 21:17ff.). Levine puts it this way: 'The deity had made a vital concession to the Israelites by consenting to dwell amidst the impurities endemic to the human situation (Lev. 16:16). If his continued residence was to be realised, Yahweh required an extreme degree of purity (Exod. 25:8).'[144] The Qumran sect took this demand to an extreme and was unlikely to have made the same concession as the Tannaim who believed that the *Shekinah* dwelt with Israel despite sin and uncleanness;[145] but, as Abelson points out, 'wherever Shekinah and sin are antithetical the reference is either to the sin of an individual or of a section of Israelites'.[146] Qumran, of course, saw the whole of Israel, apart from itself, as deprived of the presence of God, and, as we shall see, dealt in its own way with the sin of the individual.

In the eyes of the Qumran community, the worship of the Jerusalem Temple was now invalidated, the priests had become polluted (CD 5.6, 7; 20.22; 1QS 5.19, 20) and God was, as a result, no longer present there. The community itself had now assumed the role of the dwelling place of God and its major concern, as we are attempting to show, was to maintain a high degree of purity similar to that required of the Temple.

The Qumran community saw itself as 'a house of holiness for Israel and a foundation of the holy of holies for Aaron' (1QS 8.5, 6, own translation) and as 'a dwelling place [ma'on] for the holy of holies' (1QS 8.8). Here the community is compared to the Temple and is described as being made up of Aaron and Israel, of both priestly and lay elements, which are here equated with the Holy Place and the Holy of Holies of the Temple, the central and most sacred portions.[147] *Ma'on* is used in Psalm 26:8 and 2 Chronicles 36:15 to refer to the Temple as the dwelling place of God and 1QM 12.2 speaks of the angels in God's 'holy abode' (*ma'on qodesh*) in heaven (cf. 1QSb 4.25).[148] We may therefore take the use of this word in 1QS 8.8 as another indication that the community believed that the presence of God was among them.

A further indication of the community's awareness of the divine presence is seen in the insistence that there always be someone involved in the study of Torah (1QS 6.6-8; cf. Ps. 1:2). It is a frequent theme of rabbinic literature that when Torah is being studied the *Shekinah* is present. This is elucidated in M. Aboth 3.6: 'When ten sit together and are occupied with Torah the *Shekinah* rests among them'[149] and is backed up by a scriptural reference to Psalm 82:1, which reads 'God has taken his place in the divine council [*ba'adat el*].' Both *'adat* and, in 1QM 4.9 *'adat el*, are used as self-definitions of the community and we would not be overstating the fact if we suggest that a view similar to that of the later rabbis was taken towards Torah study at Qumran. We should also add that Torah study stands as one of the major tasks that the community carried out along with prayer and perfection of way.

The members of the Qumran community believed themselves to be living in the last days of the present aeon, but to them, in a special sense, the new age had already begun.[150] They were already members of the new[151] covenant and they now constituted the basis of a new Temple. To them a passage such as Ezekiel 37:26f. pointed to what was, for them, a reality: 'I will put my sanctuary for ever in their midst. They shall live under the shelter of my dwelling' (NEB).[152]

On the edge of the change of the aeons the community formed the foundation of the new Temple, its priests were to minister in it and through the ablutions that it practised the community prepared a pure dwelling place for the divine. This nucleus of the new Temple knew that the presence of God having left the defiled Temple now dwelt with them in their pure sanctuary which they had prepared in the desert.[153]

The Scrolls speak extensively of the 'spirit of holiness' and of God's spirit (1QS 3.7; 4.21; 8.16; 1QH 7.6; 9.32; 12.12; 14.13; 16.12, CD 2.12), and although the term is used in many ways it is particularly 'a manifestation of God's grace'[154] and as such an indication that the community was aware of God's presence. The concept of God's spirit as a sign of his activity in the world is not foreign to the biblical record (cf. Ps. 51:11; Haggai 2:4, 5).[155] The ideas of ablution, God's presence and the gift of the spirit are brought together in Ezekiel 36:25-7, and this passage serves as a model for the community's view that God was present amongst them: 'I will sprinkle clean water upon you, and you shall be clean from all your uncleannesses, and from all your idols I will cleanse you. A new heart I will give you, and a new spirit I will put within you. . . . And I will put my spirit within you, and cause you to walk in my statutes and be careful to observe my ordinances.' This is expressed somewhat differently in 1QS 3.7f. where the cleansing is brought about by the spirit of holiness which prepares the way for a sprinkling of water which in turn enables one to walk perfectly in God's ways. The gift of the spirit is expressed quite fully, however, in the Hymns (1QH 7.6; 12.11f.; 17.26f.). In 1QH 16.11, 12 the holy spirit is said to purify: 'Therefore I implore Thee by the spirit which Thou hast given [me] to perfect Thy [favours] to Thy servant [for ever], purifying me by Thy Holy Spirit, and drawing near to Thee by Thy grace according to the abundance of Thy mercies.' We have seen, then, that washing is required for the maintenance of the purity which enables God's presence to dwell in the community, while at the same time man's own purification comes about by the work of the holy spirit.

Finally we note in this context that the Temple Scroll also manifests an awareness of the divine presence among the community, which identifies itself as the Israelites: 'Thus I, YHWH, dwell among the Israelites, therefore sanctify yourselves and be holy, and you shall not make among yourselves any abomination' (11Q Temple 51.7-10).

Perfection and holiness at Qumran

The notions of perfection and holiness help to define the self-understanding of the Qumran group. Both concepts are used in the community's self-designation and in descriptions of the manner in which they conducted themselves. In addition the use of the terms 'perfection' and 'holiness' reveals the community's concern with purity.

In 1QS 9.5 'perfection of way' is clearly shown to be a 'delectable free will offering' in place of the Temple sacrifice. As an adjective *tamim* has connotations of sacrifice although, in a sacrificial sense, it is used in the Bible only of animals who are unblemished and fit for use as sacrificial offerings.[156] There is no reason to doubt that the community was aware of this meaning when it referred to itself as 'the men of perfect holiness' (1QS 8.20; CD 20.2, 5, 7) who sought to live perfectly before God (1QS 1.8). Klinzing notes this connection of *tamim* with sacrifice in 1QS 9.4f. and remarks 'Dass diese Bedeutung auch hier mitschwingt, machen der Parallelismus mit dem Opferbegriff *terumah* und die einander entsprechenden Ausdrücke *lemishpat, tsedeq tamim* und *ratson* wahrscheinlich, die alle etwas über die Beschaffenheit des Opfers und seiner Darbringung aussagen.'[157]

Given this connection of *tamim* with sacrifice the concept of perfection in the Scrolls can be seen to be closely tied to the community's concern with purity. Purity is a prerequisite of perfection. 'Perfection of way' presupposes purity as did the 'perfect' sacrifices of the Temple. It is in this way that the sacrifices were replaced at Qumran. The same prerequisite for temple sacrifices was required by the community, namely purity, and from this purity stemmed perfection of way as 'a delectable free will offering'.

A man is only able to 'walk perfectly' (1QS 3.9), a phrase which frequently occurs to describe the way of life of the members (1QS 1.8; 2.2; 8.21; 1QSb 1.2; 5.22; CD 1.20-1; 2.15), after purification, and he who fails to turn towards God is considered to be 'unclean' (1QS 3.5) and cannot 'be reckoned among the perfect' (1QS 3.3). Certain misdemeanours cause a man to become unclean and to be excluded from the pure activities of the community, but when 'his way becomes perfect' (1QS 8.25) he is readmitted and is considered clean (cf. 1QS 9.2).

In the final war which must be conducted in purity (Deut. 23:10-14) the participants must be 'perfect in both body and mind' (1QM 7.5). In contrast, the lame, blind, those crippled or afflicted with bodily blemishes or smitten with bodily impurity were prevented from marching out to war (1QM 7.4, 5). Here *tamim* is clearly used in the context of purity.

The notion of perfection at Qumran is closely connected with that of 'holiness'.[158] The community, as we have seen, describes itself as 'the men of perfect holiness' (CD 20.2, 5, 7; 1QS 8.20) and as those who 'walk in perfect holiness' (CD 7.5). The members are called 'the holy ones' (1QS 5.13, 18; 8.17; 9.8) and the community itself is described variously throughout the Scrolls as 'the community of holiness' (1QS 9.2); 'a council of holiness' (1QS 5.2; 8.21); 'the holy congregation' (1QS 5.20; 1QSa 1.9, 12); 'the foundation [*sôd*] of the holy' (1QH 4.25); 'a holy thing separated from the peoples' (1Q34bis 3.11.6; *DJD*, p. 154); 'a holy people' (1QM 14.12; 4QpPs37 2.7–8); 'the people of the saints of the covenant' (1QM 12.1) and 'the saints of his people' (1QM 6.6; 16.1).[159]

Qodesh and its derivatives in the biblical tradition are applied to those places, objects and things that belong to Yahweh.[160] This includes most especially the Temple and the sanctuary in particular. 'Holiness', then, refers to those objects and persons separated from the profane of the world. As the 'saints' or 'holy ones', the members of the community see themselves as separated from the polluted world around them. They consciously maintain this separation through the stringent application of the purity laws in order to create 'a holy of holies' for Aaron and a 'house of holiness' for Israel (1QS 9.6; cf. 1QS 5.6; 8.5f.) where their sacrifice of praise and perfection of way can be offered.

4. Exclusion from the community: sin and impurity at Qumran

The Dead Sea Scrolls show without a doubt that an examination of the concept of purity cannot be carried out in the realm of the cult to the exclusion of a consideration of morality. The concern with purity that was manifested at Qumran covered both the cultic and the moral life to the extent that the two areas were intermingled and at times indistinguishable. If this in fact is the case then it is even wrong to speak of either 'cultic' or 'moral' purity as such. With reference to ancient Judaism in general Jacob Neusner finds this qualifying of purity in such a way to be problematic and he refuses to prefix the word 'purity' with 'ritual'. He writes in the foreword to his *Idea of Purity in Ancient Judaism*:

> The one translation here avoided is '*ritual* purity' and '*ritual* impurity', for attaching the adjective 'ritual' raises two problems. It first requires the definition of 'ritual' and implies a distinction between 'ritual' and something-other-than-ritual – 'substantive', 'real', or 'moral', for example. So that the distinction in our culture will carry in its wake the assertion that 'ritual' stands against 'real' or 'substantive', 'meaningful' or 'actual' as though for the ancient Israelite 'ritual impurity' were somehow not real or substantive or actual, as if it bore no material meaning. But if impurity has concrete and important effects in practical, everyday affairs, and if a concrete act ('ritual') of purification has to be undertaken to remove those effects, then it hardly constitutes something not real, substantive or actual.[161]

To illustrate that it is particularly inappropriate to put much weight on the distinction between 'ritual' and 'moral' purity at Qumran we note first that when the community laid down punishments for those members who were guilty of certain misdeeds, exclusion from the 'purity' was often a common factor. Full members of the community that sinned were regarded as unclean and were removed from the 'purity' for a time. The fact that transgression brought about uncleanness is demonstrated in 1QS 5.13, 14: 'They may not enter into the water so as to touch the Purity of the holy men, for they shall not be purified unless they turn from their evil; for all who transgress his word are unclean.' The sin of the individual, whatever it was, made him unclean[162] and thus unfit to participate fully in the life of the community.

Furthermore, it may well be, as Forkman suggests, that 'separation from the Purity is less of a punishment than a safety measure to prevent the holy premises from becoming bespotted by someone who might turn out to be unclean'.[163] This appears to be the case in CD 9.16ff., where the individual who has sinned against Torah in an offence which is punishable by death is excluded from the 'purity' if two witnesses fail to make the same testimony against him. The case is not proven against him (cf. Deut. 17:6-7), but the man is excluded from the 'purity' to prevent any chance of his polluting the community.

The Damascus Document requires the witnesses in a case against a member to be 'trustworthy', and we are reminded of the use to which this term was put in matters of purity in the context of the *havurot*.[164] The same term is used in the passage that follows. This again reflects the notion that sin makes a man unclean and in this case unfit to act as a witness: 'No man who has wilfully transgressed any commandment (*mitsvah*) shall be declared a trustworthy witness against his companion until he is purified and able to return' (CD 10.2, 3).

The passage 1QS 8.16-18 gives further indication that no distinction was made between what may be called moral and ritual purity at Qumran, but rather wrongdoing of any kind offended against the purity of the community, and steps had to be taken to protect this purity: 'And any man of the men [4QSd omits 'of the community'] within the covenant of the community who deliberately turns away from any *mitsvah* shall not touch the Purity of the men of the community and shall not know anything of their counsel until his deeds are purified from all evil so that he walks in perfection of way.'

Exclusion from the 'purity', which seems to have involved the separation of the offending individual from the pure objects and persons of the community and from the common meal, is what is prescribed here. The member is excluded for any high-handed offence against any *mitsvah*, which we take here to refer not so much to biblical commandments themselves as to rules of the community derived from Torah,[165] which would have included, in particular, rules concerning purity and which are described elsewhere as *mishpatim*. Any infringement of these rules results in the offender becoming impure in relation to the rest of the membership, which in turn requires him to pass a period of time before he can again attain the level of purity expected of full members. This passage, 1QS 8.16f., is an illustration of what is laid out in 1QS 5.13f. The man who has been excluded from the 'purity' must first turn from his wickedness (5.14) and have his deeds purified before he can be made clean by a bath and again touch the 'purity'. Similarly, the individual who has wilfully transgressed a commandment must turn from his wickedness in order to be purified and become trustworthy again.[166]

In contrast to the regulations of 1QS 8.16f., deliberate or deceitful transgression of the Torah of Moses is punished by complete expulsion from the community (1QS 8.21-4). This regulation, because of its severity, is often taken to refer to a group within the community different from that referred to in 1QS 8.4b-19,[167] or, alternatively, the increased severity is understood to be the result of conflation into the present text of 1QS of a regulation from a different period of the sect's history.[168] We prefer the first alternative; namely that the punishments described in 1QS 8.21 to 9.2 applied to the fifteen individuals, twelve laymen and three priests 'perfect in all that has been revealed from the whole Torah', that are mentioned in 1QS 8.1f. They were expected, like the priests of the Bible (Lev. 10:1f.; 21:1; Ezek. 44:13ff.), to be far more circumspect in their observance of Torah than the rest of the membership. These men, then, who 'are set apart [*badal*] as holy within the council of the men of the community' (line 11) are the same as 'the men of perfect holiness'[169] in 1QS 8.20 who are punished severely by complete exclusion for high-handed or treacherous breaking of *Torat Mose*.[170] Temporary exclusion, for two years, is prescribed for those who sin inadvertently. The remainder of 1QS 8.4b-19, then, would 'refer to ordinary members of the community'[171] who, if they deliberately transgress any *mitsvah* are excluded temporarily from the 'purity'.[172]

The issue here is the maintenance of the purity of the community. Much is expected of the fifteen men who are set apart within the community and when they sin their punishments are severe. The transgressions of all members, however, bring impurity upon both the sinners themselves and the community and exclusion, temporary or permanent, is one of the means of dealing with this pollution. The community took these measures because it saw itself as the Temple, 'a house of holiness for Israel and a foundation of the Holy of Holies for Aaron' (1QS 8.5, 6), and as such had to maintain itself in a pure condition in order to guarantee the divine presence.[173]

The question of the effect of impurity on the Temple is brought out by Jacob Milgrom. He schematizes what he calls 'the dynamic, aerial quality of biblical impurity' by showing how it pollutes the sanctuary in stages.[174] The unintentional sin of the individual pollutes the outer portions of the sanctuary, while that of the High Priest or the entire community pollutes the Holy of Holies itself.[175] Both these defilements can be purged by the blood of the purification offering (*ḥaṭṭa't*, cf. Lev. 8:15; 16:14-19). This is also brought out clearly by Baruch Levine, who writes: 'The offences of the people, individual and collective, and of the leaders of the people diminish the purity of the sanctuary. This is the sense of Lev. 16:16: ". . . Thus he shall purge the sanctuary of the impurities of the Israelites, and of their transgressions whatever their offences."'[176] Intentional, wanton and unrepentant sin, however, cannot be atoned by the usual means of purification. Such sin 'not only pollutes the outer altar and penetrates into the shrine but it pierces the veil of the holy ark and *kapporet*, the very throne of God'.[177] The sinner himself cannot make amends by the usual purification offering and is banished (Num. 15:30-1).

At Qumran, where the traditional sacrifices could not be offered,[178] unintentional transgressions of Torah pollute the community but could be atoned for, or cleansed, by 'prayer rightly offered' and 'perfection of way' (1QS 9.5; 5.6; 8.10),[179] while the unintentional sinner was excluded from the pure things of the community until he was purified by perfect behaviour (1QS 8.24, 26).

Deliberate and deceitful transgressions of Torah by the group of fifteen present a greater threat to the community, just as the unclean priest did to the Jerusalem Temple (Lev. 22:3, 9). But at Qumran no sacrifice existed to deal with it. The deliberate sinner at Qumran is expelled, and the community can have no further dealings with him or his belongings (1QS 8.21-4). The impurity suffered by the community in this case could be atoned for by the 'men of perfect holiness' who 'shall atone for guilty rebellion and for sins of unfaithfulness' (1QS 9.4).[180]

Let us now look at the more detailed regulations concerning the sort of behaviour that renders members unclean and results in their exclusion from the 'purity', as they appear in the Community Rule.

The whole matter is discussed in 1QS 6.24ff. under the heading 'these are the rules (*mishpaṭim*) by which they shall judge at a community [court of] inquiry according to the cases' (1QS 6.24).[181]

The first of these cases applies to the man who lied deliberately in matters of property. This situation is also mentioned in CD 22.3 (cf. CD 14.21), and the outcome is the same in both cases: he is excluded from the 'purity'. The Community Rule adds that he is also punished by having a quarter of his food allowance denied him.[182] Disrespectful behaviour towards a fellow member, especially one of higher rank, is punished in a similar way (1QS 6.25-7).[183]

Complete expulsion is laid down for the individual who blasphemes. Under biblical law (Lev. 24:15, 16) this was punishable by death, but here the guilty party is turned out of the community never to return. It appears that the member who cursed God brought a high degree of impurity upon the community; hence the severe sanctions put upon the offender.

Less severe from the point of view of the community is the sin of the man who has spoken against 'one of the Priests inscribed in the book' (1QS 7.2). Whoever these priests are,[184] this certainly shows the high status which the sacerdotal ministry had at Qumran, for, as a result of the offence, the culprit has to be separated from the 'purity'.[185]

Exclusion from the 'purity' is ruled for the member who unjustly and deliberately insults his companion (1QS 7.4, 5; cf. Lev. 6:1-5) and for one who speaks evil of another member (1QS 7.15, 16; cf. Lev. 19:16). Should one slander the community, complete and final exclusion is ordered (1QS 7.16, 18). The severity with which those who do harm to the community are punished gives expression to the sanctity of the community as a whole. A reference to Proverbs 11:13 may also be implied here. The saying in Proverbs reads: 'He who goes about as a talebearer [cf. Lev. 19:16] reveals secrets [*sôd*] but he who is trustworthy in spirit keeps a thing hidden.' The community was concerned that its teachings not be revealed to outsiders. In 1QH 5.24-5 we have a reference to those members of the community who 'have rebelled and have murmured around about me; they have gone as talebearers before the children of mischief concerning the secret which Thou hast hidden in me'. The secret to which the psalmist refers is probably the revealed teachings of the law which the community has received. The talebearers and murmurers, in revealing these secrets to outsiders, have as a consequence caused trouble for the community. We have, in 1QS 7.16f., a reaction by the community to these slanderers.[186] Their presence is no longer allowed to pollute the sacred precinct.

In addition, it should be noted that in the second strophe of Proverbs 11:13, the man who does not divulge a secret is described as 'trustworthy in spirit'. We have seen that the term 'trustworthy' is used in the Scrolls in the traditional sense in connection with a witness in a legal case, but we have suggested, although it does not appear in such a context, that it also describes the individual who is reliable regarding the sect's own rules, especially those concerning purity. A further quality expected of members would be to keep the knowledge of these rules, their counsel, and their judgement, to themselves (cf. 1QS 5.11, 12; 6.22, 23). Here the 'trustworthy' of Proverbs 11:13 describes that quality.

Speaking with an evil tongue had always been considered, in the tradition, in terms of impurity in the form of leprosy. The idea stemmed from the incident of Miriam and Aaron murmuring against Moses.[187] The member of the Qumran community who goes about as a talebearer, then, brings about impurity upon himself and the community and must be removed.

Apart from those who have been expelled permanently, transgressors are able to return eventually in order to take a full part in the life of the community again. 1QS 7.18–20 illustrates the case of the return of the penitent who has rebelled (or deviated, cf. M. Ab. 5.22) against the authority of the community. He has become like an outsider in that he has walked in the stubbornness of his heart (1QS 1.6; 2.14, 26; 3.3; 7.24; 9.10; CD 2.17; 3.5, 11; 8.8; 19.19, 20; 20.9; 1QH 4.15). Only time will allow him to reach the standard of purity required of a full member. For the present he is just like a new member (cf. the regulations for new members, 1QS 6.13ff.) and is treated as such and has to undertake a new 'probationary period'. After being excluded from the pure things of the community for one year and from the 'drink' for two, he may, after his case has been considered, be readmitted and continue to take a full part in the life of the community by being allowed to offer his own counsel regarding its legal traditions (*mishpaṭim*, cf. 1QS 6.22).[188]

The reception of the penitent back into the community after his apostasy can only be made if he has been a member for less than ten years. 1QS 7.22 shows the severity with which the community treats the long-standing member who leaves and lives like an outsider. Under no circumstances is he allowed to return, and it appears that he is considered to carry with him a high degree of impurity, for any member who has contact with him is similarly expelled.

The theme that runs through all the regulations in 1QS 6.24 to 7.25 is that the infringement of the rules of the community is liable to make the offending individual unclean while at the same time the community suffers from defilement because of that man's sin. This is shown by the fact that sins against the community are punished by isolating the offender from the pure things. Until he has turned from his wickedness, he cannot be cleansed by water or touch the 'purity' (1QS 5.13, 14). While on the one hand repentance is a prerequisite for his return to the full life of the community, his uncleanness prevents such a return for at least one year. This period spent in separation is in place of the purification sacrifice that would normally be made by the offender at the Jerusalem Temple. As Milgrom points out in the case of the Temple, 'his inadvertence has contaminated the sanctuary and it is his responsibility to purge it with a *ḥaṭṭa't*.'[189] These inadvertent sins pollute what the Qumran community saw as the sacred portions of the Temple which they identified as the community itself. Inadvertent sin affects the purity of the sacred precincts. The sinner cannot carry out the required sacrifice in order to cleanse the sanctuary. All that can be done under the present circumstances, until the real Temple is constituted, is to remove the offender, while the communal life of praise and perfection of way substitutes for the purification sacrifice whereby the sanctuary, for now represented by the community, is cleansed.

What this meant for the individual thus excluded from the 'purity', in practical terms, was that he had to live on the periphery of the life of the community for a while. He would not have been in complete isolation, for he was likely not to have been the only penitent, and he would have had the company of the novices who were at various stages of their probationary period and with whom he shared a similar degree of impurity. He was himself made just like a novice again and like them he had to pass through the various levels of purity and examinations before regaining his full position within the community. We can see here again the Qumran parallel with the life of the Temple. The inadvertent sinner as such was not excluded completely from the Temple. It was, in fact, expected that he would bring his offering into the Temple. The Qumran covenanter who had been excluded from the 'purity' for his sin did not need to move outside the community proper, only away from what was considered to be the Qumran parallel to the priestly court; namely the life of prayer and way of perfection which substituted for sacrifice.

The sin of the transgressor, because it threatened the purity of the community and thus the continued presence of God, meant that the sinner, for the present, could have no part in the expiatory acts that were performed in the name of Israel and Aaron. Like an unclean priest he was banned from partaking in these atoning activities of the community which were carried out by those full members, both priestly and lay, that represented the Holy Place and the Holy of Holies of the Temple.

Thus, we can see that it is inappropriate to put any weight on the distinction between 'moral' and 'ritual' purity at Qumran. If one slanders one's brother or touches a corpse, one has transgressed and is unclean, one's sin pollutes the community, and means have to be taken to cleanse the community and prevent further contamination. The religious activities of the community and the exclusion of the offender are the acts by which these two objectives were carried out.

The relationship between sin and impurity in the Dead Sea Scrolls is further exemplified by the use of *kipper*. In many cases *kipper* is used in the sense of 'cleansing from impurity'. This is the case in 1QS 11.14 where it is used in parallel to *tahar*, 'to cleanse';

> In [*be*] the greatness of His goodness
> He will pardon [*kipper*] all my sins.
> Through [*be*] His righteousness
> He will cleanse me [*tahar*] of the uncleanness [*niddah*] of man.

And in 1QH 4.37:

> Thou wilt pardon iniquity,
> and through Thy righteousness Thou wilt purify
> man of his sins.[190]

Atonement, as expressed by *kipper*,[191] is linked to purification in the mind of the Qumran community. The individual who persists in walking in the stubbornness of his heart cannot enter the community. Nothing can change this situation unless there is a change in the individual himself; 'he shall neither be purified by atonement nor cleansed by purifying waters' (1QS 3.4).

The use of *kipper* with the idea of cleansing from impurity is not strange to the biblical tradition. The verb is used to describe the cleansing rite carried out by the priest in the ritual of the *hatta't* or purification offering. Here the individual has offered the sacrifice for inadvertent sin. He is not impure himself but his sin has polluted the sanctuary and it is the task of the sacrifice to purify the altar (Lev. 8:15; 16:14–19). Milgrom, who has done much to clarify our understanding of biblical impurity, points out that 'in the context of the *hatta't*, *kipper* means "purge" and nothing else, as indicated by its synonyms *hitte* and *tihar* (e.g. Lev. 14:51f.; Ezek. 43:20, 26)'.[192]

This particular use of *kipper* frequently has men as subject and an altar or sacred place as object (cf. Lev. 16:20, 33; Ezek. 45:20). We find in the Community Rule occasions where the community or at least certain of the membership appears as the subject of the verb *kipper*. An example of this is 1QS 5.6. While there is some question as to whom the 'they' of the sentence 'they shall atone for all those in Aaron . . . and those in Israel' refers, the 'they' are surely those in the community who offer sacrifice by praise and walking in perfection of way (1QS 9.5). Their 'acceptable sacrifice' purifies the whole community, which is represented by Aaron and Israel, from the pollution it suffers through those members who go astray and through the novices who come in from the outside world in order to prepare themselves for membership.

Just as sin and uncleanness were seen to have the effect of polluting the various sections of the sanctuary in the Temple in Jerusalem[193] and threatening the continued presence of God, so the Qumran community as Temple offered its own sacrifices in its own way in order to preserve itself from pollution and to provide the divine with a suitable dwelling place.

In the other examples where the community is the atoning agent we see their expiatory role extending further afield and pointing towards the future. The community is 'to atone for the land' (1QS 8.6, 10; 9.4; 1QSa 1.3; 1QM 7.2). The land of Israel is being polluted by those who occupy it by 'guilty rebellion' and 'sins of unfaithfulness' (1QS 9.4), whose 'deeds are defilement [*niddah*] before him, and all their possessions unclean [*tame*']' (1QS 5.19, 20). In the future, however, after the destruction of the wicked (1QS 5.19) the land will need to be cleansed so that the sect, in the presence of God, may dwell in it.[194] For the present the community atones for the land. It cleanses it from the impurity caused by the sins of those who now inhabit it and will, after the final war against 'the sons of darkness', need to cleanse it from the impurity caused by the bodies of those fallen in the battle (1QM 7.2; cf. Ezek. 39:12, 14, 16). Only then can God again dwell in the land (cf. Num. 35:34) and the community take possession of the land of Israel in which the new Temple will be located.[195]

The community expected that, at the *eschaton*,

> God will then purify every deed of man with his truth; He will refine for Himself the human frame by rooting out all spirit of falsehood from the bounds of his flesh. He will cleanse him of all wicked deeds with the spirit of holiness; like purifying waters He will shed upon him the spirit of truth [to cleanse him] of all abomination and falsehood. (1QS 4.20-1)

This eschatological cleansing would involve the whole man both body and soul. There could be no purification of the body unless the soul was directed towards fulfilling God's will. This is also stressed for those who were contemplating joining the community: 'And when his flesh is sprinkled with purifying water and sanctified by cleansing water, it shall be made clean by the humble submission of his soul to all the precepts [*hoq*] of God' (1QS 3.8, 9). Thus the Qumran sect made little or no distinction between ceremonial and moral transgression; both caused the individual to become impure and in turn to pollute the community. Nor was any distinction made between inner and outer purity; the whole of man was made impure by sin.

5. Conclusions

We have shown that questions regarding purity played an important part in the life of the Qumran community. We need to ask now why this concern loomed so large. To be sure differences in the interpretation of the purity laws served to distinguish all Jewish religious groups during the time of the Second Temple[196] and these differences tended to centre around these groups' respective attitudes to the Temple. Any attempt to provide an answer to our question must stem from the observation, made particularly clearly by Gärtner and Klinzing and shown also in this study, that the Qumran community saw itself as embodying the Temple and conducted itself accordingly. At the same time it viewed the role of the Jerusalem Temple as invalidated by the sinful ways of the people who brought their offerings to it and the impurity of the priests who officiated there. The membership of Qumran, both lay and priestly, now represented the Temple. It appears that in particular they saw themselves, in their special expiatory role, as constituting the two innermost and holy areas of the Temple: the Holy Place and the Holy of Holies.

All those who enter the community to partake fully in its life must come up to the standards of purity required of those sacred precincts. The demands of purity that were made on the members were as stringent as those laid down for those who were called to minister in the Temple in Jerusalem. In particular those at Qumran were to distinguish between the sacred and the profane, the pure and the impure.

The overriding reason behind these requirements for purity was that the community, as Temple, was now the dwelling place of God and his continued presence demanded a high level of purity. In his heavenly abode God was well protected from impurity 'and this condition was to be reproduced as nearly as possible in his earthly residence'.[197] It is the Qumran angelology that clearly expresses the heavenly bond of the community. Just as the angels are present with God in heaven so they are with him in his earthly abode, the Temple. Neither God nor his angels dwell any longer in the Jerusalem Temple: they are now in the midst of the community. The community then joins in the worship of God with the angels, 'the Holy Ones', 'the Sons of Heaven' (1QS 11.7-9; 1QH 3.21, 22; 6.13; 1QM

12.1ff.) and with them share in God's presence as long as the pure surroundings prevail.

> Thou hast cleansed [*ṭahar*] a perverse spirit of
> great sin that it may stand[198] with the host
> of the Holy Ones,
> and that it may enter into community [*beyaḥad*]
> with the congregation of the Sons of Heaven. (1QH 3.21, 22)

It is the angels who signify the divine presence, and we see this explicitly stated in another verse from the *Hodayot* which echoes the previous passage:

> For Thou wilt bring Thy glorious (salvation)
> to all the men of Thy Council,
> to those who share a common lot
> with the Angels of the Face. (1QH 6.13)

The Angels of the Face are those who, according to the tradition, have direct access to the presence of God.[199] It is with these angels that the community enjoys the presence of God and the community here makes the claim that it too partakes in the same privileges as the Angels of the Face.

This bond that the community has with the angels serves as what seems to be the rationale behind their concern with purity. They are of course following the biblical injunction regarding the purity of the Temple, but in one or two places the angels in their midst provide, as it were, the reason for the strict purity. At the end of passages that list those who were banned from the community or, in the case of the War Scroll, from the battle lines, come references to the angels.

> And no man smitten with any human uncleanness shall enter the assembly of God; no man smitten with any of them shall be confirmed in his office in the congregation. No man smitten in his flesh, or paralysed in his feet or hands, or lame, or blind, or deaf, or dumb, or smitten in his flesh with a visible blemish; no old or tottery man unable to stay still in the midst of the congregation; none of these shall come to hold office among the congregation of the men of renown, for the Angels of Holiness are [with] their [congregation]. (1QSa 2.3–9)[200]

Other passages of the same type end in a similar way. 'For there shall my Holy Ones be' (4QFl 1.4); 'For the Holy Angels shall be with their hosts'

(1QM 7.6, cf. 'for the Holy Angels are among their battle lines', 4QMa),[201] and 'For the Holy Angels are in the midst of it' (4QDb).[202]

The eschatological Temple, the camps during the war against the Sons of Darkness and also the present community may admit no one who is suffering from any impurity or who is in danger of becoming impure because, it is stated, the angels are resident amidst the community. This is nothing more than saying that the rules of purity must be kept because God is present and he will only remain present as long as his dwelling place is kept pure.[203]

3

PURITY AND THE CULT IN THE LETTERS OF PAUL

1. Introduction

Much of Paul's use of purity terminology centres upon his view that the believers constitute the Temple of God and as such enjoy the presence of God in their midst. In order to retain this presence (expressed variously as 'God's Holy Spirit', 'God's Spirit', 'Christ') this Temple must remain pure. This means that its members, the individual believers, must preserve strict standards of behaviour. Immorality results in an impurity which is unacceptable to God's presence. In his correspondence with the Churches in his charge, Paul strives to uphold conduct befitting those who would wish to maintain their membership in the Temple of God. In his letters Paul reveals an awareness of the inter-connection of sinful behaviour, uncleanness and the requirements for God's continued presence among his people. He uses the language of the Jewish cult which, centred as it was upon the Temple in Jerusalem, sought to ensure that the holy precincts were not contaminated by the entrance of those considered impure (Num. 19:13; M. Kelim 1.8) nor polluted by the wanton sins of the people. The continued presence of God in the sanctuary depended on the maintenance of the purity of the sanctuary and its surroundings. Wanton sinners were excluded and the impurity with which their sins polluted the sanctuary was removed by the expiatory blood rites (Lev. 16:16f.).[1]

In keeping with this tradition Paul, who views the assembly of believers as constituting the Temple of God, urges the Christian Churches to rid themselves of the sinful and expel those guilty of gross immorality. Despite the onslaught of uncleanness brought about by these acts the purity of the Churches was sustained by the perfection and blamelessness of its members who offered themselves as acceptable sacrifices.

For Jews, in the days of the Temple, the purity laws served to maintain a suitable dwelling place for the divine in the sanctuary. For Paul the same language of purity was used to describe the conditions that were required to keep God's spirit active within the Church.

We shall observe in our study of Paul's description of the Church as

Temple and believers as both priests and sacrificial offerings that his vocabulary, imagery and thought forms which are centred around the concept
of purity are generally informed by the LXX cultic vocabulary, a fact
which supports our contention that purity was important and not peripheral in Paul's thought. However, unlike Qumran, Paul does not have a
systematically-worked-out and harmonized theory according to which the
rites of the Bible are transferred to the Christian community, nor does his
Temple have a specific physical location. The Christians are the sacrifices,
the priests who bring them, *and* constitute the Temple whose precincts
must be kept pure. In no logically-worked-out system can they be all this
at once. The point is that the language of the Temple, sacrifice and purity
pervades Paul's letters and frequently influences the way he thinks about
himself, his converts and their behaviour.

2. The Christian community as the Temple

Gärtner[2] has shown quite convincingly that one need not look to the
influences of Stoicism and the works of Philo[3] in order to understand the
manner in which Paul uses the Temple as a description of the Christian
community. It was one of Gärtner's major concerns to illustrate the resemblance of what he calls the 'temple symbolism' of the Qumran sect to
Paul's use of the Temple. While that is not our present task we do certainly
acknowledge that Paul's description of the Church as the new Temple does
'resemble the temple symbolism and overall ideology of the Qumran community'.[4] Furthermore we agree with Gärtner and hope to show in more
detail than he was able that 'The resemblance does not stop with the
assertion that the community is to be identified with the temple of God;
it extends to the emphasis on the "dwelling" of God in the community, the
holiness which results, the exhortation to purity, and finally the warning
to beware of those who threaten the life of the community.'[5] We shall
argue, in the light of this, that cultic language is used by Paul in order to
elucidate the community's self understanding and that the language of
purity permeates Paul's writing and is by no means 'occasional'.[6]

Paul expressly identifies the Christian community with the Temple of
God in 1 Corinthians 3:16-17 and 2 Corinthians 6:14 to 7:1.[7] In another
passage he appears to describe the individual believer as 'a temple of the
Holy Spirit' (1 Cor. 6:19). There may also be an allusion to the Church as
the Temple of God in 1 Corinthians 9:13-14 where Paul equates the apos-
tolate with the priest's service at the altar.

The theme of the presence of God within the believing community is
clearly demonstrated by Paul in his Corinthian correspondence. We have

seen that similar ideas were expressed in Judaism. Gärtner has pointed to
this with respect to Qumran, and it was the Pharisees who were responsible
for the extension of the purity rules of the Temple to the homes of the
laity and who held that 'one must eat his secular food, that is, ordinary,
everyday meals, in a state of purity *as if one were a Temple priest*'.[8]

1 Corinthians 3:16f. and 2 Corinthians 6:16ff.

In order to counterbalance what he sees as a schism within the Church at
Corinth (1 Cor. 3:4) Paul develops his theme of the Church as a building
after dropping his first theme of the Church as a plantation or field. Paul
is first the master builder who laid the foundation which has now been
built upon by others. In verse 11 the foundation is specified by identifying
it with Jesus Christ.[9] The section is wound up by an appeal to unity by
reminding the Corinthians that they are 'God's temple' within which there
can be no divisions: 'Do you not know [οὐκ οἴδατε] that you are God's
temple [ναὸς Θεοῦ] and that God's Spirit dwells [οἰκεῖ] in you?[10] If anyone destroys God's temple, God will destroy him. For God's temple is
holy, and that temple you are' (1 Cor. 3:16, 17).

The phrase οὐκ οἴδατε, which Paul uses elsewhere,[11] suggests either
that the statement he is about to make is self-evident or that it is a basic
tenet of his teaching which the readers have already received. In two other
places statements connecting the believers in some way to the Temple are
prefixed by this same phrase (1 Cor. 6:19; 9:13).[12]

Paul chooses the Greek ναός for Temple in 1 Corinthians 3:16, 17;
6:19 and 2 Corinthians 6:16, rather than ἱερόν. This is significant. In the
LXX ἱερόν refers to the Jerusalem Temple in general and includes all its
parts[13] and its use in the New Testament reflects this understanding.[14]
Paul uses it in 1 Corinthians 9:13[15] in what appears to be a reference to
the Temple as an institution. On the other hand the LXX has ναός as a
translation for words which refer to the most sacred parts of the Temple.
Usually ναός translates *hekal*, the Holy Place of the Temple (e.g. 1 Kings
6:17; 2 Chron. 4:22; Ezek. 8:16; 41:1ff.), occasionally *'ulam*, the porch
or vestibule (1 Chron. 28:11; 2 Chron. 8:12; 15:8; 29:7, 17) and, in Psalm
28:2, the Holy of Holies.[16]

The Church appears, then, in Paul's view, to constitute the most sacred
portions of the Temple, those areas where only the priest in a state of
purity may enter; the porch (*'ulam*), the Holy Place (*hekal*) and, for the
High Priest on the Day of Atonement, the Holy of Holies (*qodesh haqo-
dashim*).[17] It is within this ναός that God's spirit dwells. Paul is thus able
to say that 'God's Spirit dwells in you'. As the *Shekinah* dwelt within the

inner sanctuary of the Temple, so now Paul, by identifying the Temple with the Church, can say that the Church enjoys God's presence. This of course means, as Gärtner put it, 'that God's *Shekinah* no longer rests on the Jerusalem Temple, but has removed to the Church. It seems likely that Paul had the *Shekinah* in mind when writing "God's Spirit dwells in you".'[18] This is a significant point; for, as we shall see, Paul transfers much more than the indwelling of God to the Church, although this is perhaps the most important point and much follows from it: for now, the priestly office and the accompanying purity regulations are applied to the Church.

The statement in 2 Corinthians 6:16 'For we are the temple [ναός] of the living God' may, as Hurd suggests, be the first time in his Corinthian correspondence that Paul identifies the Christian community with the sanctuary.[19] It would then be to this verse that the other statements to that effect, prefixed by 'do you not know', refer. It is here that a scriptural justification is given suggesting that Paul thought that if, at this point, this important fact concerning the community as Temple was not self-evident to his readers, then there was plenty of evidence for it in the various biblical texts that he brings together in verse 16. These are not direct quotations from the LXX.[20] Paul adds ἐνοικήσω ἐν αὐτοῖς, 'I will live in them', to the verb ἐμπεριπατήσω, 'walk among', of Leviticus 26:12. This gives a far stronger sense to the idea of the indwelling of God. Following the Greek of Ezekiel 37:27 he gives the passage an eschatological tone. As with Ezekiel, who speaks of the hope of God taking up his dwelling among his people, the pronouns are changed from the second person of the original verse in Leviticus to the third.[21] Paul's scriptural citation reads: 'I will live in them and move among them, and I will be their God, and they shall be my people' (2 Cor. 6:16). For Paul this promise has now been fulfilled, the Messianic age has begun and the gift of the Spirit has been received.[22] The Church has become the people of God and God dwells among them for they are now God's Temple.

2 Corinthians 6:14ff. is full of problems, not the least being that of the question of authenticity. It has also the theme of purity running through it and will receive a more thorough examination, with this wider context in mind, below. For now we note that it gives us an example of the Pauline theme of the Church as the Temple within which God has his dwelling.

By saying that 'God's Spirit dwells within you' (1 Cor. 3:16), 'your body is a temple of the Holy Spirit within you' (1 Cor. 6:19) and, in the context of the Church as Temple, 'I will live in them' (2 Cor. 6:16), Paul is transferring the idea of God's presence from the physical Temple to the believers and the community to which they belong.[23] His use of οἰκέω 'dwell' and ἐνοικέω 'live (in)' in 2 Corinthians 6:16 finds no equivalent use in the LXX²⁴ but οἰκέω is used by Paul to express the same idea of the indwelling of the spirit in Romans 8:9, 11: 'you are in the Spirit, if the Spirit of God really dwells in you. . . . If the Spirit of him who raised Jesus from the dead dwells in you.'²⁵ In the synoptic Gospels the cognate noun οἶκος 'house' is used to refer to the sanctuary.²⁶ We may take it then that Paul is here expressing the view that God's Spirit,²⁷ which previously had its special dwelling in the sanctuary of the Jerusalem Temple, now lives within the Church, which is described by Paul as God's Temple.

A threat of destruction follows Paul's statement regarding the indwelling of the Spirit of God within the Church (1 Cor. 3:17): 'If any one destroys God's temple, God will destroy him. For God's temple is holy and that temple you [pl.] are.'²⁸ In the tradition of *lex talionis*²⁹ those who corrupt or bring down³⁰ the house of God will in turn suffer destruction by the hand of God.³¹ Paul is saying that an offence against the holiness with which the Church is imbued threatens this very holiness and with it the continued presence of God's Spirit. This cannot be tolerated. While φθείρω and, as we shall see, ὄλεθρος 'destruction' in 1 Corinthians 5:5 do not mean complete annihilation³² and exclusion from the kingdom of God, the consequences are dire enough.³³ While the exact nature of these consequences is not clear it would most certainly entail exclusion from the believing community.³⁴

1 Corinthians 6:19

While both 1 Corinthians 3:16 and 2 Corinthians 6:16 refer to the community of believers as the Temple of God ('you are God's temple [ναὸς θεοῦ ἐστε]', 'we are the temple of the living God [ναὸς θεοῦ ἐσμεν]'), 1 Corinthians 6:19 appears to indicate that the individual is also 'a temple of the Holy Spirit'. Like 1 Corinthians 3:16, the statement 'your body is a temple of the Holy Spirit' (τὸ σῶμα ὑμῶν ναὸς τοῦ ἐν ὑμῖν ἁγίου πνεύματός ἐστιν) is prefixed by οὐκ οἴδατε, which again suggests that the Corinthians were well aware of the fact of the statement that follows. Paul is using the theme of the Temple here in order to underline the fact that purity is required in the life of the Church. His particular concern in 1 Corinthians 6:12ff. is sexual immorality. He is saying that πορνεία, if allowed to persist, harms both the perfection of the Church (1 Cor. 6:15, 16) and the body of the immoral man (verse 18) who is a member of the Church.

Paul's statement in 1 Corinthians 6:19 has been taken as an example of Hellenistic influence on the thought of Paul. The indwelling of the divine within man is certainly to be found in Greek thought, and both Vielhauer³⁵ and Wenschkewitz[36] provide references to show this, but as McKelvey[37] has pointed out, there are distinct differences between the way that Paul speaks of the individual as a Temple of God's Spirit and the Stoic and Philonic view that man has God living within him. As we have noted, Paul's prime concern here is with the purity of the Church which is threatened with the defilement of sexual immorality.[38] His starting point, then, is the community, and the individual is seen as a constituent part of that community. Philo, on the other hand, would start with the individual, but for Paul this is secondary to his concern for the unity of the community.[39] Furthermore it would be foreign to Greek thought to visualize the body as God's Temple as Paul does. For Philo only the soul or mind could be seen as a suitable abode for the divine.[40] As Gärtner observes: 'It is not easy to say how the individual Christian can be called a temple in which God dwells with his Spirit.'[41]

R. Kempthorne has attempted to avoid this problem of Paul's apparent contradiction.[42] He argues that 1 Corinthians 6:19 is no different from Paul's other Temple verses (1 Cor. 3:16; 2 Cor. 6:16) and that Paul is here, as in the other places, referring to the community of believers in general, the body of Christ (1 Cor. 10:17; 12:12ff.), as the Temple of God. He takes up C. F. D. Moule's suggestion[43] that verse 18bc is in fact a dialogue. Verse 18b is taken as a Corinthian 'libertine' slogan: 'Every other sin which a man commits is outside the body.' Verse 18c is Paul's reply: 'The immoral man sins against his own body.' Paul is arguing against Corinthians who are saying, with reference to the individual who commits an immoral act with an outsider (e.g. a prostitute), that he does no harm to the body which is the Church. Paul counters this by saying that any act of immorality by a member of the Church is an offence against the Church.

This interpretation is arrived at by Kempthorne by taking the τὸ ἴδιον σῶμα, 'his own body', to refer to not just the body of the individual but to *his* body which is the Church. This requires that the word ἴδιος be used not only in 'the specific sense of "private", "personal", "individual"' but as a possessive adjective[44] which in this case is translated simply as 'his'.

Paul is saying in verse 18c that the immoral man is sinning both against his own body and the body of the Church of which he is a member. If we accept this understanding of the use of ἴδιος in verse 18 then it is possible to see the following Temple verse as no different from 1 Corinthians 3:16 or 2 Corinthians 6:16. Paul uses ναός in verse 19 in the same way as he does elsewhere. The singular τὸ σῶμα ὑμῶν fits in well with our corporate understanding of ναός here. On the other hand, an individual understanding of this verse, as Kempthorne points out,[45] would really require the plural 'your [individual] bodies', as in verse 15. Kempthorne overcomes

the difficulty one meets here of ὑμῶν qualifying 'the body' by noting that
in the context it is not hard to take ὑμῶν as a descriptive or appositional
genitive: 'the body of which you are members', especially if there has been
a corporate allusion in τὸ ἴδιον σῶμα.[46] We arrive, then, if we follow
Kempthorne's suggestion, with this rendering of 1 Corinthians 6:19: 'Do
you not know that the body to which you belong is the[47] temple of the
Holy Spirit which is within you (ἐν ὑμῖν cf. I Cor. 3.16).'

We have then, in this verse, a further example of Paul's view of the
Church as the Temple in which he emphasizes the important part that the
individual members, as part of that community, must play in keeping it
pure and holy.[48]

The 'real' Temple

It is quite usual for scholars to see Paul's use of the concept of the Temple
as merely metaphorical.[49] What they mean by this, one presumes, is that
Paul found the idea of the Temple a useful image on which to base *some*
of his teaching,[50] that the Temple is put forward just for *heuristic* purposes and that it no longer holds deep religious significance but performs,
for the present, a useful role as a metaphor. This is not the case. The concept of the Temple, for Paul, is more than just a metaphor. It may be pre-
sumed that Paul, as a Jew, fully recognized the significance of the Jerusalem Temple in his former religious life and we shall show that the temple
concept in fact remained important for him. Any attempt to diminish this
importance results in a misunderstanding of Paul's later use of the concept of the Temple as well as of the cult. In the Jewish tradition, out of
which Paul came, the Temple in Jerusalem was regarded as the special
dwelling place of God, and his continued presence was secured by the
expiatory sacrifices that were offered there.[51] These sacrifices were
required to maintain the purity of the sanctuary, which was threatened
by the defiling force of the sins of the people. In Paul's mind the Christ
event had changed all this. The community of believers now constituted
the Temple and in these eschatological times was assured of God's Spirit
and his presence among those who were 'in Christ'.

Christ's death had atoned for the sins of men (Rom. 3:22ff.; 4:24-5;
5:6-9; 1 Cor. 15:3), but also it meant that the believer in dying with
Christ had died both to the power of sin and the old aeon (Rom. 6:5-11;
Gal. 1:4).[52] The sacrifices of the Jerusalem Temple belonged to the old
aeon; these now were of no avail for, as a new being, the believer partici-
pates in the body and blood of Christ (1 Cor. 10:16f.) and with fellow
believers shares in the reality of being God's Temple.

Paul's actual attitude to the Jerusalem Temple remains somewhat ambiguous. While we can be confident that he considered the cultic life of the Jerusalem Temple to be invalid as a means of justification because of the Christ event, there is evidence that he still looked upon it as an important religious centre for Jews. We can therefore surmise that when he 'in order to win Jews . . . became as one under the law' (1 Cor. 9:20), he showed some respect to the sanctuary in Jerusalem. Not that it provided a means of salvation any more than circumcision or keeping kosher did, but for Jews it played a central role in their religious lives and, provided that no one believer would be offended or weakened in his faith, Paul would have shown deference to that tradition. In this connection we would note, with Davies, that for Paul 'Actual Temple practice is not frowned upon, but supplies a model for Christian forms. There is no hint of criticism of the priesthood or the Temple system',[53] and 'Like the sectarians at Qumran and the Pharisees themselves, Paul might well have been able to recognise the Temple in Jerusalem even while he had substituted for it the new shrine of the Church.'[54] Paul posits that the religious community of which he is now a member enjoys the presence of God and like those at Qumran would deny that the *Shekinah* still dwelt in the sanctuary at Jerusalem. The Church is the Temple and it is the Church as Temple that Paul now serves.

We shall see below that Paul depicts himself as a priest offering up a sacrifice (Rom. 15:16; cf. Phil. 2:17) and expects to be supported as such (1 Cor. 9:13f.; Phil. 4:17f.). Service to the Gospel is likened to that of the priests in the sanctuary (Rom. 14:18). Paul appeals to the community in Rome to present their bodies as a living sacrifice, holy and acceptable to God in spiritual worship and like the priests to remain apart from the profane world:[55] 'do not be conformed to this world' (Rom. 12:2). Paul's use of cultic terminology including, as it does, the concept of purity, enables him to expand on the theme of the believing community as the Temple and in so doing dispels any thought that he is using the concept of the Temple *merely* as a metaphor for the Church. Rather it is the expression of the deep reality that he felt regarding the nature of the Church.

God is with the Christian community alone, for, with the Christ event, all attempts to do God's will are invalidated unless such attempts are 'in Christ'. So now God dwells with the community of Christian believers which is made up of those who have been washed, sanctified and justified (1 Cor. 6:11). Only thus purified can they enter the Temple of God and offer their bodies as a living sacrifice. All those who find themselves in this community must then conduct themselves in such a manner as to enable God's presence to remain with them. It is with a concern that such a standard of purity will be maintained in the Churches and thus enable them to continue to enjoy God's presence that Paul directs his attention to the personal conduct of the individual members. They must not be allowed to defile the sacred precincts. If they do, steps have to be taken to restore the community's purity.

Central then for Paul in the life of the Church is his view that the community is the Temple, and as such he serves it. It is from this that his use of the concept of purity stems. Before looking more closely at the way Paul elucidates his understanding of the community by the concept of purity we must examine in more detail the ramifications of Paul's view of the community of believers as the Temple. We see this in his use of cultic language and the manner in which he sees both his and the believers' service to the Church as having priestly dimensions, while at the same time he expresses this same service in terms of a sacrificial offering.

3. Paul as priest to the Christian community

A temple requires a priest and for the Church which is the Temple Paul serves in this capacity.[56] Paul compares one aspect of his work of proclaiming the Gospel to that of the priests who serve in the sanctuary (1 Cor. 9:13,14). Like the priests, Paul argues, his work as an apostle deserves by right some material reward. His calling parallels that of 'those who are employed in the temple service' (οἱ τὰ ἱερὰ ἐργαζόμενοι) and 'those who serve at the altar' (οἱ τῷ θυσιαστηρίῳ παρεδρεύοντες)[57] and who have a 'share in the sacrificial offerings' (verse 13). As such Paul believed he could get his living by the Gospel. The οὐκ οἴδατε with which verse 13 begins heralds another self-evident fact to Paul's readers that the gifts that are offered at the Temple become the property of the priests. From the Jewish point of view this would be known from Numbers 18:8-20; but, as Conzelmann points out, 'the rule is valid, incidentally, not only for the Jews; it belongs to the basic stock of cultic regulations in general'[58] and thus has relevance to both Jewish and Gentile readers of the letter.[59]

That Paul saw himself as being involved in a priestly service to a temple is brought out by his use of ἱερόν, which refers to the Temple in a general sort of way and which can mean any temple and not specifically the Jewish one, rather than the more specific ναός which he uses elsewhere and which, as we have seen, refers to the sanctuary of the Jewish Temple. Also, the verb παρεδρεύω, which has the meaning of 'serve regularly at the altar',[60] suggests this same fact.[61] His use of θυσιαστήριον does, however, bring the context back to the milieu of the Jewish cult, for this word usually translates *mizbeaḥ* 'altar', in the LXX and is rarely to be found outside Jewish and Christian circles.[62]

David Daube has indicated that, in contemporary Judaism, Torah would have been taught without charge.[63] It is suggested, then, that Paul is not envisaging his ministry as one of teaching but views it in priestly terms. He is not so much to be compared to a rabbi teaching a 'new Torah'[64] but to a priest ministering in the new Temple and as such, by right, deserving support from that Temple. Paul is not making an apology for claiming support[65] as he would if he saw his ministry in terms of teaching, but he is emphasizing that the preaching of the Gospel is a liturgical task (cf. Rom. 1:1, 9)[66] and that those who perform it deserve the rewards that accrue from that particular service.

A far stronger indication that Paul considered himself performing a role that was in place of that enacted by the priests in the Temple in former times is given in Romans 15:16. He describes himself as being called 'to be a minister [λειτουργός] ... to the Gentiles in the priestly service [ἱερουργέω] ... so that the offering [προσφορά] of the Gentiles may be acceptable [εὐπρόσδεκτος], sanctified [ἀγιάζω] by the Holy Spirit'.

This verse is full of cultic terminology, but we concentrate here on the first half where Paul is describing himself. Paul uses the noun λειτουργός in three different places in his letters. In Romans 13:6 the usage is purely secular and refers to government officials who, in their capacity as representatives of the divine will and authority, are 'ministers of God' (λειτουργοί). In Philippians 2:25 Epaphroditus is described by Paul as 'minister to my need'. These two similar understandings of λειτουργός are reflected in this word's use in the LXX. It is most frequently used to describe a servant who acts either in a personal[67] or official[68] capacity. The corresponding word for servant, διάκονος, could also be used, as, in fact, it is, by Paul in Romans 13:4 to describe the same officials.

The same word also has a definite cultic use in the LXX. In both Isaiah 61:6[69] and Ben Sira 7.29, 30 it appears in parallel to the word 'priest' (ἱερεύς):

With all your soul fear the Lord,
and honour his priests [ἱερεύς].
With all your might love your Maker,
and do not forsake his ministers [λειτουργός]. (Sir. 7.29, 30)

Ezra 7:24 has the phrase 'servants [λειτουργός] of this house of God' and in Nehemiah 10:39 λειτουργός appears as a member of a list of cultic functionaries.[70] Paul's self description, then, as λειτουργός has unquestionable cultic connotations.[71] Paul sees his mission to the Gentiles as a priestly one. The priests who once served God in the Temple are now replaced by those who are ministers of Christ Jesus in proclaiming the Gospel. The priestly service is no longer involved with animal sacrifices but with the offering of the faith of converted believers.[72] Paul, by using the participle of the verb ἱερουργέω,[73] emphasizes this priestly role which he now firmly believes he is carrying out. In the LXX[74] the verb appears only in 4 Maccabees 7:8.[75] This is the story of the martyr priest Eleazar who went to his death refusing to pollute himself by eating the flesh of pigs. The example that he set is put forward as the ideal for those 'whose office is to serve the Law'[76] (τοὺς ἱερουργοῦντας τὸν νόμον, cf. 4 Macc. 3:20). The priestly ideal for Paul is ἱερουργοῦντα τὸ εὐαγγέλιον τοῦ θεοῦ, and he too is willing to accept a martyr's death rather than compromise his calling in pursuance of this same ideal.

Konrad Weiss remarks: 'Wie konkret Paulus seine Rolle als Priester gesehen hat, wird durch Phil. 4.17f beleuchtet.'[77] Let us examine these verses: 'Not that I seek the gift; but I seek the fruit which increases to your credit. I have received full payment, and more; I am filled, having received from Epaphroditus the gifts you sent, a fragrant offering, a sacrifice acceptable and pleasing to God' (Phil. 4:17, 18). The sacrificial references of verse 18b are widely recognized as such but verses 17 and 18a are usually taken to manifest allusions to the world of commerce.[78] A close examination of verses 17 and 18a, however, shows that allusions to the priestly cult are just as dominant, if not more so. This fact is often obscured in the translations where the terse phrases of verses 17 and 18a require some expansion in order to make sense in English. This expansion is done by further emphasis on the commercial aspect with the result that the only reference to the sacrificial cult appears to be in verse 18b. However, a reading of the Greek shows that Paul makes his first reference to the cult in verse 17a with the use of δόμα and continues in that vein through to the end of verse 18.

We shall show here the correctness of Weiss' observation and present an alternative to the exclusively monetary understanding of these verses. As minister (λειτουργός) to the Gentiles Paul would, by right, be entitled to their gifts (δόμα) but he says he would prefer 'the fruit' (καρπός). In the LXX δόμα is sometimes used to refer to gifts of a secular nature.[79] But, considering Paul's later reference to sacrifice, this is not what he has in mind here. The δόμα in verse 17 refers to those gifts that are offered in the Temple. These are the holy gifts, δόμα τῶν ἁγίων, of Exodus 28:38 that are offered to the Lord.[80] The LXX translates the Hebrew *tenuphah* 'wave offering' as 'gift' in Leviticus 7:30. In Numbers 18:11 δόμα is linked with the offering of the first fruits to read: καὶ τοῦτο ἔσται ὑμῖν ἀπαρχὴ δομάτων αὐτῶν, and refers to the gifts that are to be given to Aaron and his descendants. We note again Ben Sira's summary of the responsibilities one has towards the priests: 'Fear the Lord and honour the priest, and give him his portion, as is commanded you: the first fruits [ἀπαρχή], the guilt offering, the gift [δόσις][81] of the shoulders, the sacrifice of sanctification and the first fruits of the holy things [ἀπαρχὴν ἁγίων]'[82] (Sir. 7.31). The connection of the first fruits with the gift offering is shown up in the *Alexandrinus* version of the LXX which has καὶ τὰ δόματα ὑμῶν inserted in Deuteronomy 12:11 immediately following the reference to the first fruits. A similar insertion is made in the LXX of Leviticus 28:2.[83]

Paul describes his first Gentile converts as ἀπαρχή in Romans 16:5 and 1 Corinthians 16:15 and it is in this context that we see one dimension of his use of δόμα in Philippians 4:17. Paul's rhetorical statement, 'Not that I seek the gift', in addition to the material benefits accruing to him, refers also to what he considers to be the 'fragrant offering' that he, as a priest, is presented in the form of converts to the faith (cf. Rom. 12:1f.).

Another dimension suggested by the LXX background of δόμα points directly to the priestly function of Paul. Numbers 18:1ff. describes the duties and obligations that are laid upon Aaron and his descendants. The priesthood is given to Aaron as a gift (Num. 18:7). This does not fit in exactly to the context of what Paul is saying here but it does point again to the cultic use of δόμα. Of more relevance is Numbers 18:6 where the Levites are given to Aaron as a gift: 'And behold, I have taken your brethren the Levites from among the people of Israel; they are a gift [δόμα] to you, given to the Lord, to do the service [λειτουργεῖν τὰς λειτουργίας] of the tent of meeting [τῆς σκηνῆς τοῦ μαρτυρίου].' In the same way it may be suggested that Paul, the priest to the community, sees the new believers not only as a gift to be offered as an acceptable sacrifice in the Temple of the Church but also as a gift to him as co-ministers with him (cf. Phil. 4:15; 2:30) in the priestly service of the Gospel. Just as the Levites who worked with the descendants of Aaron in the Temple were a gift to Aaron so are the converts to the Church at Philippi Paul's gift.

A further occurrence of δόμα in a cultic setting gives us an understanding of Paul's use of the word 'fruit'. Numbers 28:2 provides an interesting parallel with Philippians 4:17f. Let us compare the Hebrew of Numbers 28:2 with the Greek of the LXX:

MT *et qorbani laḥmi le'ishai reaḥ niḥoḥi*
LXX τὰ δῶρα μου δόματά μου καρπώματά μου εἰς ὀσμὴν εὐωδίας

The LXX omits the reference to bread, *lehem*, and inserts 'my gift' after δῶρα, *qorban*, and thus avoids the anthropomorphic 'bread of God'.[84]

In both Numbers and Philippians we have δόμα and ὀσμὴν εὐωδίας, 'pleasing odour'. Furthermore one can perhaps detect a play on words here with Paul's καρπός, 'fruit' and the κάρπωμα, 'burnt offerings', of Numbers 28:2.[85] While this latter claim may be somewhat tendentious, δόμα has clearly been shown to have predominantly cultic connotations in the LXX and its use here in Paul requires it to be understood in a similar way.

We take the 'fruit' of verse 17 to refer to the offering of the believers, particularly the Gentile converts who as a result of Paul's ministry have been brought into the Church (cf. Rom. 1:13; Phil. 1:22). The use of the term καρπός for the Gentiles who are now being brought into the community of the believers (Rom. 3:21f., Gal. 3:25f.) is particularly fitting and belongs to the cultic scenario of these verses. The Gentiles are like the fruit in the Promised Land, which for a set time is forbidden to the Israelites and, according to Leviticus 19:23 (LXX), until it is thoroughly cleansed of its impurity is not to be used.[86] In the fourth year all the fruit is considered holy, and is given as a gift to the priests[87] and is worthy of praise to the Lord. It is of particular interest to note that the Hebrew of verse 23 describes the fruit of the trees as 'uncircumcised' and thus not to be eaten until the proper time. This time has come, for Paul, with the Christ event. The fruit, the Gentile believers, can be offered. By Christ's death it has been cleansed and, although literally uncircumcised, is holy to the Lord.[88]

Likewise the first of the fruit, ἡ ἀπαρχὴ τῶν καρπῶν (Deut. 26:2 LXX), is to be brought to the sanctuary and given to the priest. So the members of the Church are called ἅγιοι (Phil. 1:1) and Paul thanks God for the 'partnership in the Gospel' which he shares with them. The Gentile converts are ἀπαρχή in Romans 16:5, 1 Corinthians 16:15 and in Philippians 4:16f. and are the 'fruit' which are brought and received by Paul into the community, the place where God dwells (cf. Deut. 26:2).

The LXX background to the verb πλεονάζω (Phil. 4:17) allows for it too to have a connection with the cult. We have already alluded to the gift of the Levites to Aaron (Num. 18:6) and compared it to the gift of the converts to Paul. In Numbers 3:44ff. we find πλεονάζω used in a context which deals with the excess of the firstborn, who had been redeemed by the gift of the Levites, over the actual number of Levites who had been offered to the service of God. To make up for the imbalance a gift of money was given to Aaron and his sons. 'So Moses took the redemption money from those who were over and above [πλεοναζόντων] those redeemed by the Levites' (Num. 3:49). Here we again find a term which does not require us to confine it to a secular context[89] but which leads us towards a cultic understanding of Philippians 4:17f.

A further parallel to the idea of the priest receiving gifts in abundance is found in Isaiah 61:6:

> but you shall be called the priests [ἰερεύς] of the Lord,
> men shall speak of you as the ministers [λειτουργός] of our God;
> you shall eat the wealth of the nations [ἔθνος],
> and in their riches [πλοῦτος][90] you shall glory.

While we accept the translation of εἰς λόγον ὑμῶν (Phil. 4:17) as 'to your credit' we question the necessity of taking the 'credit' here in purely commercial terms. The verb λογίζομαι, to which λόγος is related[91] is used in the LXX to denote the crediting of sacrificial offerings on behalf of the donors (Num. 18:27, 30; cf. Lev. 7:18), and the computing, by the priest, of the value of certain houses and fields during the Jubilee year. The value of the field, for instance, in the Jubliee year is given 'as a holy thing to the Lord' (Lev. 27:23).[92] We may compare what we read in Leviticus 27:21–23 with Paul's description of the Church as God's field (γεώργιον) in 1 Corinthians 3:9 and notice how fitting that imagery is in the context of Philippians 4:17f. The law of Jubilees states that the field, ὁ ἀγρός, which when released in the Jubilee year became 'holy to the Lord', is possessed by the priest and is regarded as if it were set apart, ὥσπερ ἡ γῆ ἡ ἀφωρισμένη (verse 21). Paul makes no direct reference to the concept of the Jubilee (ἄφεσις, the usual Greek word for the year of release, is lacking in Paul) but the view that Christ's coming had heralded a time of release became current in the early Church.[93] The teaching regarding the Jubilee year seems to lie behind Paul's view of the Church; not only is it God's field, it is holy, set apart (Rom. 12:2), and is Paul's gift. It is this gift, the Gentile converts of the Church, which is the credit (λόγος) to those of the Philippian community.

Paul reiterates that he has received these gifts in abundance and goes on to say that he has received them by the hand of Epaphroditus (δεξάμενος παρὰ Ἐπαφροδίτου τὰ παρ' ὑμῶν, Phil. 4:18) and he calls these gifts 'a fragrant offering, a sacrifice acceptable and pleasing to God'.[94] Epaphroditus is Paul's fellow worker, a minister (λειτουργός) to Paul's need (χρεία) (Phil. 2:25) and was active among the Philippians. At one time he had become ill and close to death in attempting to make up what was seen as the lack of 'service' (λειτουργία) on the part of the Philippians (Phil. 2:30). In Philippians 4:17f. this deficiency has been rectified, the 'need' of Philippians 2:25 has been provided (cf. Phil. 4:16) through (παρά) the priestly service of Epaphroditus.[95] This 'need' is described now, by Paul, as a gift, and comes from the Philippians in the form of the sacrificial offering (λειτουργία) of their faith (cf. Phil. 2:17).

Apart from the obvious reference to the sacrifice in verse 18 there is one further cultic term which is generally overlooked. Paul's δεξάμενος, 'having received', comes from the verb δέχομαι and has a cultic background in the LXX.[96] Perhaps the most significant for our purposes is the use of the verb in the *Codex Alexandrinus* version of Exodus 29:25 where δέχομαι translates the Hebrew *laqah*.[97] Exodus 29:25 deals with the wave offering in the ceremony of the consecration of the priests. In verse 24 the offerings are put in the hands of Aaron and his sons who then 'wave them for a wave offering before the Lord' (RSV). The LXX translates wave offering (*tenuphah*) as ἀφόρισμα, i.e. something set apart and appointed for God. Now, Paul sees himself as one set apart (ἀφορισμένος) for the Gospel of God (Rom. 1:1) and as one whom God has set apart (ἀφορίσας, Gal. 1:15); and in 2 Corinthians 6:17, citing Isaiah 52:11, he calls on believers to separate themselves (ἀφορίσθητε) from the world. In Exodus 29:25 LXX (A version) Moses receives this ἀφόρισμα and burns it with the burnt offering as a 'pleasing odour' (ὀσμὴν εὐωδίας) before the Lord: 'it is an offering by fire to the Lord [κάρπωμά ἐστιν κυρίῳ]'.[98]

This brings us to Paul's description of what he has received as a 'fragrant offering, a sacrifice acceptable and pleasing to God'. The phrase 'fragrant offering' is the same ὀσμὴ εὐωδίας which we see used frequently in the LXX and in the Hebrew Bible for *reah nihoah* as a description of the odour that ascends to God from the sacrifices of the Temple. Of the many occurrences of ὀσμὴ εὐωδίας[99] one stands out as being particularly relevant for our purposes. It appears in Ezekiel 20:41: 'For ... there I will accept them, and there I will require your contributions and the choicest of your gifts, with all your sacred offerings. As a pleasing odour, I will accept you, when I bring you out from the peoples' (Ezek. 20:40, 41).

Here the prophet speaks of God's acceptance of Israel who will serve him (δουλεύσουσιν)[100] and be to him as a pleasing odour. Here the people themselves are depicted as the offering, just as in the letter to the Philippians, but God also requires their material offerings in the form of τὰς ἀπαρχὰς ὑμῶν καὶ τὰς ἀπαρχὰς τῶν ἀφορισμῶν, literally: 'your first fruits and your set-apart first fruits'.[101]

If we understand the gift which Paul receives as being not only something tangible but also the faith of the new converts as well as the converts themselves that have been brought into the Church as a result of the 'good work' (Phil. 1:6) of the Philippians, namely their service (λειτουργία, Phil. 2:30) of proclaiming the Gospel, we see the appropriateness of Paul's language here. Like Paul himself the members of the Church are set apart (ἀφορίζω) from the world and dedicated to God. They are, in fact, like the wave offering which the LXX describes also by the use of ἀφορίζω, ἀφόρισμα. They are shared by both God and the 'priest'.[102]

Paul is not speaking here merely of material rewards for his labours. It would be going too far, however, to rule them out entirely; for Paul speaks of the support that, like that given to the priests, is due to those who preach the Gospel (1 Cor. 9:13f.). To Paul, then, are brought the gifts as they were to the priests in the Temple, and the gift that he welcomes most is the fruit that is brought in all its perfection in the form of new members of the Church. It is this 'fruit' (καρπός) which like the burnt offering (κάρπωμα) is a pleasing odour to God.

We have in Philippians 4:17 and 18 an abundance of cultic terminology which serves to depict Paul as (in Weiss' words) 'Priester der christlicher Kultgemeinde'.[103] He receives gifts like a priest which he then offers up as an acceptable and pleasing sacrifice. We are hard put to deny that the Philippian Church provided material support[104] but this, and the fact that the Philippians have carried out their ministry in providing Paul with new converts, enables Paul to see himself in the priestly role in the service of the Church which is the Temple of God. Offerings are brought to this Temple, but these are not the bloody sacrifices of the old Temple. Instead there takes place a 'spiritual sacrifice'.[105] But even this sacrifice requires that the offering be both 'acceptable' and 'pleasing' as were the animal sacrifices of old. The language of these verses in Philippians sums up this particular understanding of sacrifice. The priest receives the gift and the fruit which are set aside and dedicated to God. The intangible offerings, those of the new believers, are like the burnt offerings and are devoted to God while the tangible are given to the priest for his physical support.

So Paul, in thanking the Philippians for their gift in Philippians 4:10-23, rejoices that they have provided for his need. He expresses some reserve in asking and receiving material aid: 'Not that I complain of want' (verse 11), 'Not that I seek the gift' (verse 17); but of the gift of themselves which he considers to be of far greater value he is explicit and in so doing uses the language of the sanctuary. This language is neither metaphorical nor allegorical.[106] Now that the Jerusalem Temple has been replaced as the dwelling place of God the offerings of the Christians are real enough for Paul and require certain conditions now that they are taking place in God's Temple, the Church.

These conditions are described in the language of the old cult. One of these conditions, as we shall see, is the purity that is required of those who minister within it and make their offerings there. Paul himself is set apart for this service to the Gospel (Rom. 1:1, 9)[107] and his fellow workers such as Epaphroditus are ministers (λειτουργός) also (Phil. 2:15). So the offering is made, to be sure, not with the ritual and in the surroundings of the Jerusalem Temple, for these things no longer have salvific value. But still God requires and receives this offering and although it is of a different dimension it is no less real both in its offering and in its effect. It is required by God and in return Paul states: 'my God will supply every need of yours' (Phil. 4:19).[108]

Finally, to conclude our examination of Paul's priestly role in serving the Christian community, we take a close look at three passages in which Paul appears to be alluding to his sacerdotal role in the Church.

Paul introduces himself to the Roman Church (Rom. 1:1) by describing himself as 'a servant [δοῦλος] of Jesus Christ called [κλητός] to be an apostle, set apart [ἀφωρισμένος] for the gospel of God'. Given the use of δοῦλος and δουλεύω for cultic service in the LXX Weiss asks 'ob sie nicht auch bei Paulus in entsprechenden Zusammenhangen einen kultischen Beiklang haben.'[109] While δουλεύω is used predominantly in the LXX in a secular context it also occurs in sentences with God as the object.[110] Furthermore it is used occasionally within a specifically cultic context. In 2 Chronicles 30:8 it is reported that Hezekiah called the people to come to the sanctuary and serve the Lord, and Manasseh after restoring the altar in Jerusalem commanded Judah 'to serve . . . the God of Israel' (2 Chron. 33:16).[111]

While in most cases δουλεύω translates the MT *'avad*, Isaiah 56:6 is one of the exceptions. This familiar passage tells of the foreigners who will minister [*sharat*] the way Israelites do and whose burnt offerings will be accepted at the Lord's altar. (A theme not irrelevant to our understanding of Paul.) In the LXX the foreigners are to serve (δουλεύω) in what is clearly meant to be a cultic manner: 'And the foreigners who join themselves to the Lord, to minister [δουλεύω] to him, to love the name of the Lord, and to be his servants [εἶναι αὐτῷ εἰς δούλους καὶ δούλας] . . . their burnt offerings and their sacrifices [θυσίαι] will be accepted [δεκταί][112] on my altar [θυσιαστήριον]' (Isa. 56:6, 7).

We have already noted some of the verbal parallels between Philippians 4:17f. and Ezekiel 20:40, 41 (LXX) and we return to the latter verses once more to see that the verb δουλεύω, which translates *'avad*, is used again in a cultic context. Here the prophet calls upon the 'house of Israel' to 'serve' God for ever,[113] bring their gifts and offerings and be accepted themselves as a pleasing odour (ὀσμὴ εὐωδίας).

In the LXX the words δοῦλος, δουλεύω then, apart from their secular use, are applied to prophets or certain individuals (e.g. Jacob, Isaac, David) while Isaiah 56:6 envisages non-Jews who will bring their offerings to the Temple and be the Lord's servants.[114] There may be a suggestion, then, of priestly service when Paul uses δοῦλος with ἀφορίζω, 'set apart' in Romans 1:1.[115]

In the contrast that Paul sets up in 1 Thessalonians 1:9 between the worship of idols and the service of 'a true and living God' his use of δουλεύω as an antithetic parallel to the cult of idols suggests that he views this service to God as cultic.[116] The Thessalonians have switched their allegiance from the idols to which they offered sacrifice to the God whom they now serve by offering themselves. They are now made holy by God himself and in spirit, soul and body are kept sound and blameless (ὁλό-κληρος καὶ ἄμεμπτος) just like sacrificial offerings.[117]

One other use of δουλεύω by Paul is worthy of mention. This comes in Romans 14:18: 'he who thus serves Christ is acceptable [εὐάρεστος][118] to God and approved by men'. By a life of 'righteousness and peace and joy in the Holy Spirit' (verse 17), the believer serves Christ and presents himself to God as a worthy offering acceptable as a sacrifice (cf. Rom. 12:1f.; Phil. 4:18).

The verb ἀφορίζω is used in Numbers 8:11 in connection with Aaron's designation of the Levites as a gift to God from the people of Israel to do the work of the Lord[119] and in Leviticus 20:26 of God's separating Israel from the other nations so that they may be his own possession. It is also used of the distinction that has to be made between the clean and the unclean in Leviticus 20:25.[120] We note with Cranfield[121] that ἀφορίζω is frequently used in connection with ἅγιος or ἁγιάζω. In Leviticus 20:25 the holiness of Israel goes hand in hand with its separation from the nations and Ezekiel 45:4 has οἶκος ἀφορισμένος used for *miqdash*, sanctuary.

In the case of ἀφορίζω in Romans 1:1 Paul describes himself as being set apart for the Gospel and he differentiates between the profane and the holy service he is called upon to perform. He is both separated from the unclean world and dedicated to holy office.[122]

The manner in which Paul performs this office is described by his use of the verb λατρεύω in Romans 1:9. This verb is used throughout the LXX for the service which man renders to the divine. Sometimes it is used with reference to the worship of 'other gods' but generally it is in the context of the cultic ministry to the God of Israel (e.g. Exod. 3:12; 10:7ff. etc.) and occasionally, more specifically, the sacrificial ministry in Numbers 16:9, where it translates *sharat*, and in Joshua 22:27b, which reads: 'that we do perform the service of the Lord [λατρεύειν λατρείαν κυρίῳ] in his presence and with our burnt offerings [καρπώμασιν] and sacrifices and peace offerings [θυσίαις τῶν σωτηρίων]'. The Joshua passage refers to the altar which the Transjordanian tribes erected 'not for burnt offering nor for sacrifice but to be a witness [μαρτυρία]'[123] to future generations that they indeed did have a 'portion in the Lord [μερὶς κυρίου]'. The Church to which Paul ministers has no burnt offering but it too knows that God dwells with it (cf. Joshua 22:31) and it has the assurance that it receives the inheritance (κληρονομία, cf. Rom. 4:17; Gal. 4:7),[124] for in its own way, with Paul as its priestly minister, it performs the service of the Lord with its own 'burnt offerings and sacrifices and peace offerings' (cf. Rom. 12:1; 15:16; Phil. 4:18).[125]

Paul's phrase ἐν τῷ πνεύματί μου (Rom. 1:9) should not be taken as an attempt to spiritualize his work as servant of God and thus deprive it of its cultic context. We should understand Paul's use of 'spirit' here as a living and present reality which enables him to accomplish his ministry.[126]

4. The believer as both sacrificial offering and priest

Having shown that Paul frequently depicts himself as priest to the Christian community by his use of language that, within the LXX, is explicitly cultic, we turn to examine the way in which he sees the Christians themselves both as 'living sacrifices' offered to God within the Temple which is now represented by the Church and as priests themselves.

Perhaps the best example of this first view is expressed by Paul in Romans 12:1, 2:

> I appeal to you therefore, brethren, by the mercies of God, to present [παρίστημι] your bodies as a living sacrifice [θυσία], holy [ἅγιος] and acceptable [εὐάρεστος][127] to God, which is your spiritual worship [λογικὴν λατρείαν]. Do not be conformed [συσχηματίζω] to this world but be transformed by the renewal of your mind, that you may prove what is the will of God, what is good and acceptable [εὐάρεστος] and perfect [τέλειος].

As Sanday and Headlam point out παρίστημι is 'a tech. term (although not in the O.T.) for presenting a sacrifice'[128] but the verb is closely related to παριστάνω[129] which Paul uses in Romans 6:13 ('but yield yourselves to God') and which itself has a cultic background in the LXX. In the LXX, however, παριστάνω is never used in the way Paul uses it in Romans 6:13. It usually translates, in a cultic setting, *'amad* in such phrases as: 'to stand ['amad] before the congregation to minister to them' (Num. 16:9). But in Deuteronomy 21:5 it refers to the Levites whom God had chosen 'to minister to him' and translates *sharat*. Nevertheless, despite Paul's individual use of παρίστημι, the context clearly shows that the verb describes the offering that is to be made of the bodies of those Christians in Rome as a living sacrifice.

Θυσία is the usual word for sacrifice in the LXX, and the sacrifice of which Paul is speaking differs here from that of the Jewish cult in that the offering is living and involves no slaughter. It is similar to sacrifices offered in Judaism in that the offering is called upon to be both 'holy' and 'acceptable'.[130] Ἅγιος has a wide and varied use in Paul's letters. It is significant that it is usually Paul's habit to call all those to whom he writes 'the holy ones' (RSV has 'saints') (Rom. 1:7; 1 Cor. 1:2; 2 Cor. 1:1; Phil. 1:1; 2 Thess. 1:10), a suitable title for those who are called upon in Romans 12:1 to become sacrificial offerings. Israel was called upon to be holy (Lev. 11:44, 45; 20:26; Deut. 7:6; 14:2, 21) and the sacrifices in the Temple were 'the holy things' (Lev. 21:22; 22:6, 7, 12, 13f.; Deut. 12:26; Lev. 27:9, 10, 14 [house], 21 [field]; Num. 6:20; cf. Num. 16:3). Paul uses this understanding of holiness to bring together the idea of those called to be 'holy ones' who are in the Church gathered together to enjoy God's presence[131] with the view that those same holy ones offer themselves as a gift offering[132] through him[133] to God.

The offering that Paul requires the Romans to make is described as a λογικὴ λατρεία. It is usual to translate λογικός as 'spiritual' in the sense of 'metaphorical' as opposed to 'literal'. Thus the sacrifices of the Christians do not have the reality of the sacrifices of Judaism but are on a higher spiritual plane. This is true to a certain extent but we must not overlook λογικός as meaning 'rational'[134] as well as 'spiritual'. This would mean that Paul is saying that these sacrifices are now more fitting in the light of the Christ event and the life of the Spirit in which believers now live. The sacrifices of the Temple in Jerusalem are now of no use. The offerings made by the Christians are the only ones God will accept. It is in this sense that they are 'rational': in the light of the aeon in which believers now live these sacrifices are the only ones that, as it were, make sense.

Paul uses λατρεία only here and in Romans 9:4. In Romans 9:4 he laments the unbelief of Israel and the loss he feels now that they have forfeited their privileged position before God which they previously had by virtue of their birth. Among the privileges that were granted them was 'the worship', or 'the temple service'[135] which has now been transformed and inherited by those who are 'children of the promise' (Rom. 9:8), the Christian fellowship which is made up of both Jew and Greek. Their worship involves the offering of themselves; and in Romans 12:1 Paul uses the same term λατρεία, for now the Church, as the Temple of God, performs the sacrificial worship.[136]

Paul pursues the idea of sacrificial worship in the next verse. He calls upon the Roman Church not to conform itself to this world but to be changed so that their minds too be made as a suitable offering. The συσχηματίζω of verse 2[137] continues the theme of holiness and separateness which is required both of the offerings made to God and of those who actually make the offering. In this case the offerer and the offering are identical. In the same way as Paul sees himself as set apart for the service of the Gospel (we have already seen the sacrificial setting of this idea) so must the believer, in setting forth himself as a living sacrifice, be distinct from the world around him so that his whole being, both mind and body, may be made a suitable offering, holy, acceptable, good and perfect.[138]

We have already noted that Paul, in Romans 15:16, describes himself as being involved in the priestly service of God's Gospel. He continues in this same verse to show that his priestly role is in order that (ἵνα) 'the offering [προσφορά] of the Gentiles may be acceptable [εὐπρόσδεκτος], sanctified [ἁγιάζω] by the Holy Spirit'.

Paul's word for offering, προσφορά, although not frequent, is explicitly used for a sacrificial offering (e.g. Ps. 40:6; 1 Esd. 5:52; cf. 1 Kings 7:48) although as a rule the LXX prefers to translate the MT *minḥah* by θυσία or δῶρον. An interesting use is made of προσφορά in Ben Sira. The word always occurs in a cultic setting and in this context illustrates some useful parallels to Paul's use in Romans:

> The offering [προσφορά] of a righteous man [δίκαιος] anoints the altar,
> and its pleasing odour [εὐωδία] rises before the Most High.[139]
>
>   (Ben Sira 35.6)

> ... all the sons of Aaron in their splendour with the Lord's offering [προσφορά] in their hands, before the whole congregation of Israel [ἐκκλησίας Ἰσραηλ].
> Finishing the service [λειτουργός] at the altars, and arranging the offering [προσφορά] to the Most High, the Almighty,
> he reached out his hand to the cup and poured a libation[140] of the blood of the grape ... a pleasing odour [ὀσμὴν εὐωδίας] to the Most High, the King of all. (Ben Sira 50.13–15)

The use of προσφορά firmly places it in the cultic vocabulary of Judaism. Paul uses it in Romans 15:16 for the sacrificial offering of the Gentiles, the same idea that he expresses in Romans 12:1f. and Philippians 4:17f. and alludes to elsewhere.[141]

In contrast to προσφορά, εὐπρόσδεκτος is not found in the LXX. Paul uses it here and in Romans 15:31, 2 Corinthians 6:2, 8:12, but only

Romans 15:31 may have any cultic connection.[142] The word is, however, clearly related to δεκτός[143] which Paul uses in Philippians 4:18 and which in the LXX refers to the sacrifices.[144]

This acceptable offering of the Gentiles is to be sanctified by the Holy Spirit. Paul uses the verb ἁγιάζω elsewhere to describe the preparation one undergoes prior to entering the fellowship of the Church. The members of the Corinthian Church are 'sanctified in Christ Jesus' and become 'the holy ones' (1 Cor. 1:2). Later in the same letter Paul reminds the Corinthians that they were washed, sanctified and justified (1 Cor. 6:11). In order to enable the offspring of couples where one spouse is an unbeliever to be considered holy and acceptable to the Church Paul rules that the unbelieving spouse is sanctified through the belief of the marriage partner (1 Cor. 7:14). While the concern of Paul and the Corinthians appears to be centred around the requirements of Church membership the Church in Thessalonica was caught up with speculations about the *eschaton*. In 1 Thessalonians Paul lessens this speculation somewhat but prays that at the *parousia* God may sanctify them 'wholly' (ὁλοτελής) and that their 'spirit and soul and body be kept sound [ὁλόκληρος] and blameless [ἄμεμπτος] at the coming of our Lord Jesus Christ' (1 Thess. 5:23). Just as those who enter the Church must be purified and made holy,[145] so those who are eagerly awaiting the end must likewise be made holy and be like the sacrificial offering, sound and blameless at that time.

In the LXX ἁγιάζω is used on various levels in a cultic setting. The first-born (Exod. 13:2) and, then, in their place, the Levites (Num. 3:12–13; 8:17–18) are sanctified and set apart for God. The Aaronic priesthood is sanctified (Exod. 29:1, 44; 30:30; Lev. 8:30) and the offerings (ἀπαρχή) brought to the priests are also described as 'sanctified things' (ἁγιαζόμενα, Num. 5:9; 18:8, 29). Israel itself, in Ezekiel's prophecy, is to be made holy in the sight of the nations (Ezek. 20:41) and in particular when God dwells in their midst (Ezek. 37:28). This background is reflected in Paul's thought. We have noted that Paul sees himself as the priest who, set apart for the service of the Gospel, is in receipt of the first converts (ἀπαρχή) and accepts, in God's name, the holy ones (ἅγιοι) as a sacrifice. The Gentiles, in offering themselves, must be, like the Levites who serve in the Temple, purified and sanctified and set apart for God.[146] The Church now proceeds with the awareness that as the Temple of God it enjoys God's presence and as such is made holy.

We have already seen that it is unnecessary to confine our understanding of Philippians 4:17 to material gifts sent to Paul. We have argued that these verses, given the preponderance of cultic terminology, can be seen to refer to the same offering that Paul mentions in Romans 12:1f. and

15:16: the offering by the new converts of themselves. This offering, which comes about through the (priestly) ministry of Epaphroditus, is presented to Paul who, as a priest, accepts the gift which like the burnt offering of the Jerusalem Temple is a fragrant offering, which is then further described as a sacrifice, acceptable and pleasing to God.

Elsewhere in Philippians Paul refers to the sacrificial offering of the faith of those who are in the Church. In what may be a reference to what he sees as his own fate[147] Paul says in Philippians 2:17 'even if I am to be poured out as a libation in addition to [ἐπί] [148] the sacrifice and priestly service [λειτουργία] of your faith' (my translation). Paul has already called upon the Philippians to be blameless (ἄμεμπτος) and innocent (ἀκέραιος) and without blemish (ἄμωμος) (all cultic terms to describe the cultic offering) in contrast to the 'crooked and perverse generation' among whom they live (verse 15). As such they are suitable as a sacrificial offering to God and, in verse 17, this is how Paul depicts them, combining, at the same time, the view that they are also priests.[149] It is their faith which is the source of both this offering and their priesthood.[150] The offering is that of themselves and is made by themselves acting in faith. This is their worship by which they glorify God (cf. 1 Cor. 6:20).

Paul uses the verb λατρεύω, which is usually translated 'worship'; but this has to be clearly defined, for λατρεύω is used in the LXX for 'to serve' or 'to worship' cultically and especially by sacrifice.[151] In Philippians 3:3 Paul is contrasting those who seek to have Gentile converts circumcised with those who 'are the true circumcision, who worship [λατρεύω] God in spirit, and glory [καυχώμενος] in Christ Jesus'. Paul's use of λατρεύω here shows him again emphasizing the specifically sacrificial worship that Christians perform.

We noted in our study of Paul's view of the Church as the Temple of God that Paul reminds the Corinthians of this fact in 1 Corinthians 6:19. We were led to understand Paul, following Kempthorne's suggestion, as saying two things here: both the individual in his own body and the Church as the body of Christ were the Temple of the Holy Spirit. God's presence is experienced both within the believing community and within the individual believer. Paul follows his statement to this effect by exhorting the Corinthians: 'So glorify [δοξάσατε] God in your body [ἐν τῷ σώματι]' (1 Cor. 6:20).[152] This sentence, then, gives weight to the argument that, in verse 19, Paul is referring to the 'body' of which the individual is a member. He uses the plural imperative for the verb and has 'body' in the dative singular. The Corinthians are to glorify God in their body which is the Church.

By his use of the verb 'to glorify' Paul brings in a word that has associations with the cult. There are cultic connotations in Isaiah 43:23 LXX 'you have not glorified me by your sacrifices' and in Leviticus 10:3 LXX 'I will show myself holy among those who are near me, and before all the people I will be glorified.' Paul is saying that the believers must worship God and glorify him in the Temple of the Church just as it was previously believed that God was honoured by sacrifice in the Jerusalem Temple. This same idea is seen in Paul's letter to the Romans. As the Temple of God the Roman Church is called upon to live in harmony and so be able 'with one voice [to] glorify the God and Father of our Lord Jesus Christ' (Rom. 15:16).

We note finally Paul's use of ἀπαρχή, 'first fruits', to refer to converts in Romans 16:5 and 1 Corinthians 16:15.[153] This is a particularly fitting choice of words given our understanding of Paul's use of cultic language elsewhere in his letters to elucidate his view that converts to the faith should offer themselves as a sacrifice to God. By calling converts 'first fruits' Paul is underlining the fact that they are to consider themselves a special gift for both Paul and God, to whom Paul gives priestly service.

In the biblical tradition regarding the priests' portion, in Numbers, the first fruits of what the people give to God are kept by the priests (Num. 18:11 LXX) and out of these gifts the sanctified portion is given by the priests to the Lord (Num. 18:29 LXX). In Ezekiel 20:40, a passage we have had cause to examine previously, we find an interesting combination of the sacrificial terms which Paul uses in his letters. The prophet looks forward to the time when all Israel will serve (δουλεύω) God who will expect their first fruits (ἀπαρχή), their selected gifts (ἀπαρχὰς τῶν ἀφορισμῶν) and their holy things (ἀγιάσμασιν). As we have already noted, regarding verse 41, it is not these material gifts that are emphasized so much as the house of Israel itself which is accepted as a 'pleasing odour'.[154]

Given these precedents Paul can play on the word ἀπαρχή. To be sure it refers to those who are the first converts, the first to be baptized, but its cultic and, in Judaism, more usual meaning is not to be overlooked.[155] These first converts are like the special gifts of which Ezekiel speaks. In the same way they are the holy ones (cf. ἀγιάσμος) who have been sanctified (cf. Rom. 15:16; 1 Cor. 1:2; 1 Thess. 5:23) and who are accepted as a pleasing odour (Phil. 4:18).

5. Christ as *kapporet*

Linking the concept of the Church as Temple, and Paul and the believers as priests and sacrificial offering, is the idea that Christ is also both a sacrificial offering and the place of offering. This is expressed in Romans 3:24,

25: 'Christ Jesus, whom God put forward as an expiation by his blood, to be received by faith'. We shall posit here that Paul does indeed mean, by his use of ἱλαστήριον, translated by the RSV as 'expiation', the *kapporet* or cover of the ark, upon which the sacrificial blood was sprinkled. At the same time Christ is seen as the sacrificial victim. Although this particular understanding of Romans 3:24f. is not universally accepted[156] it does have a long history.[157] There is, however, no need to rehearse this history here.[158] We look instead at the consequences such an interpretation has when it is viewed alongside Paul's use of the concept of purity.

We have noted already the observations of Levine regarding the divine presence in the Temple and the necessity for a high degree of purity[159] and Milgrom's description of biblical impurity as having a 'dynamic, aerial quality'.[160] In connection with this we read in Leviticus 16:15 that blood was sprinkled upon the *kapporet* because the sins of the people had polluted the dwelling place of God, the Holy of Holies. Milgrom gives the following description of the rite:

> The wanton and unrepented sin not only pollutes the outer altar and penetrates into the shrine but it pierces the veil to the holy ark and the *kapporet*, the very throne of God. . . . Since the wanton sinner is barred from bringing his *ḥaṭṭa't* (Num. xv, 27-31), the pollution wrought by his offense must await the annual purgation of the sanctuary on the Day of Atonement, ... Thus the entire sacred area, or more precisely, all that is most sacred is purged on Purgation Day (*Yom hakippūrîm*) with the *ḥaṭṭa't* blood.[161]

Thus the *kapporet*[162] is cleansed by the blood and God's presence is guaranteed.[163]

It is now possible to apply these aspects of belief regarding purity and sacrifice to Paul's teaching that the community of believers constitutes the Temple and that as such, in order to benefit from the presence of God's spirit, that community must remain pure.

We recall that the community is described as ναός, which in the LXX usually translates *hekal*, the inner sanctuary or Holy of Holies, within which the *kapporet* was located. It is in this sense of *kapporet* that Paul describes Christ as ἱλαστήριον.

Paul's understanding of Christ's death, as expressed in Romans 3:25, is that it parallels and replaces this redemptive act carried out by the High Priest on the Day of Atonement (cf. Heb. 9:6-14 where Christ as High Priest offers his own blood). For Paul, Christ's death enables man's sinful nature to be expiated, not for just one year, but for all time. The blood of Christ which was shed cleanses the impurity which Christ, as *kapporet*, received as a result of the wanton sinful nature of man.[164] As the sanctuary was purged by the sprinkling of blood on the *kapporet*,[165] so Christ as ἱλαστήριον, displayed publicly,[166] and not concealed from view in the inner sanctuary, is cleansed by his own blood and man's sin is forgiven.[167] This is not all, for God's presence is now assured in the figure of Christ who lives on within the Church,[168] which is the Temple.

The paradox of Christ as both the offering and the object on which the blood of the victim is sprinkled need not be seen as unduly problematic: one does not always look to Paul for consistency.[169] Paul is saying here that all men have sinned (Rom. 3:9-22, 23) with a 'high hand' and deserve to be cut off (cf. Num. 15:30). No offering is sufficient to atone for their offence, just as the purification offering could not be offered by a wanton sinner. Paul's conviction that both Jews and Gentiles are called to be God's people necessitates the openness of the sacrifice which purges these transgressions. The sacrifice of the Day of Atonement will not suffice, God himself must intervene. So it is 'by his grace as a gift'[170] that he publicly offers Christ as a sin offering (purification offering, cf. Rom. 8:3; 2 Cor. 5:21).[171] Whereas it was the function of the priesthood to maintain the purity of the Temple by regular purifications so that God would not abandon the sanctuary,[172] now the once and for all purificatory sacrifice of Christ brings forth the guarantee that God will be forever present within the community.

6. Conclusions

By describing the Christian community as the Temple of God, Paul transfers from the Jerusalem Temple many concepts that pertain to that institution. Of primary importance is the idea that the divine presence now dwells wherever those who are 'in Christ' gather. Whereas God's Spirit previously had its special dwelling in the sanctuary of the Temple in Jerusalem, it is now, in Paul's view, with the Church, which is described by Paul as God's Temple. Furthermore, Paul uses language which suggests that he sees himself performing a priestly duty for this Temple and, in addition, sees the individual believers as not only performing a priestly function but also, paradoxically, presenting themselves as sacrificial offerings.

All of this has been made possible, in Paul's mind, by the sacrificial death of Christ which has put an end to the efficacy of the atoning sacrifices of the Jerusalem Temple and has enabled God's Spirit to be forever present within the believing community. However, just as conditions were laid down for the maintenance of the divine presence in the Holy of Holies in Jerusalem, so Paul sets out stringent conditions for the Christian community in order to preserve purity and thus maintain God's presence. It is to an examination of these conditions that we must now turn.

4

PURITY AND MEMBERSHIP OF THE CHURCH

1. Introduction

Having established that Paul teaches that the Church is the Temple of God and as such is ministered to in a priestly fashion by its members, as well as having brought to it offerings in the form of converts who offer themselves as living sacrifices, we need now to return directly to an examination of Paul's use of the concept of purity, a concept essentially connected to Temple life, the priesthood, and the sacrificial system.

As we noted above, the Temple or, more specifically, the sanctuary within the Temple, was acknowledged as the place where God had his special dwelling. The continued presence of the divine within the Holy of Holies could only be guaranteed by keeping the sanctuary and its precincts pure. Thus the Jerusalem Temple was separated from the outside world and protected from the impurity that abounded around it. Only Jews could enter its inner portals and only priests, in a state of purity, 'charged with assuring the purity of the sanctuary',[1] could minister in its inner precincts. The sacrifices themselves were directed towards maintaining the divine presence and 'most cultic activity was motivated, directly or indirectly by this objective, especially the process of ritual expiation . . . most particularly the blood rites designated by the verb *kipper*'.[2] Furthermore all sacrifices that were to be offered on its altars had also to come up to a high standard of purity. If, following the Christ event, according to Paul, the rites of the Jerusalem Temple no longer led to salvation and the community of believers now constituted the Temple within which God's spirit dwelt, we maintain that along with a reinstated priesthood and sacrificial system, albeit of a different order, Paul now pursues the view that this new Temple was subject to the requirements of purity that would ensure the retention of the divine presence, and makes these requirements manifest in his letters. Given the centrality of the purity regulations, their close link with the cult as it is depicted in Leviticus and their role in the everyday life of Judaism, we seek now to show that Paul would not have ignored them while at the same time exhibiting a concern for Temple,

79

priesthood, and sacrifice. We have already shown that Paul viewed the death of Christ as an expiatory sacrifice and expressed it in terms that recall the expiatory blood rites of the Temple (Rom. 3:23ff.) and we go on to show now, through an examination of Paul's letters, that a concern with the concept of purity played a role in his thought greater than heretofore acknowledged. Not only is this concern bound up, as is to be expected, and as indeed we have shown, with his view of the Church as the Temple, but also we shall demonstrate that the purity rules that were incumbent on observant Jews in their everyday life continued to exert an influence on Paul's ongoing attempt to maintain the moral order of the Church.

This last point needs to be pursued especially in the light of Carrington's suggestion that Paul saw the Church as a 'neo-levitical' community.[3] As W. D. Davies writes, 'Paul's advice to the Thessalonian Christians (I Thess. 4.1–12) . . . and other references in other Epistles reveal that he thought of Christians as forming a community that was "holy", apart from the world and dedicated to God which had therefore to observe certain rules.'[4] We must ask therefore what connection these 'certain rules' had with the purity regulations under which Paul, as a Jew of the Diaspora, had lived.[5] Anything from his Jewish heritage that caused division between Jewish and Gentile Christians would be abandoned. Therefore little emphasis is placed on the food laws, but aspects of the purity rules as they touched on family life, his attitude towards idolatry and the manner in which he describes sinful acts in general reflect an ongoing concern with the idea of purity.[6]

We set out now, then, to examine further the role of the concept of purity in Paul's letters. Our first task is to show how an understanding of what it means to be a member of the Christian community can be elucidated by examining the very terms of membership from the point of view of purity. In view of Paul's attitude to the Church as the Temple we shall show how he speaks of what it means to enter this Temple, maintain oneself within it, and what it takes to get oneself expelled from it, in terms of purity.

The community, as described by Paul, sees itself, for the purposes of its own organization, as a group separated from the rest of the world. On joining this community of believers one is cleansed, and in order to maintain this membership one has to remain in a state of purity and be 'holy'. Furthermore, acts of impurity that offend the sanctity of the body of Christ are met with condemnation and, in extreme cases, expulsion. However, unlike Qumran, contact with outsiders does not necessarily convey impurity.

As we saw above, it appears likely that, in Paul's time, the purity laws governing food had been applied to the laity with the consequence that they determined with whom one shared food. In fact, as we have already seen, the whole question of table fellowship was partly responsible for bringing about the split of Christianity from the rest of Judaism, as well as the cause of division within Christianity itself.[7] Paul himself gives guidance regarding the sharing of food with members of the brotherhood guilty of some form of impurity.

A reading of Paul from the point of view of the concept of purity also throws light on perennial problems of Pauline interpretation such as the role of women in the Church, Paul's attitude to marriage and the position of the offspring of the union of a believer with an unbeliever.

We shall also note that throughout his letters Paul frequently makes use of purity terminology taken from the sacrificial cult to describe both himself and other believers. Furthermore the obvious allusions to purity in 2 Corinthians 6:14-7:1 will be seen to be perfectly in tune with Paul's use of the concept of purity elsewhere and will give no cause to seek an extra-Pauline source for this passage.

2. Washing, sanctification and justification: entrance into the religious community

We have already noted in our study of Paul's cultic terminology that he viewed Christians as having been sanctified and that he called them the 'holy ones'. One aspect[8] of the process of becoming a Christian then was for one to be made holy and to be separated from the present age (Rom. 12:2). Membership of this present age (cf. Gal. 1:14) involves submission to the power of the sins of the heathen. For Paul the 'holy ones' are contrasted with the unrighteous (ἄδικοι, 1 Cor. 6:1), and in both Hellenistic and Palestinian Judaism a connection was seen between those who were considered unrighteous and the impure. Philo equates the unrighteous with uncleanness: 'For the unrighteous [ἄδικος] and impious man is in the truest sense unclean [ἀκάθαρτος]'. He goes on to explain why this is so: 'he puts everything into chaos and confusion'.[9] In Philo's view wickedness breaks up the unity of God's creation as do all acts of uncleanness.[10]

In the Psalms of Solomon we find that the unrighteous have no place amid a holy and pure people. Jerusalem is purged (καθαρίζω) of Gentiles (17.22) and the holy people (λαός ἅγιος) who have been sanctified (ἁγιάζω) by God will no longer have the unrighteous in their midst (17.26, 27).[11]

In 1 Corinthians 6:9-11 Paul reminds the Corinthian Church 'that the unrighteous [ἄδικοι] will not inherit the kingdom of God' and continues:

Do not be deceived; neither the immoral, nor idolaters, nor adulterers, nor homosexuals, nor thieves, nor the greedy, nor drunkards, nor revilers, nor robbers will inherit the kingdom of God. And such were some of you. But you were washed, you were sanctified, you were justified in the name of the Lord Jesus Christ and in the Spirit of our God.

It appears that Paul considered that a few of the Corinthians were guilty of some of these predominantly Gentile sins. However, they have passed from this sinful state to membership in the Church.

Paul is here clearly speaking, with his use of ἀπολούω, in 1 Corinthians 6:11, of a cleansing of past transgressions. Such sins as immorality and idolatry, in particular, would have been viewed by Paul, as a Jew, as the very epitome of uncleanness.[12] Gentile converts, in order to come into the community, needed to have such impurity removed, for they were entering what Paul saw now as the Temple of God. It is not necessary, however, to view this cleansing as a requirement for Gentiles alone.[13] Paul's concern was that all those entering the Church, whether Jew or Gentile,[14] were cleansed of their past allegiance to sin. He perhaps expected, as a Jew, that among the Gentile converts would be many who were guilty of transgressions that few Jews, if any, would have committed.[15] But this was not the point. All those who became believers were a 'new creation' (2 Cor. 5:17), their old life had been left behind, they *all* needed to be washed, sanctified and justified, for they were transferring their allegiance to a different Lord.[16] They were once under the control of 'the god of this world' (2 Cor. 4:4) but now they 'belong to Christ Jesus' (Gal. 5:24) and 'are called to be holy ones' (Rom. 1:7; 1 Cor. 1:2).[17]

Thus we can say, with Sanders, that ἀπολούω is used here as a 'transfer term'.[18] In order to pass from the old life to the new, in order to be made fit to enter the Temple, which, like the old, demanded that all who performed their service in it be pure, one had to be made pure and holy and be justified.

All three verbs that appear in verse 11 refer back to the initial act of cleansing[19] which is expressed first by ἀπολούω, a word that Paul uses only here and which appears in only one other place in the New Testament.[20] The same verb is found only once in the LXX (Job 9:30),[21] where it translates the Hebrew *raḥats*, which is used predominantly in the Hebrew Bible in a cultic setting to describe the washing of both persons and objects who have contracted some form of impurity or who are to perform some specific task in the Temple.[22] *Raḥats* is usually rendered in the LXX by λούω.[23]

Despite the rarity of ἀπολούω in the New Testament it is used quite frequently by Philo and Josephus. Philo uses it to describe the washing an individual must undergo after touching a corpse (*Spec. Leg.* III.206) and before entering the Temple (*Spec. Leg.* III.89; cf. also *De Somn.* I.148, II.113). In Josephus it is the word used to describe the bathing of the Essenes (*Bell.* II.129, 149, 150), washing before meals (*Ant.* II.163) and ablutions after sexual intercourse (*Apol.* II.203). Both the context and the contemporary use of this word allow us to conclude with some certainty that Paul had in mind a cleansing from impurity which anyone entering the Church had to undergo.

It seems widely agreed[24] that 1 Cor. 6:1 is associated with baptism.[25] While it is true that Paul says that it is by Christ's death that man's past sins are expiated (Rom. 3:23–5; 4:24, 25; 1 Cor. 15:3)[26] at the same time he is able to view the actual passing from the realm of a life ruled by sin to one under Christ as a purificatory act made viable by baptism. We would conclude, then, that in his use of ἀπολούω he understands one dimension of baptism to entail a cleansing from past transgressions.[27]

Having been cleansed from his past sins the believer is now fit to 'inherit the kingdom of God'. He was once unrighteous (ἄδικος), he has now been 'justified'. Paul's use of δικαιόω in verse 11 probably refers back to the ἄδικοι[28] of verse 9 and leads us to assume, given that 'justified' here seems to be a parallel expression to 'washed',[29] that, for Paul, the unrighteous are, in fact, unclean.

The unrighteous, according to Paul, will not inherit the kingdom of God. It is only with this washing, sanctification and justification that comes through baptism that the individual can be placed in a position where he can have some assurance of salvation. Cleansed from his past transgressions he is expected to maintain this state of purity so that he is 'sound and blameless at the coming of our Lord Jesus Christ' (1 Thess. 5:23). As a believer he is set apart from the world, and his life within the Church is to be guided by the fact that his behaviour be not 'conformed to this world' (Rom. 12:2).

One way in which this purity was maintained was through the guidance leaders like Paul gave the Church from time to time. With W. D. Davies we would assume that 'the Church, like every new sect within Judaism, had to draw up rules for the moral guidance of its members and had to define its position'.[30] It was in view of this that Paul saw the Church as a 'neo-levitical' community,[31] a community pure and holy, a sanctuary of God in which his spirit dwelt.

The presence of God's spirit within the Church depended, as did that of the *Shekinah* within the Temple, on the purity of the environment.[32]

The relationship between the presence of God in the Temple and purity is, as we have already noted with reference to the Qumran community, discussed by Levine. We look again at his comments on this matter:

> One becoming impure as the result of an offense against the deity introduced a kind of contagion into the community. The more horrendous the offense, the greater the threat to the purity of the sanctuary and the surrounding community by the presence of the offender, who was the carrier of the impurity. The person required purification if the community was to be restored to its ritual state, which, in turn, was a precondition set down by the resident deity for his continued presence among the people. The deity had made a vital concession to the Israelites by consenting to dwell among the impurities endemic to the human situation (Lev. 16:16). If his continued residence was to be realized, Yahweh required an extreme degree of purity (Ex. 25.8). In his heavenly abode, Yahweh was well guarded from impurity, and this condition was to be reproduced as nearly as possible in his earthly residence.[33]

It is the concept described here that determined much of the teaching and disciplinary measures of Paul and his Churches. Uncleanness of any form was not to be tolerated; for, as Paul reminds the Corinthians: 'you are God's temple and . . . God's Spirit dwells in you' (1 Cor. 3:16).

3. Preparation for the *eschaton*: the maintenance of purity

It is Paul's constant concern throughout his letters, but more especially in the Philippian and Thessalonian correspondence, that members of the Churches in his charge maintain an acceptable standard of behaviour so as to be ready at the final day. In describing the state in which he hopes that day will find them he uses terms that are frequently related to the concept of purity and which in many cases are words that are used in the LXX to describe the conditions for those who wish to enter the Temple and of the offerings that are to be sacrificed there.

In Philippians 1:10, 11 Paul prays that the Philippian believers 'may be pure [εἰλικρινής][34] and blameless [ἀπρόσκοπος] for the day of Christ, filled with the fruits of righteousness',[35] and in Philippians 2:14-16 he writes:

> Do all things without grumbling or questioning, that you may be blameless [ἄμεμπτος] and innocent [ἀκέραιος], children of God without blemish [ἄμωμος] in the midst of a crooked and perverse generation,

among whom you shine as lights in the world, holding fast the word of life, so that in the day of Christ I may be proud that I did not run in vain.

Paul uses here three terms to describe the state of preparedness in which the Church at Philippi is to maintain itself. Ἄμεμπτος is used in the LXX to describe the righteous state of man before God. It is used of Abraham (Gen. 17:1; Wisd. 10:5), Moses (Wisd. 18:21), the Holy people (of Israel) (Wisd. 10:5) and of Job. The most frequent occurrence of the word is, in fact, in the book of Job where it appears in parallel to δίκαιος (Job 9:20; 12:4; 15:14; 22:19) and καθαρός (Job 4:17; 11:4; 33:9) and translates *tam* (Job 2:3; 9:20), *ṭahar* (Job 4:17) and *bar* (Job 11:4). Paul uses it elsewhere in Philippians 3:6; 1 Thessalonians 3:13 and in an adverbial form (ἀμέμπτως) in 1 Thessalonians 2:10 and 5:23. Both 1 Thessalonians 3:13 and 5:23 refer to the *parousia*.

The next word, ἀκέραιος, has a similar meaning but not such a widespread usage. It means literally 'unmixed' and is used by Paul to mean 'innocent', 'guileless' (cf. Rom. 16:19).

The third word of this group (ἄμωμος) makes the link with the cult. It appears extensively in Exodus, Leviticus, Numbers and Ezekiel (LXX) as a translation of *tam* and is applied to animals that are offered for sacrifice 'without blemish'.[36] In what appears to be an attempt to describe the moral state of man it is used in David's song of deliverance:

I was blameless [ἄμωμος] before him, and I kept myself from guilt.
Therefore the Lord has recompensed me according to my righteousness,
    according to the cleanness of my hands in his sight.
                                        (Ps. 18:23, 24; 2 Sam. 22:24, 25)

In addition Psalm 15:1-2 describes qualities that are required of those who wish to enter the sanctuary:

O Lord who shall sojourn in thy tent?
Who shall dwell on thy holy hill?
He who walks blamelessly [ἄμωμος], and does what is right [ἐργαζόμε-
    νος δικαιοσύνην],
and speaks truth [ἀλήθεια] from his heart.[37]

The term ἄμωμος appears again in a cultic context in Psalm 101:6 where the use of the verb λειτουργέω reminds us of the liturgical service rendered by believers (Phil. 2:17, 30; cf. Rom. 15:16).

I will look with favour on the faithful in the land,
    that they may dwell with me;

he who walks in the way that is blameless[38]
shall minister [λειτουργέω, MT *sharat*] to me.

Similar ideas are expressed in 1 Thessalonians, a letter which reveals an even stronger eschatological consciousness. Paul hopes that the Lord 'may establish your hearts unblamable [ἄμεμπτος] in holiness [ἁγιωσύνη] before our God and Father, at the coming of our Lord Jesus Christ with all his saints' (1 Thess. 3:13), and in the conclusion to his letter he writes 'May the God of peace himself sanctify you [ἁγιάζω] wholly; and may your spirit and soul and body be kept sound and blameless [ἀμέμπτως] at the coming of our Lord Jesus Christ' (1 Thess. 5:23).

Paul, in calling on those at Philippi and Thessalonica to be blameless and innocent and without blemish, utilizes terms, taken from the cultic language of purity, which embrace the whole realm of the believer's life in Christ. This life is to be beyond reproach in all respects. Like Job they are to be righteous and pure. They are to be innocent and free from guilt and if they are to present themselves as a holy and acceptable sacrifice to God (Rom. 12:1), they must be, like the sacrificial offerings of the Jerusalem Temple, free from blemish. Thus the Church, in the time that remains for it in this age, keeps itself pure so that God's spirit can remain active within it.

4. Cleansing the community: keeping the Church pure

The most striking example of Paul's concern for the purity of the Church in the face of what he sees as gross uncleanness, and which leads him to call for severe disciplinary action to protect the Church, is the case of the Corinthian who has been openly 'living with his father's wife' (1 Cor. 5:1). All of chapter 5 of this letter to the Corinthians is a fine example of Paul's utilization of the concept of purity in order to regulate the life of the Christian community.

The offending member has to be expelled so that he does not further contaminate the community. 'Let him who has done this be removed from among you' (verse 2) and 'Drive out the wicked person from among you' (verse 13). The Corinthian Church is reminded of Paul's previous instructions[39] regarding the presence of immorality within the community: 'I wrote to you in my letter not to associate with immoral men' (verse 9), by which he means specifically those within the Church who are guilty of immorality. With such people table fellowship is to be avoided: 'not even to eat with such a one' (verse 11). It is, Paul insists, the duty of the Church not so much to concern itself with the behaviour of outsiders, but to take all possible measures to maintain a standard of correct behaviour within its own ranks. The purity of God's Temple is of paramount importance.

Within the disciplinary instructions of verses 1-4 and 9-13 lies a short passage in which Paul moves towards a theoretical basis for the teaching of this chapter. He speaks in terms of the Passover sacrifice in which all leaven is removed from the household, the lamb sacrificed and unleavened bread consumed. He identifies the paschal lamb with Christ and the bread, made without any trace of leavening agent, with the believers. But also, and we have already noticed this tendency in Paul, he sees the believers not only as the object of the celebration (unleavened bread), but also as those who are celebrants at the festival. These two levels are expressed in this way: first, 'you really are unleavened' (verse 7) and secondly, 'Let us, therefore, celebrate the festival . . . with the unleavened bread of sincerity and truth' (verse 8).

Let us examine this chapter in more detail and discover the pervading concern that it exhibits. 'It is actually reported that there is immorality [πορνεία] among you, and of a kind that is not found even among pagans [ἔθνος]; for a man is living with his father's wife' (1 Cor. 5:1). We need not concern ourselves too much with the nature of this apparently incestuous relationship which was being allowed to persist in the Corinthian Church.[40] The sin was of a sexual nature, as Paul's use of πορνεία denotes (cf. 1 Cor. 6:13) and as such was unclean. Elsewhere Paul links sexual immorality with impurity (2 Cor. 12:21; Gal. 5:19). He uses ἀκαθαρσία as a broad term which can mean impurity of any kind[41] but links it specifically with πορνεία.[42]

The same sin that is condemned by Paul is described as being of a most serious nature and as such unclean in the Book of Jubilees:

> they shall surely die together, the man who lies with his father's wife
> and the woman also, for they have wrought uncleanness on the earth.
> And there shall be nothing unclean before our God in the nation . . .
> and it is unclean, and there is no atonement forever to atone for the
> man who has committed this, but he is to be put to death and slain,
> and stoned with stones, and rooted out from the midst of the people of
> our God. (Jub. 33:10-13)

The fact that Paul indicates, most certainly in a rhetorical tone, that such immorality that exists in the Corinthian Church 'is not found even among pagans' has led to the suggestion that Paul is here chastising Jewish Christians who have taken the rebirth of baptism to have had an annulling effect on all previous relationships and thus allow the convert to marry whomever he wishes.[43] In any case, it does not require a Jewish readership to appreciate the point that Paul is making here (cf. 1 Cor. 6:4ff.), namely, that the community as Temple must not tolerate such impurity in its midst.[44]

Paul, however, is adamant. He chastises the Church for condoning such a relationship and orders the offender to be expelled from the community. 'Let him who has done this be removed from among you' (verse 2b). Paul uses the word αἴρω here, which literally means 'to carry' or even 'to lift up' and as such is frequently applied to inanimate objects.[45] Because of the seriousness of the offence in this case and the resultant impurity that the man's continued presence brings to the community, Paul may have in mind here Leviticus 10:4, 5 where, in the LXX, αἴρω is used to denote the carrying out of the dead bodies of the two laymen who had attempted to act as priests but had been consumed by the fire of the presence for their presumptuousness. They had, as laymen, brought impurity into the sanctuary and as a result were destroyed. Their remains, also impure, but even more so, were carried (αἴρω) 'from before the sanctuary out of the camp'. So Paul calls on the Corinthians to remove, from the Church, the man who has been polluting the community, a community which has to be kept pure if it is to remain the sanctuary in which God's spirit dwells.[46]

The severity of the sin in this case is demonstrated by the severity of the judgement which the assembled Church is to pass on the individual: 'you are to deliver this man to Satan for the destruction of the flesh, that his spirit may be saved in the day of the Lord Jesus' (1 Cor. 5:5). The suggestion is made by Forkman that in order to protect the sanctity of the Church the fornicator is to be removed from one realm to another. He is to be taken from under the lordship of Christ and put again under the authority of Satan.[47] Forkman, who surveys the many attempted interpretations of this difficult verse,[48] concludes that what we see here is a reversal of the baptismal process:[49]

> The one who was baptized in the name of Jesus was transferred from the domain of Satan to that of Christ, from the sphere of death to that of life; for his old man, his flesh, must die, and his new man, his spirit, must live. Now, when the life of the fornicator stands in obvious and conscious contrast to the character of the church, he must once again, in the name of Jesus, be given over to Satan, from where he once came.[50]

It is quite possible to understand Paul as seeing this assigning to Satan as the equivalent to the cutting off from the people ordained for such an offender in Leviticus 18:29, or the physical death laid out in Jubilees

33:13.[51] However, unlike the finality of the punishments that are set out in both Leviticus and Jubilees, Paul sets forth for this individual the hope of salvation. In terms of salvation his baptism remains efficacious.

It should be noted that the threat of destruction in 1 Corinthians 5:5 and 3:17 ('If anyone destroys God's temple, God will destroy him'), is not as strong as such statements that Paul makes regarding inheritance of the kingdom, e.g. 'the unrighteous will not inherit the kingdom of God' (1 Cor. 6:9; cf. Gal. 5:21). Destruction in 1 Corinthians 5:5 allows for salvation, so 'that his spirit may be saved'. The threat is directed towards one who is 'in Christ', one who is a constituent member of the Temple of God. On the other hand those who do not enjoy this membership, those who have not been washed, sanctified and justified, have no part in the inheritance of the kingdom of God. Salvation is denied them.

When Paul speaks of delivering a man to Satan for the destruction of the flesh this does not then entail a removal of the benefits of baptism.[52] The statement comes rather as an expression of Paul's concern to maintain the purity of the community and this concern is further expressed in his use of the imagery of leaven which has to be cleansed out. Those who are not believers, the unrighteous, the unclean, present no threat to the sanctity of the Church. Even when their sins appear comparatively trivial, e.g. dissension, envy (Gal. 5:20, 21), they cannot look forward to salvation, for, as the argument in Galatians shows, these are works of the flesh while 'those who belong to Christ Jesus have crucified the flesh with its passions and desires' (Gal. 5:24). Paul's use of the language of destruction in 1 Corinthians 3:17 and 5:5 is didactic. It is his intention to point to the sacredness of the community and the importance of maintaining its status as the dwelling place of God. Sin, any sin, endangers its holiness,[53] and this fact is brought out by the seriousness of the statement in 1 Corinthians 3:17. The Corinthian Church needs to be further reminded, in even stronger terms, of this point, for they are openly allowing impurity to persist in their midst. Paul's statement in 1 Corinthians 5:5 is directed towards this fact and the rest of the chapter reveals that this concern is not so much with the fate of the offender but with the maintenance of the purity of the community.

For Paul, salvation, expressed in terms of the word σώζω, is either held out to be a future hope (Rom. 5:9, 10; 10:9) or as an ongoing process (1 Cor. 1:8; 2 Cor. 2:15).[54] In fact salvation, σωτηρία, takes on an eschatological tone in Romans 13:11 and is to come 'through sanctification by the Spirit' (2 Thess. 2:13). The salvation of the spirit of the fornicator is to come 'in the day of the Lord Jesus' and it is Paul's concern that, at the *eschaton*, believers be sanctified, sound and blameless (1 Thess. 5:23).

There is a difference, of course, between what Paul writes in 1 Thessalonians regarding the preparation for the *parousia* and the salvation that awaits the spirit of the man who has been delivered to Satan. Paul prays in 1 Thessalonians 5:23 for the purity of the spirit, soul and body (σῶμα) of the believer at the coming of the Lord while in 1 Corinthians 5:5 he mentions only the spirit of the man, his flesh (σάρξ) having been destroyed. This contrast however need not present too much difficulty, for Paul's use of σάρξ elsewhere (Rom. 2:28; 8:4ff.; Gal. 3:3; 4:23, 29; 5:17; Phil. 3:3) allows us to take him to mean that while the man's removal from the Church is a necessity because of his impurity it is not his body (σῶμα)[55] that is to be destroyed but rather the propensity he has exhibited to live in the realm of flesh (σάρξ) rather than spirit, which is the prerequisite of the believer. Removed from the pure environment of the community his fleshly nature can be destroyed so that at the *eschaton* he also will be, as Paul writes in 1 Thessalonians 5:23, sound and blameless in spirit and, we may presume, in body and soul.[56]

To be sure life outside the community would subject the individual to suffering[57] and eventually death (Rom. 8:7, 13), for this is the fate of all those who live in the realm of Satan. But death also comes even to those who are in Christ (Rom. 8:10), for all men are subject to mortality. The difference is, however, that those in Christ are assured that their spirits will live. 'But if Christ is in you, although the body [σῶμα] is dead because of sin, the Spirit is alive because of righteousness' (Rom. 8:10).[58]

It is in the light of what Paul says in Romans 8:10 that we can understand his statement in 1 Corinthians 5:5. Expelled from the community of believers the man guilty of fornication will suffer from the vicissitudes of life in the world which for him will be the more trying because he is isolated from the fellowship of which he once was a member (cf. 1 Cor. 5:11). Foremost in Paul's mind is the maintenance of the purity of the Church. With this man's removal it is again pure and can function as a dwelling place for God's spirit. Paul does not, however, neglect the individual. Through his baptism he remains 'in Christ'[59] and although outside the Church and in the realm of Satan, where he will most likely die, his spirit will be saved at the last day.[60]

Having dealt with the offending party Paul now turns his attention to the Church; for its continued existence as the body of Christ is his major concern. They have allowed impurity to dwell in their ranks and have been unconcerned by it. We may even assume that they have been proud of the freedom that they have allowed their members by permitting them, in their new life in Christ, to maintain relationships[61] that even under the old dispensation would have been anathema. In their arrogance and boasting they have ignored, or even taken advantage of, what they had learned from Paul. As a community that enjoys the presence of God's spirit certain standards have to be maintained in order to preserve, within that community, an environment that allows for such a presence.

This is something that the Corinthian community should have already known and Paul re-emphasizes its importance by speaking in terms of the leaven which at Passover[62] has to be removed from the household so that the festival is celebrated with only unleavened bread:

> Your boasting is not good. Do you not know [οὐκ οἴδατε] that a little leaven leavens the whole lump? Cleanse out the old leaven that you may be a new lump, as you really are unleavened. For Christ, our paschal lamb, has been sacrificed. Let us, therefore, celebrate the festival, not with the old leaven, the leaven of malice and evil, but with the unleavened bread of sincerity and truth. (1 Cor. 5:6–8)

Paul cites what is probably a proverb:[63] 'a little leaven leavens the whole lump' and makes the thrust of this chapter unambiguous: by allowing one impure person to remain in their midst the community as a whole is tainted. They have no alternative before them, for, just as the Jewish home at the time of Passover has to be cleansed of all leaven (a traditional sign of impurity)[64] so the Church, as God's building (1 Cor. 3:9), had to remove that which would otherwise invalidate what Paul sees as the ongoing celebration of the Church's own passover, its life in Christ[65] in which redemption is offered (cf. M. Pes. 10.5) to all who participate.

Paul calls upon the Corinthians to 'cleanse out [ἐκκαθαίρω] the old leaven'. This verb, which is used only here in Paul and only once elsewhere in the New Testament (2 Tim. 2:21), does not have an extensive use in the LXX (Deut. 26:13; Josh. 17:15; Judg. 7:5) and then not exactly in the same way as Paul uses it. The similar verb ἐκκαθαρίζω appears in Judg. 20:13, not in a cultic sense but with similar connotations to those of Paul. The tribes of Israel call upon the Benjaminites to 'put away [ἐκκαθαρίζω LXX, *ba'ar* MT] evil [πονηρία, cf. 1 Cor. 5:13] from Israel'. The Hebrew *ba'ar* means to burn or consume with fire[66] and this is what normally has to be done with the leaven that is found within the confines of the home at Passover.[67] Both Philo[68] and Josephus use the verb ἐκκαθαίρω but not extensively. Josephus talks of the sacrificial victim being carefully cleansed (*Ant.* III. 227) and of God desiring to purge the sanctuary by fire (*Bell.* IV. 323).

The use of the verb ἐκκαθαίρω indicates the presence of something unclean which needs to be removed and here Paul is clearly pointing to the fornicator who must be excluded so that the community as the 'new lump' and 'unleavened' can function as intended.

Windisch, commenting on ζύμη (leaven) in 1 Corinthians 5:6, describes Paul here as changing the cultic command into a moral injunction[69] and sees this as 'an important example of the translation of cultic concepts into ethical'.[70] This is not the case; for there is a cultic element still in the forefront of Paul's thinking. He is dealing with what he considers to be the Temple of God, the Church, and as such it has cultic demands, namely the necessity of purity within its precincts. To point out the fact that the purity that Paul calls for stems from what the modern mind sees as moral questions (sexual immorality, greed, etc.) only clouds the issue. Such a division between the realm of the cult and that of morality was not apparent to the semitic mind.[71] The important thing was that vice, in any form, was seen to be impure and thus inappropriate for the household of God.

Paul makes no attempt in his exhortation to be completely coherent. We have noticed this elsewhere. While he maintains throughout these verses the idea that the old leaven of 'malice and evil' is the impurity that threatens the Church he identifies first the community itself as the new dough which is unleavened and then goes on to call upon the Church to 'celebrate[72] the festival . . . *with*[73] the unleavened bread of sincerity and truth'.

What Paul is, in effect, saying here is that the Christians are living, as it were, during the festival of Unleavened Bread which follows the slaughter of the paschal lamb, who in this case is Christ. Just as Jewish homes during the festival remained cleansed of leaven so must the community of believers (God's building, 1 Cor. 3:9) during the time that remains until the *eschaton* be likewise cleansed. As the 'new lump', 'the unleavened', they constitute the household of God which is cleansed of all leaven and, at the same time, as members of that household, they celebrate the festival. Paul uses the verb ἑορτάζω, 'to celebrate'; a word which, along with ἐκκαθαίρω, is to be found only here in Paul.[74] The so-called 'un-Pauline' character of much of the vocabulary and semitic style of the language of this passage leads Jeremias to the conclusion that 1 Corinthians 5:7b-8 'is probably based upon an early Christian passover *haggadah*'.[75] It is, however, in keeping for Paul to make use of cultic terminology and in particular the language of purity especially when he is making a point regarding church discipline and unity.[76] Ἑορτάζω is used in the LXX as a translation of *ḥagag*, the usual word to describe the keeping of a pilgrim feast such as Passover,[77] and Paul's use of this verb is certainly not out of place at this point.

For the Christians this festival continues until the coming of the Lord and they are to continue to celebrate their new life in Christ 'with the un-leavened bread of purity [εἰλικρίνεια] [78] and truth' (my translation). The uncleanness has now been excluded from the Church, just as the leaven was removed and burnt in preparation for Passover. The Church now, by virtue of celebrating its own Passover, exists in a covenantal relationship with God. Christ, its own paschal lamb, has been sacrificed and it lives as if during the festival. Its members, in Paul's words, are the new dough, the unleavened bread untainted by the old, the presence of which would pre-vent the proper celebration of the festival. [79] We should also add that to speak of the celebration of a festival would of necessity mean that it was understood that the divine was especially present.

Paul may have moved away for a moment, in 1 Corinthians 5:6–8, from his view of the Church as the Temple and have introduced the theme of the community as God's building. Passover is celebrated in the home and it is from the home that the leaven is excluded. So in this passage the believing community becomes the household of God [80] which keeps itself pure until the end and celebrates with joy the paschal sacrifice of the crucified Christ.

1 Corinthians 5:9–13 continues with the theme of the purity of the Church. From the specific case of verses 1–5 Paul turns to the general prob-lem of dealing with impurity within the community. A previous letter (2 Cor. 6:14ff?) has pointed out that believers should not associate with immoral men. Paul's intentions here were misunderstood, for he has to tell the Corin-thians that he was not referring to immoral men in general but in parti-cular to those members of the Church who commit immoral acts. An act of immorality within the Church causes it to be polluted. So as to avoid the polluting effect of evil-doers within their ranks Paul calls on the Church 'not to associate [συναναμείγνυμι] with anyone who bears the name of brother if he is guilty of immorality [πόρνος] or greed [πλεονέκτης], or is an idolater, reviler, drunkard, or robber – not even to eat with [συνεσθίω] such a one' (1 Cor. 5:11). This is clearly a call for purity. The verb συνανα-μείγνυμι, which means literally 'to mix up together' [81] is used only twice in the LXX but in both cases it translates *balal.*

The verb *balal* (in the *hithpoel* form), which is translated as συνανα-μείγνυμι in Hosea 7:8, appears elsewhere in the form φυράω. [82] Connected with this verb is the noun φύραμα which is usually translated 'mixture' or 'dough', the word Paul uses to describe the Christians in 1 Corinthians 5:7. The believers themselves are mixed (Gentiles and Jews) but it is a new mixture of the spirit and not of the flesh. The old mixture, or lump of dough, contained impurity, malice and evil, and is thrown out. [83]

The word συναναμείγνυμι itself occurs in passages that show concern for the purity of the people of Israel. In Hosea's diatribe against Israel the prophet says 'Ephraim mixes himself with the peoples' [84] (Hos. 7:8) and in Ezekiel 20:18 (LXX) we find a reminder of the ordinance of God against which Israel has now rebelled: 'Do not walk in the statutes of your fathers, nor observe their ordinances and in their ways do not mix and defile yourselves'[85] (my translation). This latter verse links the act of mixing with defilement. By mixing themselves up with the way of life of their forebears the people of Israel polluted themselves.

This is also the thrust of Paul's exhortation. By associating with fornicators, idolaters and the like, the Corinthians are bringing defilement upon themselves and the Church. In order to prevent further the polluting effect of such people they are to disassociate themselves from them and not even to share their food with them.[86]

We have already remarked that table fellowship provided a dividing line between those that were 'in' and those that were 'out' in first-century religious groups. The verb $\sigma\upsilon\nu\varepsilon\sigma\vartheta\iota\omega$ is used only occasionally in the LXX,[87] but its use is significant and relates directly to what Paul is writing to the Corinthians. Jethro, the non-Israelite priest, offered sacrifices to God and then ate with Aaron and the elders 'before God' (Exod. 18:12). The significance of this passage for our understanding of Paul is the fact that an outsider performs an exclusive liturgical service and that the food that he shares with Israelites is eaten in the presence of God.[88] We have already seen that Paul envisages the Gentile converts in his Churches making an offering which he describes in cultic terms and that the community exists as a dwelling place of God whose presence is especially felt when the fellowship meets together. One would not eat, then, with the evil man because of the impurity which he represents. We should add that whenever the community met together it was 'before God' and, we should note, eating together here is not confined to the eucharist.[89]

Table fellowship is to be denied to those whom Paul's list in 1 Corinthians 5:11 typifies. From this list we should note three vices that within the Jewish tradition result particularly in impurity. These are: immorality (a constant concern with Paul), idolatry and slander, all of which are standard Jewish accusations against Gentiles (cf. Rom. 1:24ff.).[90]

The fact that immorality and idolatry are mentioned in both the list in verse 10 and that of verse 11 need not point only to the possible existence of such vices in the Corinthian Church;[91] rather they serve to show that Paul continues to think of impurity as endangering the Church.

Another occurrence of $\sigma\upsilon\nu\varepsilon\sigma\vartheta\iota\omega$ is in Psalm 101:5. An equivalent verb does not, however, appear in the Hebrew, for the LXX translates '*ukal*[92] as '*okel* to eat. The resultant reading (my translation) is:

He who slanders[93] his neighbours secretly, he is banished.[94]
He who is of haughty looks and of a greedy heart,
with him food is not shared [συνεσθίω].

Here we have similar vices to those included in Paul's list; slander, arrogance and greed. The peculiarity of the Greek translation allows for a parallelism: banishment is equivalent to banning from table fellowship. Paul's passage exhibits a similar parallelism between the phrases: 'cleanse out', 'do not eat' and 'drive out'.

A further link with Paul's sentiments can be found in this psalm. The incompatibility of evil and the presence of God in the Temple is expressed in verse 7:

No man who practises deceit
shall dwell in my house;
no man who utters lies
shall continue in my presence.   (Ps. 101:7)

This is exactly what Paul is saying. The evil person has no place in the Temple of God and God's presence cannot tolerate such a one.

In a place like Corinth contact with immoral men and idolaters could not be prevented and Paul, despite some initial misunderstanding, was not asking for that: 'I wrote to you in my letter not to associate with immoral men; not at all meaning the immoral of this world ' (1 Cor. 5:9, 10). What was important for him was that the believers themselves should remain pure. This was not so that both Jew and Gentile could then enjoy table fellowship – he does not see that as a problem – but because, as the Temple of God, they could only have the spirit dwelling among them if they refrained from all impurity. To be sure, Paul does not expect Christians to have close social contact with the impure by sharing their table; but that is not the main issue, it merely follows from it.[95] The main issue is that impurity cannot be allowed to remain in the Church. To share one's table with one who has been excluded from the Church would be to continue to maintain a bond that should have been severed; for table fellowship was a sign that the participants held something in common and that their values were shared. The brother guilty of immorality was, then, to be shunned more than outsiders who might still choose to join the believing community.[96]

Paul ends this chapter with a further emphasis that the Church should remain undefiled. It is not with the behaviour of outsiders that believers should concern themselves but with those within the Church: 'For what have I to do with judging outsiders? Is it not those inside the church whom you are to judge? God judges those outside. "Drive out [ἐξάρατε] the wicked person from among you"' (1 Cor. 5:12, 13). This last sentence recalls a recurring expression in Deuteronomy (e.g. Deut. 13:5; 19:19; 21:21; 22:21; 24:7): 'So you shall purge [ἐξαρεῖς] the evil from the midst of you.' It is used in Deuteronomy as a final statement regarding the punishment of the wrongdoer and is directed to the community as a whole, which has the responsibility of carrying out the judgement with its own hands. The Hebrew verb that is used here is *ba'ar* which, as we have already noted, means 'burn' or 'consume'[97] in its literal sense but used here figuratively it means 'utterly remove'.[98] In Mishnaic Hebrew the verb was used to describe the removal of leaven from the house at Passover.[99] In the formulaic statements of Deuteronomy the LXX translated *ba'ar* with ἐξαίρω except at Deuteronomy 13:5 where the verb is ἀφανίζω. When *ba'ar* appears in Deuteronomy 26:13 the LXX has ἐκκαθαίρω, the same verb that Paul has used in 1 Corinthians 5:7.

The sentence which Paul quotes in 1 Corinthians 5:13 refers, in Deuteronomy, in many cases, to those who are guilty of the particular sins which Paul lists in verses 10–11. Deuteronomy 13:5; 17:2 pertain to idolatry; 21:21, 22, 24 to sexual immorality; 21:21 to drunkenness and robbery; 24:7 to robbery and 17:12 to presumptuousness before a priest. Those guilty of these sins are to be purged from the community, from Israel itself (cf. Deut. 17:12). In the same way those guilty of these sins are purged from the Church. In both cases the purity of the religious community is at stake.

Paul, then, concludes this section with a stern warning to the Church. If they wish to maintain their relationship with God they, like the Israelites in Deuteronomy, cannot allow any form of evil to remain in their midst. Like the leaven at Passover it must be removed and utterly consumed and it is the responsibility of the community to carry out this purgation itself.

In the section before us, Paul is not concerned with sin in a general sense. That, he says, is God's problem and he writes no diatribe against the sins of the city of Corinth. His concern is with the sin that is within the brotherhood because that sin taints the Church, weakens it and will eventually destroy it. The Church will be deprived of its holiness and it will cease to function as God's Temple.

We have attempted to show that throughout chapter five of Paul's First Letter to the Corinthians the concept of purity has served as a device to regulate the morality of the Church and to emphasize that members of the Church, those who have been sanctified, the holy ones, must remain pure so that God can dwell among them. In order to elucidate these themes Paul has made use of the biblical tradition that taught that the people of

God cannot allow vice to have a place in their ranks; that such sins as sexual immorality and idolatry epitomized impurity; and that if God was to dwell among his people all traces of evil had to be removed. Paul brings all of these allusions together in this chapter and closes with a biblical quotation which sums up, in no uncertain terms, what he has been trying to say.[100]

5. Conclusions

We have attempted in this chapter to demonstrate that Paul, who regarded the Christian community as the Temple of God, applies to that community the concept of purity in a manner that is modelled on the purity regulations pertaining to the Jerusalem Temple. In Jerusalem a certain level of purity was required of all those Jews who wished to enter the Temple and more stringent standards were set for those partaking in the specific rituals. This was in order that the purity of the inner sanctuary would be maintained so that the *Shekinah* could remain there.

In a similar manner, membership of the Church, as Temple, was expressed by Paul in terms of purity. Entrance to the community was couched in terms of removal of impurity, especially in the case of Gentiles, and those within the Church, the believers, were extolled to keep themselves pure and in eschatological readiness and warned that toleration of sinful polluting activities within their ranks would mean the loss of the divine presence.

5

PURITY AND THE CONTINUING LIFE OF THE CHURCH

So far we have concerned ourselves with the concept of purity as it pertains to the ideology of the Temple. Purity, however, was a concern of observant Jews beyond the confines of the Temple. We have already noted how the Pharisees, early in the first century, were extending the purity regulations to the home. We now need to examine to what extent Paul applied the concept of purity, as he would have understood it as a Jew, to the continuing life of the Church.

1. Table fellowship and the purity of food

It is clear from what Paul says in 1 Corinthians 5:11 that believers are not to share their food with one of their number who is guilty of immorality, greed, idolatry, reviling, drunkenness or robbery. This, we have argued, is because of the impurity that such a person would have brought to the community, a point that is primarily based on Paul's view that the Church, as God's Temple, in which the spirit dwells, is holy (1 Cor. 6:17) and as such cannot be allowed to have its sanctity tainted.

It is tempting, in view of this attitude towards table fellowship, to make some comparison of the Christian fellowship of believers with the Jewish *ḥavurot* whose members kept the laws of purity and refused table fellowship to those whom they considered unreliable in regard to purity and tithing. J. M. Ford has sought to draw such a comparison in her attempt to show that in Paul's use of the term ἄπιστος (which is usually translated 'unbeliever') there are grounds to say that Paul uses this word as the opposite of ἀδελφός and that one could even translate ἄπιστος as *'am ha-arets*.[1] Such a comparison is not possible, however, in the case of the believer guilty of immorality. While table fellowship is refused to him it is not thought out of place for a believer to eat with an unbeliever (1 Cor. 10:27). We must keep the usual understanding of ἄπιστος as describing one who is not a member of the Church, either Jew or Greek, and approach the question of table fellowship with believers and unbelievers differently than Ford.[2]

A comparison of 1 Corinthians 5:11 with 1 Corinthians 10:27 gives the impression of the apparently anomalous position that Paul allows a believer to eat with an unbeliever irrespective, it would seem, of his life style, while forbidding believers to eat with their own brethren who are guilty of immorality. This anomaly can, however, be resolved in the light of Paul's understanding of the nature of the Church. The believer, as we have noted, has been washed, sanctified and justified (1 Cor. 6:11). He has passed from the realm of the flesh to that of the spirit and is a 'new creation' (2 Cor. 5:17). As such he is a member of the Church and subject to the requirements that such a membership entails.

These requirements are not those of the world but are the concern of God and the Church. That is why Paul is so much against Church members taking fellow members to court in the presence of unbelievers. Unbelievers are not competent to judge the affairs of the Church (1 Cor. 6:1ff.).

In the same way Paul insists that Christians should guard the purity of the Church and not concern themselves with what goes on outside (1 Cor. 5:12f.). In fact purity is only a matter for concern within the Church. The purity regulations which Paul lays upon the believers are for them and for them only as they relate to one another within the Church. Paul can then say that 'nothing is unclean in itself' (Rom. 14:14) and at the same time use the concept of purity to point out the uncleanness that exists in the Church and insist that it be purged. A believer can eat with an unbeliever without any qualms, for believer and unbeliever do not constitute the Church. An unbeliever makes no claim to be a member of the body of Christ; he does not bear 'the name of brother' (1 Cor. 5:11); he does not come under the judgement of the believing community and can do no harm to the holiness of the believer with whom he shares his food. Each lives in a different aeon. One is in the realm of the spirit, the other in that of the flesh. Only when one has been 'washed', 'sanctified' and 'justified' can he, through his sin, pollute the fellowship of which he is a member. In the case of the immoral man he 'sins against his own body' (1 Cor. 6:18) which means, if we are to take Kempthorne's reading of this passage,[3] that this man sins at the same time against the body of which he is a member, the Church. Paul elucidates this same idea of the interrelationship of the members of the Church elsewhere: 'For just as the body is one and has many members, and all the members of the body, though many, are one body, so it is with Christ. For by one Spirit we were all baptized into one body – Jews or Greeks, slaves or free – and all were made to drink of one Spirit' (1 Cor. 12:12, 13). Part of the point of this teaching about the body is to show that members of the Church should care for one another, so that 'If one member suffers, all suffer together; if one member is honoured, all rejoice together' (1 Cor. 12:26).

If the hurt felt by an individual member is shared by the whole community one would presume that the member who made himself impure by sinning would be seen to be in danger of imparting this impurity to his brethren. As the Temple of God the Church cannot tolerate impurity, so the sinner has to be excluded from its midst and members have to be informed that they may not eat with him. Eating with one who is a brother confirms the very bonds of brotherhood and is a sign of mutual sharing of values. This cannot be so for the member who sins, for his sin harms the very body of which he is a member; and to associate with him by sharing a meal would be a sign, and a very real one at that, of condoning his sin. To eat with an unbeliever who may also be a sinner can, on the other hand, according to Paul, do no harm to the believing community. This is because there is no claim made that the two parties, believer and unbeliever, share a common bond which is Christ.

It seems that the Corinthian Church may have taken this much further and felt that any relationship with an outsider was permissible, even intercourse with a prostitute. This is the slogan that Paul seems to quote in 1 Corinthians 6:12 and 10:23; 'All things are lawful.' Paul has to rectify this belief by defining more clearly what he had really meant. The well-being of the Church as a unified body is of prime importance. Thus food laws which would cause divisions among believers of different cultural backgrounds are rejected. Paul did not keep, nor did he expect Gentile believers to keep, the rules of *kashrut* (cf. Gal. 2:11f.). On the other hand purity laws dealing with sex are handled differently by Paul. Given its nature, sexual immorality committed by a believer impinges on the very structure of the Church (cf. 1 Cor. 6:15ff.). Thus, for Paul, sex is still subject to impurity while food laws have no validity because observing them threatens the unity of the Church.

Connected with, but not exactly identical to, the question of keeping the Jewish food laws is the issue of food offered to idols. The concern here is with idolatry rather than the nature of the food itself. We have had cause to notice that idolatry in the Jewish tradition is 'understood as a principal source of impurity'.[4] For just as 'purity is the prerequisite of the grace of God'[5] so idolatry, which is, at bottom, the rejection of God, is the epitome of uncleanness.

While Paul does not expect the Church to tolerate idolaters in its midst because of their uncleanness,[6] food itself, which may or may not have been used in the service of idols, is intrinsically harmless to the community of believers: 'Eat whatever is sold in the meat market without raising any question on the ground of conscience. For "the earth is the Lord's, and everything in it"' (1 Cor. 10:25, 26). If, however, some of the brethren have qualms about such food Paul tells the Church not to upset those who may be disturbed by eating meat offered to idols; for a Jew it may seem like idolatry, while a Gentile may believe that in eating it the deity of the idol is affirmed. So, a believer who eats the food of an unbeliever but who is told (by, we are to presume, a believer):[7] 'This [food] has been offered in sacrifice' is advised by Paul that 'out of consideration for the man who informed you, and for conscience' sake – I mean his conscience, not yours – do not eat it' (1 Cor. 10:28, 29). To proceed to eat this food would serve to break the unity one had in fellowship with the informant and thus bring disunity to the Church (1 Cor. 8:12f.) and also bring the Church into bad repute: 'so whether you eat or drink, or whatever you do, do all to the glory of God. Give no offence to Jews or to Greeks or to the church of God' (1 Cor. 10:31, 32).

Paul's concern is with the unity of the Church and it is to that end, within the Church, that he makes use of the concept of purity. Outside the confines of the Church idolatry is of little concern except where it impinges on this unity. For those outside and for those of the Church who deal with those outside 'everything is indeed clean' (Rom. 14:20). Paul makes this statement in the context of writing about food and again we see that harmony (Rom. 15:5) within the Church is foremost in his mind. Individual opinions, tastes and traditions regarding food should not cause a barrier to be set up between believers:

Let not him who eats despise him who abstains, and let not him who abstains pass judgement on him who eats. (Rom. 14:3)

... decide never to put a stumbling block or hindrance in the way of a brother. (Rom. 14:13)

If your brother is being injured by what you eat, you are no longer walking in love. Do not let what you eat cause the ruin of one for whom Christ died. (Rom. 14:15)

Do not, for the sake of food, destroy the work of God. Everything is indeed clean, but it is wrong for any one to make others fall by what he eats; it is right not to eat meat or drink wine or do anything that makes your brother stumble. (Rom. 14:20, 21)

So that peace may prevail[8] within the community Jewish food laws are abrogated: 'Let us then pursue what makes for peace and for mutual upbuilding' (Rom. 14:19).

It can, of course, be argued that Paul's attitude to the traditions of purity within Judaism can be summed up in what he says in this chapter of his letter to the Roman Church: 'I know and am persuaded in the Lord Jesus that nothing is unclean [κοινός] in itself; but it is unclean for any one who thinks it unclean' (Rom. 14:14)[9] and 'Everything is indeed clean [καθαρός]' (Rom. 14:20). These two statements give Paul's view regarding the cleanness of food for the benefit of both Gentile and Jewish members of the Church and they stem from the concern expressed in verse 13 'that no obstacle or stumbling block be placed in a brother's way', that the traditional attitudes regarding food should not cause division within the Church.[10]

Paul uses the word κοινός in verse 14, which in this case means 'profane'[11] and which is used in Revelation in the sense of 'impure',[12] and in verse 20 he uses καθαρός, which appears only here in Paul,[13] but which in the LXX is the usual translation of *taharah* and appears frequently in connection with the purity regulations of the Torah.

Our study so far has shown that this is not Paul's final word on purity, but it can be said that this is his view regarding food. All food is lawful (cf. Gal. 2:11ff.) and in the case of food offered to idols this view is maintained. Idol food, or any food for that matter, is only unclean if one does, in fact, consider it to be unclean (Rom. 14:14). If one eats food which he believes, because of his weak conscience, really is offered to an idol, then his conscience is indeed defiled (μολύνω, 1 Cor. 8:7).[14] But in the end food has nothing to do with God. 'Food will not commend us to God. We are no worse off if we do not eat, and no better off if we do' (1 Cor. 8:8). We would agree then, in conclusion, with Neusner that, for Paul, the impurity decreed by the biblical food laws, which we take to include both kosher laws and the impurity naturally associated with idolatry, was suspended.[15]

2. Sexual immorality

When it comes to matters pertaining to sex Paul remains well within the Jewish tradition and continues to view sex as subject to impurity.[16] An examination of a few passages will show that Paul, in keeping with this tradition, defines sexual immorality by use of the language of impurity.

Sexual licentiousness and idolatry[17] were considered by Jews to be the characteristic sins of the Gentiles, and we find that Paul continues to regard Gentiles in the light of such an attitude. Both idolatry and sexual immorality, in Paul's view, were the lot of the non-Jew (cf. 1 Cor. 6:9f.; Gal. 5.19-20; see also Rom. 1:23-7): 'Therefore God gave them up in the

lusts of their hearts to impurity [ἀκαθαρσία], to the dishonouring of their
bodies among themselves' (Rom. 1:24). In the LXX ἀκαθαρσία is a common term for uncleanness in general, especially in Leviticus, but it comes
to denote sexual impurity in particular.[18] In Paul's letters ἀκαθαρσία invariably denotes sexual immorality and appears elsewhere in connection
with πορνεία (immorality):

> I may have to mourn over many of those who sinned before and have
> not repented of the impurity [ἀκαθαρσία], immorality [πορνεία], and
> licentiousness [ἀσέλγεια][19] which they have practised. (2 Cor. 12:21)

> Now the works of the flesh are plain: immorality, impurity, licentious-
> ness, idolatry. . . . (Gal. 5:19, 20)

Paul expresses sexual immorality in terms of uncleanness in Romans
6:19 and uses the concept of purity to help him describe the move one
makes from the realm of flesh to that of spirit on becoming a believer:
'For just as you once yielded your members to impurity and to greater
and greater iniquity, so now yield your members to righteousness for
sanctification' (Rom. 6:19). The convert passes from uncleanness to sanctification. This is a process of purification.[20] The convert who previously
lived only for impurity which only increased his iniquity can through
righteousness be set apart and made acceptable for God's service within
the Church.[21] We should note here the pairs of opposites which in Paul's
parallelism show a characteristic lack of distinction between ritual and
ethics. Uncleanness and a life of iniquity are set over and against righteousness and sanctification respectively.
Paul uses the word 'uncleanness' as a counterpart of sanctification
(ἁγιασμός) in 1 Thessalonians 4:3, 7. The context is again sexual (cf. 1
Thess. 4:4, 5) and Paul is reminding the Thessalonian Church of instructions he had already imparted to them. These instructions, as the present
verses suggest, dealt with sexual immorality.

> For this is the will of God, your sanctification: that you abstain [ἀπέ-
> χεσθαι] from immorality; that each one of you know how to take a
> wife for himself in holiness and honour, not in the passion of lust like
> heathen who do not know God. (1 Thess. 4:3-5)

> For God has not called us for uncleanness [ἀκαθαρσία] but in holiness
> [ἁγιασμός]. (1 Thess. 4:7)

There is here a hint of the requirements of the Apostolic Decree as they
are set out in Acts (Acts 15:29 ἀπέχεσθαι . . . πορνείας) and Carrington

has argued that this is, in fact, the case. He goes further and makes the suggestion that Paul's instructions, which are referred to here, constitute the teaching he used in setting up the Church as a 'neo-levitical' community. Carrington points out the comparison that can be made with passages in Leviticus:

> In I Thessalonians . . . reference is made to a Christian law of holiness ('your sanctification . . . how you are to walk') which had already been taught to converts during a period of evangelisation which had only lasted a few weeks. It contains the exact phrase of the letter of Acts XV, 'to refrain ($\dot{\alpha}\pi\acute{e}\chi\epsilon\sigma\vartheta\alpha\iota$) from fornication'; and this is further explained as to 'know how to preserve his vessel in holiness and honour, not in passion of lust as the gentiles who know not God' (I Thess. iv, 4-5). The next verse:
>
>> Not to overreach
>> Nor defraud his brother in the matter:
>> For the Lord is the avenger . . .
>
> echoes the style and manner of Lev. XIX (cf. v. 11). This negative aspect of consecration is reinforced in a positive way by the 'called . . . unto holiness' of v. 7 and the 'brotherly love' of v. 9 which recall Lev. XIX 2 and 18.[22]

Any allusion to the Apostolic Decree in his letters would not mean, of course, that Paul accepted outright the provisions as they are set out in Acts. His concern was with the purity of the Church and it is to that end that any view he held that bore some resemblance to the demands of the Jerusalem Church as set out in Acts was maintained.[23] We have noted his attitude to food offered to idols, and 1 Thessalonians 4:3, 4 suggests that he expected converts to be aware of the rules of marriage and take wives only within the permitted degrees.[24]

We are to conclude that Paul, in keeping with the Jewish traditions, viewed sexual immorality as impure and to be avoided within the Church because of the threat that such impurity presented to its sanctity[25] and to God's presence within the community.

We are in a position now to examine specific problems which relate to Paul's view of sex and marriage and with which he had to deal in the Corinthian Church. First we shall look at the question of the status of the offspring of the marriage in which only one partner is a believer (1 Cor. 7:12ff.) and secondly the question of women's head covering during worship (1 Cor. 11:2ff.).

Mixed marriage

While Paul seems to speak with some authority on the matter of divorce in
1 Corinthians 7:10, 11 and claims that his teaching is that of the Lord, he
expresses his own view on the next topic that arises: 'To the rest I say this,
as my own word, not as the Lord's' (verse 12 NEB). Here he allows the marriage of a believer with an unbeliever on condition that the unbeliever
consents to live with the believer (verses 12-13). On the other hand he
also allows for divorce if the unbelieving partner so wishes it (verse 15).

Paul is here speaking of the current situation as it was in Corinth: 'If
it is the case that a believer is married to an unbeliever' and the unbeliever
realizes that the partner has certain obligations as a member of the Church
and consents to live with the partner then that marriage is valid in Paul's
mind and there can be no divorce. The concern that Paul reveals behind
this teaching, which comes in response to a problem that has obviously
arisen in the Corinthian Church (cf. 1 Cor. 7:1), is for the offspring of
such a union. Were the children of the marriage of an unbeliever with a
believer to be considered members of the Church or were they thought of
as illegitimate and therefore unclean (ἀκάθαρτος) and outside the Church?

After giving what he considers to be the authoritative teaching of the
Lord regarding divorce in verses 10-11 Paul's statement in verse 15 regarding separation of believer and unbeliever appears liberal in the extreme.
Agreement to live with the partner serves as the criterion. If there is agreement the marriage is valid and there can be no divorce. If there is no agreement - and this, in part, would, one presumes, entail a refusal to submit
to the way of life of the Church - then they can separate.

If there is consent to live together the resulting marriage is like all others
within the Church and 'the two shall become one' (1 Cor. 6:16). Such a
union does not therefore break the union one has with the Church. In fact,
the sanctification that one receives as a believer is now passed on to the
unbelieving spouse and the children of such a union are holy and not
unclean. The manner in which Paul expresses his thought on this matter
is indeed 'taken from the language of the Levitical purification ceremonies'[26] and indeed here 'holiness is crassly regarded as a thing; it is trans-
ferable, without faith (and even baptism) being necessary'.[27]

Paul is here making use of the concept of purity in order to elucidate
a problem that has the potentiality of causing division within the Church.
In the light of already having told them that their bodies are members of
Christ and that they cannot therefore take their bodies and make them
members of a prostitute the problem of mixed marriages creates a special
problem. A choice is given to those involved in such partnerships; separate

or remain together. Those who choose to remain together would, because of what Paul says in 1 Corinthians 6:15ff, desecrate the sanctity of the Church. To overcome this problem and to involve both partners in the body of the Church Paul makes use of the concept of purity to say that because the marriage is valid, there is consent to live together, then through union with the believer the unbeliever is sanctified. Just as the believer who has intercourse with a prostitute who is outside the Church is made impure by his actions and breaks the link that he has with the Church, so now the unbeliever who becomes the legal spouse of a believer within the Church is made pure. As a result, the children of this latter relationship are holy and not unclean,[28] and, like their parents, are part of the body of the Church. The fact remains, however, that only the one parent is a believer, but Paul does allow that the unbeliever may be converted.[29]

As justification for this teaching Paul adds: 'For God has called us to peace' (verse 15). The peace and wholeness of the Church are one of Paul's prime concerns. We have noted that he prays that the Church should be found sound and blameless and guiltless at the end time and this is not far from Paul's mind when he writes to the Corinthians; 'the appointed time has grown very short' (1 Cor. 7:29) and 'For the form of this world is passing away' (verse 31). So here again we note that, faced with the problem of the unity and well-being of the Church, Paul draws on the tradition of purity to bring home his message that as the Temple of God the Church must remain pure and holy so that the Spirit can continue to dwell within it. In answer to Conzelmann's question regarding Paul's argument in 1 Corinthians 7:14, in which he asks; 'Is this kind of thinking a foreign body in the thinking of Paul?',[30] we must answer, no, it is a familiar motif in Paul's Jewish tradition and at the same time, as part of Paul's use of the concept of purity, occurs frequently throughout his letters.[31]

The veiling of women at worship

At first glance the question of the veiling of women at worship does not appear to be a problem that could be better understood by reference to the concept of purity. In recent years, however, especially since the discovery of the Dead Sea Scrolls, new interpretations have been given to Paul's statement: 'That is why a woman ought to have a veil on her head, because of the angels' (1 Cor. 11:10).[32]

Many of these interpretations have arisen because of the occurrence of the phrase 'because of the angels' in the Qumran writings.[33] No reference in the Dead Sea Scrolls is made in this context to women but this particular clause is added to passages that seek to define the nature of the religious community. In 1QM 7.4-6 and 1QSa 2.3-11 persons afflicted with various types of bodily defects are banned from either taking part in the eschatological war, or, in the case of 1QSa, from entering the sacred assembly. While no mention is made of angels, similar bodily defects and blemishes to those mentioned in these Qumran passages prevented those descendants of Aaron similarly afflicted from rendering service to God in the Temple (Lev. 21:17-23).

Gärtner has shown and we have confirmed that the Qumran community understood itself as a temple community and limited its membership to those who came up to the standards of purity that they believed were necessary within the Temple. We have also found that purity within the community was considered a necessity because it facilitated the divine presence. Furthermore the indwelling of God within the community meant that his angels were also present and were, in fact, a sign of his presence. In the two specific cases cited above where the community was called upon to keep itself pure the reason is given that it is 'because of the angels'. Impurity among the ranks of the gathered community would 'offend the sight of the angels who were present'[34] which in turn meant that God himself would be offended and remove his presence because of impurity.[35]

In the light of the evidence of Qumran it is possible that Paul's διὰ τοὺς ἀγγέλους (1 Cor. 11:10) also refers to those angels which signify the divine presence amidst the worshipping community[36] and which at the presence of any impurity would remove themselves. Given that Paul understands the Christian community as the Temple of God within which the spirit dwells this particular interpretation of the phrase certainly appears feasible.[37] The important question remains, however, namely what is it in the uncovered heads of the women that constitutes the impurity which will offend the angels?[38]

Paul praises the Corinthians for maintaining the traditions that he had handed on to them (verse 2) but apparently some misunderstanding had arisen regarding women's head covering. The Corinthians obviously thought that a woman could worship with her head uncovered.[39] Paul had to put them right on this: 'any woman who prays or prophesies with her head unveiled dishonours her head – it is the same as if her head were shaven' (verse 5). By saying that an unveiled woman dishonours her head Paul is saying, in fact, if we follow what he said in verse 3, that she is dishonouring her husband. Just as the man who worships with his head covered dishonours his head. As Paul points out in verse 3: 'I want you to understand that the head of every man is Christ, the head of a woman is her husband, and the head of Christ is God.' We would suggest, then, that Paul expected all married women to have their hair covered or tied up[40] as a sign of respect.

Many attempts have been made to understand Paul's use of ἐξουσία in verse 10. The RSV translates it 'veil' and notes that the Greek reads '*authority* (the veil being a symbol of this)'. Kittel's interpretation of ἐξουσία as veil on the basis that Paul is, by using this word, making a play on an Aramaic word which is related to both 'hair band' and 'veil', while attractive, is expecting too much linguistically of Paul's Corinthian readers, although much of what we have seen of Paul's Corinthian correspondence does suggest that allusions to the Jewish tradition are not completely lost on his readers.[41]

Perhaps one of the more successful attempts to explain Paul's use of the word 'authority' comes from Morna Hooker. She makes the important point, which is often overlooked, that this whole passage must be seen in the context of worship and in her interpretation of ἐξουσία she incorporates Paul's use of 'image' and 'glory' in verse 7.

Man, Paul explains, 'is the image and glory of God; but woman is the glory of man'. Man should not, then, particularly in worship, hide the glory of God which is his head. 'Since he is the reflexion of God's glory, any attempt to disguise this fact in worship, where God is expressly glorified, would be shameful.'[42] As for the woman, 'the glory of man', she must have her head covered 'not because she is in the presence of men, but because she is in the presence of God and his angels and in their presence the glory of man must be hidden'.[43]

Annie Jaubert in her discussion of the veiling of women[44] does not think that it is probable that Paul is concerned with ritual impurity but remarks that:

> Le contexte de I Cor. XI montre qu'il voyait une indécence dans le fait que la femme ait la tête découverte. C'est sur ce plan qu'il intervient, lui qui considérait la communauté comme le temple de Dieu (I Cor. III.16, II Cor. VI.16). L'étalage de la chevelure féminine lui paraissait intolérable dans un lieu de prière. Et sur ce point au moins il partageait les idées de son milieu.

With Jaubert we would place Paul's concern here firmly within his concept of the Church as the Temple of God and would agree with her that Paul viewed a woman with uncovered hair as a sign of immodesty out of place in an environment in which God was being worshipped. We would go further and suggest that Paul's concern here was that a woman with uncovered hair was like a woman with loosened hair.[45] For a woman's hair to be loosened is a sign of an adulteress (Num. 5:18) and Paul is sensitive to this tradition and feels that a woman with uncovered hair will bring shame upon herself and dishonour her husband.[46] In addition a woman appearing as if she were an adulteress would also be considered as impure and defiled.[47] Paul wishes to have no hint of this within the pure community of the Church. In order to make this clear Paul adds: 'because of the angels'.[48] This is an indication that he insists that this be carried out, not because of some custom[49] but because otherwise the sanctity of the community as Temple is threatened. The angels, here representing God's presence, will be offended by the apparent uncleanness which is indicated by the woman's uncovered hair.

We may add that Paul's insistence that men not wear their hair long is also tied to the question of purity. Long and dishevelled hair was both a sign of mourning (Lev. 10:6; cf. 21:10)[50] and of leprosy (Lev. 13:45) which meant that a man with long hair was considered unclean; i.e. those that mourn because of corpse uncleanness and the leper by virtue of the impurity that pertains to his disease. In addition we note that priests who must remain clean in order to serve in the Temple may not allow their hair to grow long (Ezek. 44:20).

3. Corpse uncleanness

The following observations arise from a short article by J. M. Ford.[51] She finds, in the puzzling passage in 1 Corinthians 15:29 regarding baptism 'on behalf of the dead', a reference not to the act of Christian initiation but to purification after contact with a corpse. The verse reads: 'Otherwise, what do people mean by being baptized on behalf of the dead? If the dead are not raised at all, why are people baptized on their behalf?' Instead of translating οἱ βαπτιζόμενοι as 'those who are baptized', Ford prefers 'those who dip, wash or purify themselves',[52] for the same verb and its cognates are used in just this sense in other passages in the New Testament (Mark 7:4, Luke 9:38).[53] The present tense used by Paul suggests also a repeatable action, an act which he does not appear to criticize. The Greek ὑπέρ is here usually translated 'on behalf of' or 'for' but it can equally mean 'because of'[54] and τῶν νεκρῶν are 'corpses' rather than 'the dead', the departed ones to whom Paul refers in verse 29b. Ford finds reason to translate ποιήσουσιν as 'gain' or 'profit' (cf. Luke 12:33; 16:9; John 4:1) and ὅλως as 'complete', 'in all its parts', 'in its entirety'.

With this in mind we have the following rendering of verse 29: 'Otherwise, what will they gain, those who practise purificatory rites after defilement from corpses? If the dead do not rise complete with every member [i.e. with complete body and spirit] why indeed are they purified after defilement with them?' Paul is arguing here against those who, while they question his particular teaching on the resurrection of the dead, still wash after contacting corpse uncleanness. For, as Ford suggests, purification from such impurity arises from the view that within the dead body before it has decomposed[55] is the potential for the resurrected life.[56] Paul, then, is 'using an argument *ad hominem* already expressed in Pharisaic circles'.[57] If one does not believe in the resurrection of the body as well as the spirit, what is the point, Paul asks, of washing after contact with a corpse because, as Ford argues, a corpse, like sacred books, renders the hands unclean because of its intrinsic holiness.[58]

For our own purposes here we note that Paul makes no criticism of the actual act of purification. As a Jew he expects it to be carried out along with many other aspects of his life in which the biblical purity laws continue to play a part. Like those at Qumran it does not concern him that one probably cannot purify oneself with the ashes of the red heifer, for him the Christ event had made that unnecessary. The uncleanness of corpses is now part of the 'cultural baggage' which he brings from Judaism and which he finds no need to drop for it does not interfere with his work as an apostle.

4. 2 Corinthians 6:14 to 7:1 and purity

We turn now to consider the place of 2 Corinthians 6:14 to 7:1 in the Pauline corpus, a passage which abounds with purity terminology. There has been much doubt expressed on the authenticity of these verses.[59]

The vocabulary and indeed the ideas expressed here have been seen as foreign to Paul and closer to the thought patterns of the Qumran community.[60] We would contend, however, in the light of the present study, that what is written in this passage follows very closely what we learn from some of Paul's concerns as they are expressed in the rest of his letters. To be sure there are parallels to what we read in the Dead Sea Scrolls but it has already been noted that the Qumran community was not alone in seeing itself as the Temple of God and all that that meant.

While we would agree that 2 Corinthians 6:14 to 7:1 does not fit into the context of the rest of chapters 6 and 7 of this letter, we cannot allow that the verses bear little or no relationship with what Paul writes elsewhere.

The whole passage centres on the sentence 'For we are the temple of the living God' (verse 16) and is an expression of what it meant for the Church, the body of believers, to be the dwelling place of the divine. We find particularly attractive the suggestion made by J. C. Hurd and others before him[61] that this passage formed the nucleus of a 'previous letter' of Paul, a letter in which he elucidated to the Corinthians, for the first time, the idea of the Church as the Temple. It is to this passage that he is referring when he says; 'Do you not know that you are God's temple?' (1 Cor. 3:16) and 'Do you not know that your body is a temple of the Holy Spirit within you?' (1 Cor 6:19). The Corinthians should need little reminding, for they have already read what Paul had written in a previous letter, namely that they as believers constitute the Temple of God and as such should conduct themselves accordingly.

We would contend that this passage can be understood by reference to other aspects of Paul's thought exhibited elsewhere in the Corinthian correspondence. One argument against this contention is, of course, based on the occurrence of a large number of *hapax legomena*. Gordon D. Fee, while drawing different conclusions regarding this passage, sees no problem with the *hapax legomena* that we find here.[62] He points out that 'five of the alleged NT hapaxes occur in a burst of rhetoric (verses 14-16a), and it is the nature of Pauline rhetoric to have a sudden influx of *hapax legomena*'.[63] He refers to other rhetorical passages where hapaxes occur, namely 1 Corinthians 6:7-13 and 2 Corinthians 6:3-10. He concludes that 'the quantity of hapaxes in vi.14-vii.1 is therefore not a particularly unusual feature'.[64]

We would concur that the vocabulary of 2 Corinthians 6:14-16a, although unique, does not take anything away from the authenticity of this passage, particularly when we note that ideas expressed by the use of these words coincide with what Paul says elsewhere. In these verses Paul is leading up to the main point of this passage; the Church is the Temple of God and should be kept pure in order to allow the continued presence of God. He does this by using a series of contrasts, after making the initial statement: 'Do not be mismated with unbelievers.'

The verb ἐτεροζυγέω, mismate, is one of the *hapax legomena* of this passage. It occurs in the LXX only at Leviticus 19:19 in connection with the crossbreeding of different types of agricultural animals and translates two words: the Hebrew verb 'to copulate' and *kilayim* (lit. 'two kinds'). This latter word gives its name to the law of mixtures, *kilayim*, and is found only here and in the repetition of the same law in Deuteronomy 22:9, 10. The passage in Deuteronomy says nothing about the breeding of cattle, but *kilayim* is used here as it was in Leviticus 19:19 in the law forbidding the sowing together of different kinds of seeds.

The concern expressed in the law of mixtures is that the order of God's creation be preserved,[65] the rationale behind many of the biblical purity regulations.[66] We would suggest that Paul has been influenced by these verses in attempting to give expression to his concern for the purity of the Church. Our attention is drawn not to the verses in Leviticus and Deuteronomy regarding the mating of different kinds of animals (Paul is not speaking directly to the question of marriage to unbelievers) but to the idea of mixtures and in particular to the illustration provided by the sowing of different kinds of seeds in the vineyard or field (LXX has vineyard in both passages, MT has field in Lev. 19:19). Paul refers to the Church as a field in 1 Corinthians 3:9 and alludes to it as a vineyard in 1 Corinthians 9:7. He seems to have in mind, in 2 Corinthians 6:14, the law of *kilayim*[67] which warns that if two types of seeds are mixed the whole harvest would become sanctified ($\dot{\alpha}\gamma\iota\alpha\vartheta\tilde{\eta}$) (RSV Deut. 22:9: 'lest the whole yield be forfeited to the sanctuary'). Paul has no desire to have unbelievers considered to be what they clearly are not; that is, 'sanctified' (cf. Rom. 15:16; 1 Cor. 1:2; 6:11; 7:14; 1 Thess. 5:23). The Church, God's field, the vineyard, must be clearly defined. Contact with outsiders, as Paul explains in 1 Corinthians 5:11, is naturally unavoidable, but, what can be avoided, and what must be avoided at all costs, is to have within the fellowship of the believing community one who is 'guilty of immorality . . . , or is an idolater, reviler, drunkard, or robber' (1 Cor. 5:11). Such a person no longer has the right to bear the name of brother, he is like an unbeliever ($\check{\alpha}\pi\iota\sigma\tau\sigma\varsigma$, cf. the Qumran disciplinary regulations) and must be purged from the community.

Having made his initial point Paul follows it up with a string of rhetorical questions. The dualism reflects that expressed by the Dead Sea Scrolls, but need not stem directly from Qumran.[68] The final question, 'What agreement has the temple of God with idols?' (verse 16a), leads to the key statement of this passage: 'For we are the temple of the living God' (verse 16b). The emphasis in verse 16b is on 'temple' and not 'idols'.[69] Idols here are the epitome of the uncleanness from which the community must be protected.

We have previously noted that Paul backs up what he says about the Temple by a collection of biblical citations in verse 16. These we have discussed already. The next verse speaks to the consequences of becoming the Temple and of enjoying God's presence. Using Isaiah 52:11 Paul indicates that believers, as God's holy ones, separate themselves in the same way that he himself was set apart by God (Rom. 1:1; Gal. 1:15), and 'touch nothing unclean'.[70]

Paul is certainly not calling for a complete separation from the world, but from those who would call themselves brothers yet through their immorality have become unclean and threaten the purity of the Church. It appears though, from 1 Corinthians 5:9ff., that he was in fact under-

stood to be advocating a complete shunning of outsiders, a misunderstanding which he then proceeds to clarify (1 Cor. 5:11).

In keeping the confines of the religious community pure, believers maintain their status as children of God. This is the sense of Paul's use, in verse
18, of 2 Samuel 7:14: 'I will be a father to you, and you shall be my sons
and daughters' (Paul adds 'and daughters' to what is in the MT). The actual
passage in 2 Samuel is part of Nathan's prophecy and refers to Solomon,
who 'shall build a house for my name' (2 Sam. 7:13). Paul changes the
referent to God's children who now make up his house, the Temple of the
Church. Solomon is to be punished when he commits iniquity but God's
lovingkindness will never leave him (verse 15). This is reminiscent of the
thought in 1 Corinthians 5:1ff., where Paul urges the community to rid
itself of the immoral man 'for the destruction of the flesh' but adds that
his spirit will 'be saved in the day of the Lord Jesus' (1 Cor. 5:5).

The final portion of this passage sums up the consequences of what Paul
has written for the ongoing life of the community. They have the promise
of God's spirit among them, the promise of the spirit (cf. Gal. 3:14) and
must, in preparation for the *eschaton*, keep themselves both physically
and spiritually in a state of readiness (cf. Phil. 1:10; 1 Thess. 5:23).

Thus we can see that 2 Corinthians 6:14 to 7:1, while it does not fit in
with its immediate context, is in accord with Paul's view of the Church as
the Temple of God made up of those believers who have been sanctified
but who are subject to disciplining should they threaten to bring impurity
upon the community by their immorality. If they behave like outsiders
then they will be considered as outsiders,[71] but unlike the ἄπιστοι in
general they will be shunned and have no communication with the Church,
for a brother who rejects the norms of the community is under more sus-
picion than those outside who may still turn to Christ.

In conclusion we note that Paul's use of the concept of purity serves
two purposes. First it elucidates the concept of the Church as the Temple
of God within which God's presence depends on the purity of the surroundings, and secondly it serves as a disciplinary device in order to maintain ethical standards within the community. Just as the rabbis preserved,
elaborated and extended the cultic symbols of cleanness and uncleanness[72] after the destruction of the Temple, so Paul, after the earthly
Temple had been made redundant by the saving act of Christ, applied this
same symbolism to the life of the Christian community.

We find, in Paul's attempt to define the religious community, clearly
marked lines of structure both on the level of personal interaction between
members and on the wider cosmic level involving the community's relationship with the divine. It is under such conditions that Douglas has

observed that a concern with the clean and unclean will arise.[73] In showing the extent to which Paul uses the idea of purity in his letters this study has confirmed that 'rituals of purity and impurity create unity. So far from being aberrations from the central project of religion, they are positive contributions to atonement.'[74]

6

CONCLUSION

The student of religion needs to take notice and treat seriously those disciplines that are able to provide useful tools to further his study. A refusal to acknowledge that 'purity', as an anthropological concept, is worth considering on the grounds that it has no place in the 'higher religions' closes off to the researcher an avenue of approach that can lead to a fuller understanding of his subject matter. It is hoped that this study has shown that the examination of a concept overlooked by most biblical scholars, but noted by anthropologists as being of significant importance in their attempt to interpret the life of many cultures, has helped reveal a fresh understanding of both Qumran and Paul.

We have acknowledged the centrality of the concept of purity in the religious life of the community at Qumran and we have shown that Paul uses the idea of purity in his letters in a manner which had much in common with contemporary Jewish groups. This is particularly the case on the level of purity and the divine presence in the Temple. We should look finally at the specific differences between Paul and the Jewish group, upon which we have centred our attention in this study, when it comes to the matter of purity.

It has been admitted that the concept of purity in Paul is not the one central concern in his letters. Like many other topics he uses it when it suits his purposes and then goes on to treat other problems. In a similar way, the question of righteousness which has long been thought to be Paul's major vehicle for the expression of his faith is principally utilized when dealing with the problem of the relationship of Jews and Gentiles within the Church.[1] The concept of purity arises only on certain occasions. These are, for instance, when he is dealing with discipline, discussing the nature of the believing community or seeking a basis for moral behaviour. This occasionality gives no grounds for the dismissal of purity concerns in Paul, for, as this study has shown, Paul uses the concept in several key passages in his letters.

We have noted, following Gärtner and others, that both Paul and the

Qumran covenanters perceive of their respective communities as the Temple and we have gone on to show that they employ the concept of purity, drawn from the biblical tradition, to elucidate this view. While others have noted that the Dead Sea Scrolls exhibit a concern with purity, this concern has never been strongly emphasized nor, indeed, closely examined. It is to be hoped that this study has moved towards remedying that situation in demonstrating that the concept of purity is central and governs much of the Qumran community's life. It helps give them self-identity and regulates their attitudes to outsiders, newcomers and full members.

There are, however, a number of points of difference between Paul and Qumran. A major difference centres around the question of purity/righteousness terminology. Paul's use of righteousness terminology appears, for the most part, in connection with the believer's entrance into the community. The requirements for entry are couched in terms of righteousness. One becomes a member through faith and not works and is thus made righteous. Once one is in, and a member of the Church, one enjoys the gift of the Spirit. Paul then switches to purity terminology in order to lay the framework for the behaviour pattern of believers.[2] This he does, for the most part, by linking purity with the concept of the divine presence. In order to maintain the presence of God's Spirit within the Church the believing community must be maintained in a state of purity. Righteousness language meanwhile slips into the background. At Qumran entrance to the community is defined in terms of both righteousness *and* purity, and this twofold concern remains once one achieves membership.

Furthermore, Paul's Temple has no specific physical location but exists wherever the 'saints' are assembled together. Unlike Qumran, Paul does not consider that contact with outsiders conveys impurity, but he warns, in a manner which is similar to the Qumran covenanters, that contact with believers who have become impure is to be avoided.

Generally speaking, whereas at Qumran there appears to be a systematically worked out Temple/purity scheme with an almost allegorical precision no such system is to be found with Paul. However, as this study has shown, the concept of purity is by no means unimportant in Paul's mind and plays a significant part in the elucidation of his religious thought.

NOTES

1. Introduction

1 Morton Smith, 'The Dead Sea Sect in Relation to Ancient Judaism', *NTS*, 7 (1960), 352.
2 Jacob Neusner, *The Idea of Purity in Ancient Judaism* (Leiden, 1973), p. 28.
3 E.g. Tylor, Frazer, Robertson Smith, Levy Bruhl etc., see Mary Douglas, *Purity and Danger. An Analysis of the Concepts of Pollution and Taboo* (London, 1966), pp. 13ff., 136.
4 See, for example, the Order *Tohoroth* in the Mishnah.
5 Neusner, *Idea*.
6 Jacob Neusner, *A History of the Mishnaic Law of Purities*, 22 vols. (Leiden, 1974–77).
7 For the purposes of this study the following letters will be considered to be the work of Paul: Romans, 1 and 2 Corinthians, Galatians, Philemon, Philippians, 1 and 2 Thessalonians. On the authorship of the Pauline literature see the respective introduction to each book in W. G. Kümmel, *Introduction to the New Testament* (London, 1975).
8 R. J. Zwi Werblowsky, 'A Note on Purification and Proselyte Baptism', *Christianity, Judaism and Other Greco-Roman Cults*, ed. J. Neusner (Leiden, 1975), p. 201.
9 Cf. R. Bultmann, *Primitive Christianity in its Contemporary Setting*, ET (Cleveland, 1956), pp. 65f. On the purity regulations he writes that they 'went into detail to the point of absurdity' and cites as his authority W. Bousset, *Die Religion des Judentums im späthellenistischen Zeitalter*, ed. H. Gressman (Tübingen, 1926).
10 Cf. N. Micklem, 'Leviticus', *IB* 2, pp. 52ff.; E. Durkheim, *The Elementary Forms of the Religious Life* (New York, 1967), p. 339. See the comments of Douglas, *Purity and Danger*, p. 21.
11 Hauck, *TDNT* 3, p. 417: 'The requirement of cultic purity had inner value and justification as a symbol pointing to something more profound. The fault of later Jewish religion was to give this requirement preference over a more inward concern of religion, and to prove incapable of expelling the primitive element. This led to a fatal distortion and ossification.'
12 W. Robertson Smith, *The Religion of the Semites*, 3rd edn. (London, 1927).

117

13 Douglas, *Purity and Danger*, p. 12.
14 Robertson Smith, *Semites*, p. 449.
15 Ibid., p. 447, cf. p. 422.
16 Douglas, *Purity and Danger*, p. 45. See, for example, R. E. Clements, *God and Temple. The Idea of the Divine Presence in Ancient Israel* (Oxford, 1965). This author makes no mention of purity while he deals with concepts such as the divine presence and the cult which, as we shall see, have close connections with purity.
17 Mary Douglas, 'Pollution', *IESS*, 12 (New York, 1968), p. 337.
18 T. O. Beidelman, W. *Robertson Smith and the Sociological Study of Religion* (Chicago, 1974), p. 28.
19 G. W. Buchanan, *The Consequences of the Covenant* (Leiden, 1970), p. 159, cf. Neusner, *Idea*, p. 13.
20 Cf. M. Jastrow, *A Dictionary of the Targumim, the Talmud Babli and Yerushalmi and the Midrashic Literature* (Berlin, 1926), p. 1043.
21 Buchanan, *Covenant*, p. 160.
22 Cf. Deut. 7:26; 1 Kings 21:26.
23 Douglas, *Purity and Danger*, p. 129.
24 H. Windisch, *TDNT* 2, p. 903.
25 G. F. Moore, *The History of Religion*, vol. 2 (New York, 1919), pp. 42f.
26 F. Gavin, *The Jewish Antecedents of the Christian Sacraments* (London, 1928), p. 9.
27 Ibid., p. 4, citing Bousset, *Religion*, p. 199.
28 Cf. E. P. Sanders, *Paul and Palestinian Judaism* (Philadelphia, 1977), pp. 35f., 42f. To be sure, there have been welcome exceptions. For example, R. Asting (*Die Heiligkeit im Urchristentum* (Göttingen, 1930), p. 51) maintained that: 'Allerdings empfinden die Juden eigentlich keinen Wertunterschied zwischen dem Ethischen und dem Rituellen.' A more recent, sympathetic account is to be found in E. S. Fiorenza, 'Cultic Language in Qumran and in the NT', *CBQ*, 38 (1976), 159f.
29 Gavin, *Sacraments*, p. 13. Cf. M. Douglas, *Natural Symbols. Explorations of Cosmology* (New York, 1973), p. 21.
30 Douglas, *Purity and Danger*, p. viii.
31 As suggested by H. D. Betz, 'II Cor. 6.14-7.1: an Anti-Pauline Fragment?', *JBL*, 92 (1973), 98.
32 I. Epstein, *Judaism* (Harmondsworth, 1959), p. 4.
33 Douglas, *Purity and Danger*, p. 45. A recent commentary on Leviticus, G. J. Wenham, *The Book of Leviticus* (Grand Rapids, 1979), in fact acknowledges the work of Douglas in this area.
34 Douglas, *Purity and Danger*, p. 95.
35 E.g. the hare, a rodent, masticates.
36 J. Sorel, 'The Dietary Prohibitions of the Hebrews', *The New York Review of Books*, 26 (June, 1979), 24-30; ET of 'Sémiotique de la nourriture dans la Bible', *Annales: Economies, Sociétés, Civilisations*, 28 (1973), 943-55.

37   F. Jacob, *La Logique du Vivant* (Paris, 1970), p. 119.
38   Douglas, 'Pollution', p. 338.
39   Sorel, 'Dietary Prohibitions', 28.
40   Ibid., or, as Douglas would put it, dirt is matter out of place.
41   Douglas, *Purity and Danger*, p. 113.
42   Neusner, *Idea*, p. 129. Cf. M. Eliade, *The Sacred and the Profane*
      (New York, 1959), pp. 40f., 60f. After the destruction of the
      Temple this focal point is transferred to the people themselves.
      This move was prepared for by the Pharisees in their bringing of
      the Temple purity rules into the homes of the people.
43   Douglas, *Purity and Danger*, p. 53.
44   Ibid.
45   S. R. Isenberg and D. E. Owen, 'Bodies, Natural and Contrived:
      The Work of Mary Douglas', *RSR*, 3 (1977), 2. Commenting on
      Douglas, Isenberg and Owen write: 'To understand the system of
      purity rules, their logic and their function is to understand much
      about a society.'
46   Douglas, *Purity and Danger*, p. 115.
47   Ibid., p. 57.
48   J. Neusner, 'History and Structure: The Case of Mishnah', *JAAR*,
      47 (1977), 186.
49   Neusner, *Idea*, p. 108.
50   J. Neusner, 'Method and Structure in the History of Judaic Ideas:
      An Exercise', *Jews, Greeks and Christians*, ed. R. Hamerton-
      Kelly and Robin Scroggs (Leiden, 1976), p. 99.
51   Neusner, *Idea*, p. 25.
52   Ibid., p. 115.
53   Ibid., p. 28.
54   Ibid., p. 15.
55   J. Milgrom, 'Kipper', *EJ* 10, p. 1042.
56   B. A. Levine, *In the Presence of the Lord* (Leiden, 1974), p. 75.
57   Milgrom, 'Kipper', p. 1042. Milgrom argues against Levine's view
      that biblical impurity is both dynamic *and* demonic: Levine,
      Presence, pp. 101–8.
58   J. Milgrom, 'Israel's Sanctuary: The Priestly Picture of Dorian
      Gray', *RB*, 83 (1976), 398.
59   J. Milgrom, 'Sin-offering or Purification-offering?', *VT*, 21 (1971),
      237–8.
60   J. Neusner, 'History and Structure', 186.
61   Neusner, *Idea*, p. 117.
62   G. Alon, 'The Bounds of Levitical Cleanness', (in Hebrew) *Tarbiz*,
      9 (1937–38), 1–10, 179–95, ET *Jews, Judaism and the Classical
      World* (Jerusalem, 1977), p. 233; Neusner, *Idea*, p. 65; J. Milgrom,
      'Purity and Impurity', *EJ* 13, p. 1412.
63   Cf. Alon (*Jews, Judaism and the Classical World*, pp. 211ff.), who
      counters Büchler's view ('The Levitical Impurity of the Gentile in
      Palestine Before the Year 70', *JQR*, n.s. 17 (1926–27), 1–82)
      that the extension of the rules of purity to the laity took place
      only after AD 70. See also J. Neusner, 'The Fellowship (*havurah*)

in the Second Jewish Commonwealth', *HTR*, 53 (1960), 125f. This controversy is based on rabbinic sources whose dates of origin are not completely determinable. We, however, in dealing with Qumran and Paul have before us material which can be definitely dated before AD 70.

64 Neusner, 'History and Structure', 185.
65 Alon, *Jews, Judaism and the Classical World*, p. 199.
66 Cf. M. Ab. 3.3, 7.
67 B. Gärtner, *The Temple and the Community in Qumran and the New Testament* (Cambridge, 1965).
68 G. Klinzing, *Die Umdeutung des Kultus in der Qumrangemeinde und im Neuen Testament* (Göttingen, 1971).
69 G. Forkman, *The Limits of the Religious Community* (Lund, 1972).
70 Neusner, *Idea*, p. 59.
71 R. J. McKelvey, *The New Temple* (Oxford, 1969), p. 122.
72 H. Wenschkewitz, *Die Spiritualisierung der Kultusbegriffe. Tempel, Priester und Opfer im Neuen Testament* (Leipzig, 1932), p. 116.
73 M. Fraeyman, 'La Spiritualisation de l'Idée du Temple dans les Epîtres pauliniennes', *ETL*, 23 (1947), 405. For a criticism of the tendency in the study of ancient Judaism to dismiss cultic concerns and look only at what is seen as a spiritualization of these concerns see H-J. Hermisson, *Sprache und Ritus im altisraelitischen Kult* (Neukirchen, 1965), pp. 24ff.
74 See, for example, our discussion of Rom. 3:25, pp. 75-7.
75 Much has been done with the idea of the spiritualization of the Temple in the New Testament, e.g. Wenschkewitz, Fraeyman, McKelvey, but these works have ignored a concern which any Jew would have had when considering the Temple, namely purity.
76 The more important elements of the Pauline purity terminology that have LXX parallels are as follows: ἁγιάζω, ἁγιασμός, ἅγιος, ἀκαθαρσία, ἀκάθαρτος, ἄμεμπτος, ἄμωμος, ἀτιμάζω, δεκτός, εἰλικρινής, ἐκκαθαίρω, καθαρίζω, καθαρός, κοινός, μολυσμός, ὁλόκληρος, συναναμείγνυμι, τελειός.
77 O. Michel, *Paulus und seine Bibel* (Gütersloh, 1929), p. 68: 'er lebt und arbeitet nur mit seiner griechischen Bibel'.
78 E. E. Ellis, *Paul's Use of the Old Testament* (Edinburgh, 1957), pp. 150f.
79 From his comments in Gal. 1:22 it appears that Paul had little contact with Jerusalem before visiting the city after his conversion, in spite of the account in Acts of his earlier life. See E. Haenchen, *The Acts of the Apostles*, ET (Oxford, 1971), p. 625; J. Knox, *Chapters in the Life of Paul* (New York, 1950), pp. 35f.
80 Paul's obvious familiarity with the Bible is widely accepted, especially his ability to employ it in argument (e.g. in Romans and Galatians).
81 Thus, for instance, in Rom. 3:25, Paul describes Christ as the *kapporet*, the cover of the ark, which did not figure in the cultic

furniture of the Second Temple but which plays a central role in the rites described in Leviticus 16. See pp. 75-7.

2. The concept of purity in the Qumran community

1   This study will proceed on the assumption that the Essenes as described by Josephus are identical with the community at Qumran which was responsible for the Scrolls. This is now almost universally accepted. See P. Wernberg-Møller, *The Manual of Discipline* (Leiden, 1957), p. 19; A. R. C. Leaney, *The Rule of Qumran and its Meaning* (London, 1966), p. 33; M. Hengel, *Judaism and Hellenism*, vol. 2 (London, 1974), pp. 142f., n. 690; Sanders, *Paul*, p. 239; G. Vermes, *The Dead Sea Scrolls. Qumran in Perspective* (London, 1977), p. 130: 'The only remaining alternative is that the archeologists have uncovered relics of a hitherto totally unknown Jewish sect almost identical to the Essenes.' But see L. H. Schiffman, *The Halakhah at Qumran* (Leiden, 1975), p. 136: 'The Qumran sect has affinities with the Pharisaic and Essene traditions yet its separate identity must be recognized', while Yigael Yadin believes that the Temple Scroll 'corroborates the identification of the sect with the Essenes'. See J. Milgrom, 'The Temple Scroll', *BA*, 41 (1978), 119.
2   See the works of Gärtner and Klinzing.
3   We shall include in our study a consideration of the Damascus Document (CD), which is also known as the Zadokite Document, only fragments of which were found in the caves at Qumran. The complete document was discovered in the Cairo *genizah* in 1896. While it is a generally accepted view that CD belongs to the writings of the Qumran community (see Schiffman, *The Halakhah*, p. 4) it must be recognized that CD and the other scrolls were written over a period of time and of necessity reflect a historical development. We feel satisfied that in spite of a lack of overall homogeneity within and among the scrolls these documents can be used as a whole in order to determine aspects of the sect's basic theology. See Hengel, *Judaism and Hellenism*, vol. 2, p. 148, n. 739; Benno Przybylski, *Righteousness in Matthew and his World of Thought* (Cambridge, 1980), pp. 13ff.; Sanders, *Paul*, p. 239.
4   C. H. Hunzinger, 'Beobachtung zur Entwicklung der Disziplinarordnung der Gemeinde von Qumran', *Qumran-Probleme*, ed. H. Bardtke (Berlin, 1963), p. 233. Josephus, *Bell.* II. 129, 138: ... ἀπολούονται τὸ σῶμα ψυχροῖς ὕδασιν, καὶ μετὰ ταύτην τὴν ἀγνείαν.
5   H. W. Huppenbauer, '*Ṭahar* und *ṭaharah* in der Sektenregel von Qumran', *TZ*, 13 (1957), 351.
6   Klinzing, *Die Umdeutung*, p. 111.
7   J. M. Baumgarten, 'Sacrifice and Worship among the Jewish Sectarians of the Dead Sea (Qumran) Scrolls', *HTR*, 46 (1953), 148, 151.

8   C. Rabin, *Qumran Studies* (Oxford, 1957), pp. 6ff.
9   Rabin, *Qumran Studies*, pp. 7, 8. Cf. Baumgarten, 'Sacrifice and Worship', 148.
10   Ibid., p. 8.
11   S. Lieberman, 'The Discipline in the So-called Dead Sea Manual of Discipline', *JBL*, 71 (1952), 203.
12   Cf. Baumgarten, 'Sacrifice and Worship', 148.
13   D. Flusser, 'The Dead Sea Sect and pre-Pauline Christianity', *Scripta Hierosolymitana*, 4 (1965), 243; Wernberg-Møller, *Manual of Discipline*, p. 96; H. Ringgren, *The Faith of Qumran* (Philadelphia, 1963), p. 218; G. Vermes, *The Dead Sea Scrolls in English* (Harmondsworth, 1962): 'pure meal', p. 79; M. Burrows, *The Dead Sea Scrolls* (London, 1956): 'sacred food', p. 377.
14   W. H. Brownlee, 'The Dead Sea Manual of Discipline', *BASOR Supplemental Studies* (New Haven, 1951), p. 21.
15   Based, in Rabin's case, on his assumption that identifies those responsible for 1QS with the early Pharisees. See Rabin, *Qumran Studies*, pp. vii, viii. While Lieberman ('Discipline', 202ff.) points out that there are striking external similarities between the pharisaic groups and Qumran it is not necessary to go as far as Rabin and identify the two groups.
16   See Leaney, *Rule of Qumran*, p. 168 on 'those who join'. Cf. Isa. 14:1, 56:3 re proselytes 'joining' Israel.
17   Cf. 1QH 6.20, 'where no man goes who is uncircumcised, unclean or violent'.
18   The proselytes in CD 14.3ff. are recruited from the Jews. Cf. H. H. Rowley, *The Zadokite Fragments and the Dead Sea Scrolls* (Oxford, 1962), pp. 35f., n. 8; Wernberg-Møller, *Manual of Discipline*, p. 56, n. 49.
19   Cf. 4QF1 1.3f., 1QSa 2.5f., Lev. 21:17-23. While 4QF1 and 1QSa are eschatological there is no reason to believe that they did not apply to the present situation. Cf. 1QSa 2.21, 22, Gärtner, *The Temple and the Community*, p. 96; A. Jaubert, *La notion d'alliance dans le judaisme de l'ère chrétienne* (Paris, 1963), p. 199.
20   Gärtner, *The Temple and the Community*, p. 7.
21   On the titles *paqid* and *mebaqqer*, see Wernberg-Møller, *Manual of Discipline*, p. 107, n. 42.
22   Cf. 1QS 9.21, 23; CD 10.2. This word, *ne'eman*, however, is not used in exactly the same sense in the Scrolls. On 'trustworthy' as a technical term in relation to one who keeps the purity laws see G. W. Buchanan, 'The Role of Purity in the Structure of the Essene Sect', *RQ*, 3 (1960), 403.
23   Along with Leaney (*Rule of Qumran*, p. 177) we may assume that this is also understood in 1QS 6.14.
24   Rabin, *Qumran Studies*, p. 4.
25   Cf. 1QS 5.23: 'understanding and perfection of way'.
26   See M. Delcor, 'Le vocabulaire juridique, cultuel et mystique de l'"initiation" dans la secte de Qumrân', *Qumran-Probleme*, ed. H. Bardtke (Berlin, 1963), p. 123. He notes that: 'dans l'A.T. les

verbes *qarev* ou *nagash* sont employés pour exprimer le service liturgique des prêtres qui s'approchent de Dieu'. Thus it is not difficult to give a cultic meaning to those phrases in the Scrolls where these verbs are used, particularly as many of the passages refer to those who may or may not approach the Lord or the Holy Place and the offerings because of their purity or lack of it, cf. *qarev*: Lev. 9:5, 7, 8; 21:17, 18; 22:3; Ezek. 42:13, 14; 43:23; 44:15, 16, 27; *nagash*: Lev. 21:21, 23; Ezek. 44:13. See also Klinzing, *Die Umdeutung*, pp. 117f.

27 Lieberman, 'Discipline', 202.

28 See also S. Lieberman, *Greek in Jewish Palestine* (New York, 1965), p. 80: 'In my opinion, the word *ba'im* is a shortened technical term for coming to embrace a new faith (or new principles).'

29 Sanders, *Paul*, pp. 240ff.

30 Cf. CD 15.5f.; also CD 3.10–14, 1QpHab 7.4f.

31 See Hunzinger, 'Beobachtung', 235. Both *'etsah* and *mishpaṭ* express the same concept in 1QS 6.9.

32 Cf. 1QS 5.11: 'hidden things' vs. 'revealed things'.

33 It should be noted that the Scrolls are permeated by references to esoteric teachings which are jealously guarded by the community. See M. Newton, *The Concept of Secrecy in the Hodayot*, unpublished M.A. Thesis, McMaster University, 1975.

34 Rabin, *Qumran Studies*, p. 6.

35 Klinzing, *Die Umdeutung*, pp. 116ff.; Sanders, *Paul*, p. 313; O. Betz, 'Le ministère cultuel dans le secte de Qumran et dans le Christianisme primitif', *La secte de Qumran et les origines du Christianisme*, ed. J. van der Ploeg (Bruges, 1959), p. 167; Jaubert, *La notion d'alliance*, pp. 145ff.

36 Klinzing, *Die Umdeutung*, p. 41.

37 Cf. the use of 'Lebanon' in 1QpHab 12.3 as a symbol of the community and as a symbol of the Temple. See Vermes, *Qumran in Perspective*, p. 181, and *Scripture and Tradition* (Leiden, 1961), pp. 26–39, and Jaubert, *La notion d'alliance*, p. 159. For the community as a temple see 1QS 5.6; 8.5, 8, 11; 9.6; 11.8; Klinzing, *Die Umdeutung*, p. 37: 'Die Gemeinde selbst ist der wahre Tempel.'

38 Wernberg-Møller, *Manual of Discipline*, p. 124.

39 Exod. 28:43; 30:17–31; 40:31–2.

40 1 Kings 8:10–13. See below for God's presence in the community.

41 Vermes, *The Dead Sea Scrolls in English*, p. 87. Cf. Klinzing, *Die Umdeutung*, pp. 38, 41, Ringgren, *Faith of Qumran*, p. 215, Gärtner, *The Temple and the Community*, p. 20.

42 Jaubert, *La notion d'alliance*, p. 159: 'Vivre dans la communauté, ce serait pour les laïcs se conduire toujours comme dans le Temple, et pour les prêtres se considérer toujours comme dans le Saint de Saints.'

43 Cf. 1QSa 2.5–9; Lev. 21:17–22.

44 Klinzing, *Die Umdeutung*, p. 109.

45 Cf. 1QS 5.18.

46 Cf. Lev. 11:47; 20:25.

47   See O. Betz, 'Le ministère cultuel', 166ff. Note also the use made of the Ezekiel account of the Temple in 11Q Temple 12.16–17, 31–3, 48. See Milgrom, 'The Temple Scroll', *BA*, 41 (1978), 114.

48   CD 10.14 to 11.18. Schiffman, *The Halakhah*, pp. 131ff. Rabin (*Qumran Studies*, p. 86) points out that this is only a relative strictness: the sabbath rulings of Jubilees are far more rigid; but now see 11Q Temple.

49   Note that Ps. Sol. 2:38 has 'distinguish between righteous and sinners'.

50   See Rabin, *Qumran Studies*, p. 61.

51   Cf. Num. 16:21.

52   Sanders, *Paul*, p. 244.

53   Betz, 'Le ministère cultuel', p. 167. See also Klinzing, *Die Umdeutung*, pp. 130ff.

54   See 11Q Temple 22.4, 12; 57.12–15; 61.8–9. J. Milgrom, 'Studies in the Temple Scroll', *JBL*, 97 (1978), 501ff.

55   See Vermes, *The Dead Sea Scrolls in English*, pp. 23f.; Leaney, *Rule of Qumran*, pp. 71ff.

56   I.e. from the Jews. See Rowley, *The Zadokite Fragments*, pp. 35f.

57   Jaubert, *La notion d'alliance*, p. 151: 'symboliquement tous les hommes de la communauté entraient dans la grande lignée des fils de Sadoq ou tout au moins des fils de Lévi'.

58   *TDOT* 2, p. 1.

59   BDB, p. 634.

60   Neusner, *Idea*, pp. 28, 117.

61   Alon, *Jews, Judaism and the Classical World*, p. 232.

62   CD 4.18.

63   Rabin's understanding of *'arav* is followed here and elsewhere. Instead of 'mix' or 'mingle' he takes it to mean 'make common cause' or 'have contact with'. See also M. Black, *The Essene Problem* (London, 1961), p. 22.

64   Hunzinger, 'Beobachtung', p. 234.

65   Forkman, *Limits*, p. 55.

66   E. Hatch and H. A. Redpath, *A Concordance to the Septuagint*, vol. 1 (Oxford, 1897), p. 150b.

67   H. St J. Thackeray, *Josephus, the Man and the Historian* (London, 1929), pp. 77ff.

68   Wernberg-Møller, *Manual of Discipline*, p. 62, n. 52.

69   1QS 3.4.

70   A. Büchler, *Studies in Sin and Atonement in the Rabbinic Literature of the First Century* (London, 1928), pp. 294, 297.

71   Cf. Rabin, *Qumran Studies*, p. 29 and 4QSe.

72   Cf. Rabin, *Qumran Studies*, p. 8.

73   Black, *The Essene Problem*, p. 22: 'property (hon) included all that belonged to one, such as land, livestock, houses etc., as well as money'.

74   E.g. Ezek. 27:12; Prov. 19:14 etc.

75   'Men of falsehood' are understood to be not complete outsiders (Wernberg-Møller, *Manual of Discipline*, p. 135, n. 20) with

whom it would not, because of the nature of the community, be necessary to warn against contact but either those who were once members (Black, *The Essene Problem*, p. 22), or Jews who do not belong to the community (Sanders, *Paul*, p. 244).

76 1QS 9.17ff.

77 Cf. 1QS 1.11–12: 'All those who freely devote themselves to His truth shall bring all their knowledge, powers, and possessions into the community of God.'

78 Black, *The Essene Problem*, pp. 19ff.

79 This is Black's interpretation of 1QS 5.2, *leyaḥad batorah uvahon*, as a *hendiadys* rather than a basis for an argument for 'total community of possessions', p. 23.

80 Black, *The Essene Problem*, p. 27.

81 Num. 18:20, 23ff.; 26:62. Also Ezek. 44:28ff.

82 Rabin, *Qumran Studies*, p. 31; Black, *The Essene Problem*, pp. 24ff.

83 Wernberg-Møller, *Manual of Discipline*, p. 101. Lieberman 'Discipline' (203) identifies *rabim* with *yahad*. Cf. Ringgren, *The Faith of Qumran*, pp. 211f.

84 This phrase is often taken to be separate from what precedes it, see Vermes, *The Dead Sea Scrolls in English*, p. 82. This is because many commentators take *'arev* to mean 'merge' or 'mingle' and see here an example of the communism of the sect whereby the new members' property is now joined with that of the common property of the sect.

85 'Purity' sometimes actually means specifically food.

86 Cf. Lev. 20:25, 26.

87 Rabin, *Qumran Studies*, p. 9.

88 Let it be reiterated here that the ritual bath would not have been considered under the heading of 'drink'; it would not be a liquid susceptible to impurity. By their nature 'waters of impurity', the water in which the unclean person bathes, be it a menstruant or, as is often the case at Qumran, a full member who has sinned or has had contact with a novice, are not made impure.

89 J. Allegro, *The Dead Sea Scrolls* (Harmondsworth, 1956), p. 90; A. Dupont-Sommer, 'Culpabilité et rites de purification dans la secte juive de Qoumran', *Semitica*, 15 (1965), 61.

90 W. H. Brownlee, 'John the Baptist in the Light of the Dead Sea Scrolls', *The Scrolls and the New Testament*, ed. K. Stendahl (New York, 1957), p. 35.

91 R. de Vaux, *The Bible and the Ancient Near East* (London, 1972), p. 201.

92 O. Betz, 'Die Proselytentaufe der Qumransekte und die Taufe im Neuen Testament', *RQ*, 1 (1958), 218. Brownlee, 'John the Baptist' (p. 38) hints at such a procedure.

93 Betz, 'Die Proselytentaufe', 218.

94 A. Büchler, 'The Levitical Impurity of the Gentile before the Year 70', *JQR*, n.s. 17 (1926–7), 20. It is not clear at what time the Gentile became to be considered by Jews to be, by nature,

unclean. It was, however, Büchler's opinion (page 2) that this was not until after the destruction of the Temple. But see the criticism of Büchler on this point in G. Alon, 'The Levitical Uncleanness of Gentiles', in *Jews, Judaism and the Classical World* (Jerusalem, 1977), pp. 146-89 and J. Neusner, 'The Fellowship (*ḥavurah*) in the Second Jewish Commonwealth', *HTR*, 53 (1960).

95 Betz, 'Die Proselytentaufe', 218.
96 Flusser, 'The Dead Sea Sect', 243.
97 See B. J. Bamberger, *Proselytism in the Talmudic Period* (New York, 1968), for references.
98 J. Gnilka, 'Die essenischen Tauchbäder und die Johannestaufe', *RQ*, 3 (1961), 191. See also W. Paschen (*Rein und Unrein. Untersuchungen zur biblischen Wortgeschichte* (München, 1970), p. 93) and his slight modification of Gnilka's view.
99 J. Pryke, 'The Sacraments of Holy Baptism and Holy Communion in the Light of Ritual Washings and Sacred Meals at Qumran', *RQ* 5 (1964/66), 546ff. See also G. R. Beasley-Murray, *Baptism in the New Testament* (London, 1962), p. 17.
100 Pryke, 'Sacraments', 544.
101 *Bell.* II.138. See H. H. Rowley, 'The Baptism of John and the Qumran Sect', in *New Testament Essays*, ed. A. J. B. Higgins (Manchester, 1959), p. 220.
102 Alon, *Jews, Judaism and the Classical World*, pp. 172f.
103 Note, however, that no mention is made here of a bath, cf. H. Haag, 'Das liturgische Leben der Qumrangemeinde', *ArchLit*, 10 (1967), 98.
104 Rowley, 'The Baptism of John', p. 222.
105 J. Bowman, 'Did the Qumran Sect Burn the Red Heifer?', *RQ*, 1 (1958), 82. See also Brownlee, 'John the Baptist', pp. 37f., and Jaubert, *La notion d'alliance*, p. 150.
106 Bowman, 'Did the Qumran Sect Burn the Red Heifer?', 84.
107 See R. de Vaux, *Ancient Israel* (New York, 1965), p. 462. He comments that 'the rite concerning the ashes of the red heifer and the use of lustral water is rather paradoxical; it appears to have been an archaic rite which lived on side by side with the official religion; it was not even part of the ordinary life of the people'. According to M. Para 3.5 the ritual of the red heifer is said to have taken place in the last three hundred years of the Temple only five or perhaps seven times. Cf. J. Jeremias, *Jerusalem in the Time of Jesus* (London, 1969), p. 152; Klinzing, *Die Umdeutung*, p. 116.
108 J. Neusner, *A History of the Mishnaic Law of Purities*, vol. 10 (Leiden, 1976), p. 209: 'I am unable to find any reference to the rite of the red cow in the Dead Sea library.'
109 Cf. M. Mik. 1.1-8. For a cautious comment on the use of the cisterns for purification at Qumran see de Vaux, *The Bible and the Ancient Near East*, p. 201: 'There are two or three smaller pools where the steps take up more room and they are very prob-

ably baths. But again this evidence is not decisive, since archeology is unable to show whether or not the baths taken were ritual ones.'

110 See Ringgren, *The Faith of Qumran*, p. 221.
111 Lev. 12:2; 15:19ff.; 18:19; Ezek. 22:10.
112 Cf. 2 Chr. 29:5; Ps. Sol. 8:11ff. See also Ps. Sol. 2:3; Enoch 59:73; Test. Levi 16:1; Ass. Mos. 5:3.
113 Cf. Delcor, 'Le vocabulaire juridique', p. 128.
114 Neusner, 'The Fellowship', 127.
115 Cf. Lev. 22:6; Klinzing, *Die Umdeutung*, pp. 109f.
116 Ringgren, *The Faith of Qumran*, p. 220; cf. Test. Levi 8:4, 5.
117 Flusser, 'The Dead Sea Sect', p. 229.
118 K. G. Kuhn, 'The Lord's Supper and the Communal Meal at Qumran', in *The Scrolls and the New Testament*, ed. K. Stendahl (New York, 1957), p. 68.
119 Ibid.
120 J. Gnilka, 'Das Gemeinschaftsmahl der Essener', *BZ*, 5 (1961), 51.
121 Klinzing, *Die Umdeutung*, p. 50.
122 Klinzing devotes a complete section of his book to perfection of way and praise as sacrifice, pp. 93-106.
123 *Tamin* occurs frequently especially in Leviticus and Ezekiel to describe the perfection required of sacrificial offerings.
124 Exod. 30:17-20; 40:30-2; Lev. 22:6; Test. Levi 9:11-12; Jub. 21:16; M. Tamid 1.2, M. Yoma 3.2.
125 CD 10.10; cf. Test. Levi 10:11; Jub. 21:16; M. Hag. 2.6. See Gnilka, 'Gemeinschaftsmahl', 43. He refers to the purity requirements of Deut. 23:10f. which are laid out for the camp in which God walks (verse 15). This is appropriate considering the concern of 1QM and the Temple Scroll.
126 On the possibility of this referring to either the temple services in the future or symbolically to the present cultic activity of the sect, see Gärtner, *The Temple and the Community*, pp. 8f. and Sanders, *Paul*, p. 299, n. 172.
127 In view of our understanding of *sekel* 1QS 5.23 shows that a member could be advanced or moved down according to his knowledge and his observance of the purity laws.
128 J. van der Ploeg, 'The Meals of the Essenes', *JSS*, 2 (1957), 163-75. For studies of the meal itself see Kuhn, 'The Lord's Supper'; Gnilka, 'Gemeinschaftsmahl'; J. F. Priest, 'The Messiah and the Meal in 1QSa', *JBL*, 82 (1963), 95-100; M. Delcor, 'Repas cultuels esséniens et thérapeutes Thiases et Haburoth', *RQ*, 6 (1967/9), 401-25.
129 Van der Ploeg, 'The Meals of the Essenes', 171.
130 See also Haag, 'Das liturgische Leben', 101.
131 Cf. the Temple Scroll.
132 Kuhn, 'The Lord's Supper', p. 68.
133 *Bell.* II.129-31, *Ant.* XVIII.18-21.
134 See van der Ploeg's explanation of this, 168.

135 Wine, like leaven, is a fermented and thus an altered substance. Sorel, 'Dietary Prohibitions', 28: 'fermentation is the equivalent of a blemish'.
136 R. de Vaux, 'Fouilles de Khirbet Qumran; rapport préliminaire sur les 3ᵉ, 4ᵉ et 5ᵉ campagnes', *RB*, 63 (1956), 574.
137 Neusner, *Idea*, p. 136.
138 Van der Ploeg, 'Meals of the Essenes', 173.
139 See Kuhn, 'The Lord's Supper'.
140 Van der Ploeg, 'Meals of the Essenes', 171. Gärtner (*The Temple and the Community*, p. 10) seems able to isolate 'a meal which was purely sacral in character' from other meals, but presents no evidence that such a differentiation was made by the community. For a further view that the regulations in 1QS 6.4f. constitute nothing except the daily meals of the community see E. F. Sutcliffe, 'Sacred Meals at Qumran?', *The Heythrop Journal*, 1 (1960), 51.
141 Gnilka, 'Gemeinschaftsmahl', 54.
142 For meals eaten before God see Exod. 18:12; Deut. 12:7, 18; 14:23; cf. Jaubert, *La notion d'alliance*, p. 202. Note that *tirosh* is used for wine in Deut. 14:23.
143 De Vaux, *Ancient Israel*, pp. 325f.
144 Levine, *In the Presence of the Lord*, p. 75.
145 Cf. Sifre Num. *Naso* 2; Sanders, *Paul*, pp. 81f.
146 J. Abelson, *The Immanence of God in Rabbinical Literature* (London, 1912), p. 138.
147 Gärtner, *The Temple and the Community*, pp. 26f. In 4QSᵉ *ma'on* is substituted by *ma'oz*, citadel or fortress. But see the use of *ma'oz* with 'temple' in Dan. 11:31. See J. T. Milik, review of Wernberg-Møller, *The Manual of Discipline*, *RB*, 67 (1960), 413. Cf. Jaubert, *La notion d'alliance*, p. 94.
148 *Zevul* is also used in the Bible for God's dwelling in both heaven and the Temple but is used only of the heavenly abode in the Scrolls, cf. Gärtner, *The Temple and the Community*, p. 94.
149 Cf. b. Tamid 32b; b. Ber. 6a. See Gnilka, 'Gemeinschaftsmahl', 49.
150 See H.-W. Kuhn, *Enderwartung und gegenwärtiges Heil* (Göttingen, 1966); Klinzing, *Die Umdeutung*, p. 90.
151 On describing the covenant as 'new' see Sanders, *Paul*, p. 241.
152 Cf. Jub. 1:17.
153 On an interesting parallel to the idea of God's presence within the desert community see ARN 34; S. Schechter, *Aboth de Rabbi Nathan* (New York, 1967), p. 102; J. Goldin, *The Fathers According to Rabbi Nathan* (New York, 1974), p. 142.
154 Ringgren, *The Faith of Qumran*, p. 89.
155 N. A. Dahl, 'The Origin of Baptism', in *Interpretationes ad Vetus Testamentum pertinentes Sigmundo Mowinckel*, ed. A. S. Kapelrud (Oslo, 1955), p. 45.
156 F. Nötscher, 'Heiligkeit in den Qumranschriften', *RQ*, 1 (1958-9),

165; Klinzing, *Die Umdeutung*, p. 98; Exod. 12:5; 29:1; Lev. 1:3, 10 etc.
157 Klinzing, *Die Umdeutung*, p. 98. He also notes the use of *tamin* with *ratson* in Lev. 22:21.
158 See Nötscher ('Heiligkeit', 163f.) on the distinction between the two.
159 Cf. Jaubert, *La notion d'alliance*, p. 145.
160 N. H. Snaith, *The Distinctive Ideas of the Old Testament* (London, 1947), p. 43.
161 Neusner, *Idea*, p. 1.
162 Klinzing, *Die Umdeutung*, p. 13.
163 Forkman, p. 65.
164 Cf. M. Demai 2.2; Jastrow, *Dictionary*, p. 866; G. W. Buchanan, 'The Role of Purity in the Structure of the Essene Sect', *RQ*, 3 (1960), 403.
165 Rabin, *Qumran Studies*, p. 108; Leaney, *Rule of Qumran*, p. 224.
166 Wernberg-Møller (p. 130) points to the relationship of these three passages. The use of *zakar* in 1QS 8.18; CD 10.3 (cf. 1QS 3.4; 9.9) is identical to that of *ṭaher* in 1QS 5.13. Cf. A. M. Honeyman, 'Isaiah 1:16 *hizaku*', *VT*, 1 (1951), 63–5.
167 Sanders, *Paul*, p. 324.
168 Hunzinger, 'Beobachtung', pp. 242–5. See Sanders (*Paul*, pp. 323ff.) where the whole problem is discussed.
169 See Klinzing, *Die Umdeutung*, pp. 51ff.
170 Cf. 1QS 5.8 where those who join the community swear a binding oath 'to turn to the Torah of Moses according to everything he commandeth'.
171 Sanders, *Paul*, p. 325.
172 Rabin (*Qumran Studies*, pp. 108f.) proposes a distinction between the Torah of Moses, which he feels 'cannot be anything but "Biblical" law' and *mitsvah* which 'must denote a less hallowed category'. This distinction should not, however, be so clear cut as to suggest that the *mitsvot* were seen as anything but laws derived from Torah and thus God's laws.
173 Ps. 101:6, 7 displays a striking parallel with 1QS 8.21–3 and these verses in the Scrolls may reflect an awareness of the words of the psalmist. Verse 7 from Psalms reads: 'No man who practises deceit shall dwell in my house.' In the previous verse it is 'he who walks in the way that is blameless shall minister to me'. So in 1QS the individual who 'walks in the way of perfection' is expelled from the community if he transgresses the Torah of Moses intentionally.
174 Milgrom, 'Israel's Sanctuary', 393.
175 See also J. Milgrom, 'Two kinds of *ḥaṭṭa't*', *VT*, 26 (1976), 333–7.
176 Levine, p. 76. For *kipper* as 'cleanse', 'purge', see pp. 63ff.
177 Milgrom, 'Israel's Sanctuary', 393.
178 J. M. Baumgarten, review of Y. Yadin, *The Temple Scroll*, *JBL*, 97 (1978), 588.

179 Klinzing, *Die Umdeutung*, pp. 93ff.; Gärtner, *The Temple and the Community*, pp. 44f. The use of Prov. 15:8 in CD 11.20f.: 'The sacrifice of the wicked is an abomination, but the prayer of the just is an agreeable offering' shows how prayer substitutes for sacrifice, for the time being. Cf. C. Rabin, *The Zadokite Documents* (Oxford, 1958), p. 58.

180 Cf. Sanders, *Paul*, p. 303. The man who suffers from corpse uncleanness and who has not purified himself is cut off, for he 'defiles the tabernacle of the Lord' (Num. 19:13). See Levine, *In the Presence of the Lord*, p. 75, where he translates *et migdas YHWH timme* as 'he has rendered the sanctuary of YHWH impure'.

181 Leaney translates *'al pi hadebarim* here as 'on the authority of the words' and takes *hadebarim* to perhaps refer to 'the words of the scholars of the sect, their authoritative interpretations of the law' (*Rule of Qumran*, p. 200). We prefer Vermes' translation here but would note that the *mishpatim* are most likely the rules and regulations of the community which were determined by the community's own interpretations of Torah (*bemidrash yahad*). Cf. Wernberg-Møller, *Manual of Discipline*, p. 120.

182 We would, with Hunzinger ('Beobachtung', pp. 235f.), and Sanders (*Paul*, p. 285), take the punishment referred to throughout this passage as that specified in 1QS 6.25: namely, a quarter of his food is held back from him.

183 There is enough space at the end of line 27 to read 'and he shall be excluded'. Cf. 1QS 7.5 and E. Lohse, *Die Texte aus Qumran* (Darmstadt, 1971), p. 24.

184 Cf. Leaney, *Rule of Qumran*, p. 203.

185 *'al nephesh*, when translated 'for his soul's sake', is vague. See Leaney, *Rule of Qumran*, p. 203, for alternatives, e.g. 'for his life's sake'. See also Wernberg-Møller, *Manual of Discipline*, p. 114.

186 Cf. Exod. 15:24. See Leaney, *Rule of Qumran*, p. 208, for further biblical references.

187 On arrogance, cf. Mek. Ba-Hodesh 9, 'whosoever is proud of heart causes the land to be defiled and the Shekinah to withdraw'.

188 Wernberg-Møller, *Manual of Discipline*, p. 120: '*hmshpt* alludes to the common store of halakic knowledge of the community'.

189 Milgrom, 'Israel's Sanctuary', 392. Cf. M. Shev. 1.4f.

190 Restoring *weleta[har'ano]sh*, Lohse, *Die Texte*, p. 128; M. Mansoor, *The Thanksgiving Hymns* (Grand Rapids, 1961), p. 131; M. Delcor, *Les Hymnes de Qumran (Hodayot)* (Paris, 1962), p. 150.

191 Levine, *In the Presence of the Lord*, pp. 50ff.

192 Milgrom, 'Israel's Sanctuary', 391, see also Jaubert, *La notion d'alliance*, p. 166 and *TDNT* 3, p. 315.

193 Milgrom, 'Israel's Sanctuary', 393.

194 Cf. Sanders, *Paul*, p. 303, who refers to Jub. 6.2f. in this connection. Cf. Lev. 18:28; 20:22; also Sifre Num. 161; Milgrom, 'Kip-

per', p. 1043. Deut. 32:43 (LXX) has ἐκκαθαριεῖ κύριος τὴν γῆν
λαοῦ αὐτοῦ. The Qumran fragment which contains this verse is
closer to the LXX than the MT. See P. W. Skehan, 'A Fragment
of the Song of Moses from Qumran', *BASOR*, 136 (1954), 12–
15; F. M. Cross, *The Ancient Library of Qumran and Modern
Biblical Studies* (Garden City, 1958), pp. 182f. The latter
attempts a reconstruction of the original text of this verse.

195   Cf. 4QPs37 4.5; much of this *pesher* on Psalm 37 deals with both
the destruction of the wicked and the community who will possess the land in the future. See also 1QM 12.12, 4QF1 1.2, 3.

196   Morton Smith, 'The Dead Sea Sect', 352.

197   Levine, *In the Presence of the Lord*, p. 75. On the heavenly cult
and its earthly counterpart see J. Strugnell, 'The Angelic Liturgy
at Qumran', *Suppl. to VT*, 7 (1960), p. 335.

198   For the cultic understanding of this expression see Delcor, 'Le
vocabulaire juridique', p. 124.

199   G. F. Moore, *Judaism*, vol. I (Cambridge, 1927), p. 410. The idea
is drawn from Isa. 63:9 and it is expressed widely in the pseudepi-
graphal literature: Jub. 1.27, 29; 2.2; 15.27; 31.14; Enoch 6.2;
13.8; 40.2; Test. Levi 3.42.

200   Cf. Lev. 21:17–23. See J. A. Fitzmyer, 'A Feature of Qumran
Angelology and the Angels of 1 Cor. 11:10', in *Essays on the
Semitic Background of the New Testament* (London, 1971), pp.
198ff.

201   Fitzmyer, 'Qumran Angelology', p. 202.

202   J. T. Milik, *Ten Years of Discovery in the Wilderness of Judaea*
(London, 1959), p. 114.

203   Gärtner, *The Temple and the Community*, p. 33.

3. Purity and the cult in the letters of Paul

1   Levine, *In the Presence of the Lord*, pp. 75f.

2   Gärtner, *The Temple and the Community*.

3   Cf. Wenschkewitz, *Kultusbegriffe*, pp. 116f.

4   Gärtner, *The Temple and the Community*, p. 60.

5   Gärtner, *The Temple and the Community*, p. 60. See also Y.
Yadin, *The Temple Scroll* (Jerusalem, 1977).

6   Against the views of Peter Richardson, *Israel in the Apostolic
Church* (Cambridge (1969), pp. 116f. and Lloyd Gaston, *No
Stone Upon Another* (Leiden, 1970), p. 187. Cf. W. D. Davies,
Paul and Rabbinic Judaism (London, 1970), p. 232.

7   We shall deal in greater detail with this particular passage later,
because of its special nature, its use of purity terminology and
the doubts many have expressed regarding its authenticity.

8   Neusner, *Idea*, p. 65.

9   These ideas are paralleled in the Dead Sea Scrolls, which speak of
the community as a plantation, holy building and house and of
the Teacher of Righteousness as the builder of the community.

4QPs37 3.15f.; 1QS 8.5; 11.8; CD 1.7f.; 1QH 6.24; 8.4ff., 20ff.
Cf. Klinzing, *Die Umdeutung*, p. 168.
10   The reference here is to the community, the local Church and not the individual. Cf. A. Robertson and A. Plummer, *The First Epistle of St Paul to the Corinthians* (Edinburgh, 1911), p. 66; Gärtner, *The Temple and the Community*, p. 57; Forkman, *Limits*, p. 139; H. Conzelmann, *I Corinthians* (Philadelphia, 1975), p. 178.
11   Rom. 6:16; 11:2; 1 Cor. 5:6; 6:2, 3, 9, 15, 16, 19; 9:13, 24.
12   It may well be the case that the original teaching on the community as Temple was given by Paul in 2 Cor. 6:16 and that these other references to this fact refer back to an earlier correspondence which contained the categorical statement 'for we are the temple of the living God'. This would place 2 Cor. 6:14 to 7.1 as a 'Vorbrief' of Paul's Corinthian correspondence. In a footnote J. C. Hurd gives a brief survey of those who support this hypothesis, *The Origin of I Corinthians* (London, 1965), p. 236. Hurd himself believes 'that this fragment was originally part of an original letter', p. 237. In addition see the bibliographical details supplied by J. Gnilka, '2 Cor. 6.14–7.1 in the Light of the Qumran Texts and the Testaments of the Twelve Patriarchs,' in *Paul and Qumran*, ed. J. Murphy-O'Connor (London, 1968), p. 49.
13   E.g. Ezek. 45:19; 1 Chron. 29:4.
14   Matt. 12:6; 24:1; Mark 13:3; Luke 21:5; Acts 24:6; 25:8.
15   See p. 60.
16   Gärtner, *The Temple and the Community*, p. 53.
17   Cf. M. Kelim 1.8, 9.
18   Gärtner, *The Temple and the Community*, p. 58. Cf. Klinzing, *Die Umdeutung*, p. 171 and W. D. Davies, *The Gospel and the Land* (Berkeley, 1974), p. 193.
19   Hurd, *The Origin of 1 Corinthians*, p. 237.
20   Cf. E. E. Ellis, *Paul's Use of the Old Testament* (Edinburgh, 1957), pp. 178f.
21   Cf. Jub. 1:17 where the passage is similarly cited.
22   Davies, *Paul*, pp. 216f.
23   It is useful here to compare this idea to the kind of statement made in post-70 Judaism. Commenting on Exod. 20:24b ('in every place where I cause my name to be remembered I will come to you and bless you') Mek. Bahodesh 11 (II, p. 287) reads: 'the sages said: wherever ten persons assemble in a synagogue the Shekinah is with them, as it is said: "God standeth in the congregation of God" (Ps. 82:1). And how do we know He is also with three people holding court? It says: "In the midst of the judges He judgeth" (ibid). And how do we know He is also with two? It is said: "Then they that feared the Lord spoke one with another," etc. (Mal. 3:16). And how do we know that He is even with one? It is said: "in every place where I cause my name to be mentioned I will come unto thee and bless thee".'
24   Cf. Gärtner, *The Temple and the Community*, pp. 52ff., 58.

25 This verb is used also in Rom. 7:18, 20 but with a completely different subject and in the very ordinary sense, on a human level, of 'cohabit' in 1 Cor. 7:12, 13.
26 See Luke 11:51 where the parallel passage in Matt. 23:35 has ναός. Cf. Robertson and Plummer, *1 Corinthians*, p. 66.
27 On the interchanging of the word *Shekinah* and Holy Spirit in the rabbinic literature see J. Abelson, *The Immanence of God in Rabbinical Literature* (London, 1912), pp. 377ff. Abelson states that 'the two terms, having so much in common, are ofttimes used indiscriminately', while, in the earlier Tannaitic Midrashim, *Shekinah* was preferred 'when the ideas of Holy Spirit in the Christian sense were making great inroads among many people' (p. 379). Moore is of the same opinion concerning the use of the term *Shekinah* in the rabbinic literature (e.g. Mek. Baḥodesh 11 to Exod. 20:24). He writes that it 'is not something that takes the place of God, but a more reverent way of saying "God"'. G. F. Moore, 'Intermediaries in Jewish Theology', *HTR*, 15 (1922), 58. See also P. Schäfer, *Die Vorstellung vom Heiligen Geist in der rabbinischen Literatur* (München, 1972), pp. 135ff.
28 Taking ναός as the antecedent of οἴτινες. See Robertson and Plummer, *1 Corinthians*, p. 68 and Conzelmann, *I Corinthians*, p. 78.
29 Conzelmann, *I Corinthians*, p. 78.
30 See W. Bauer, *A Greek English Lexicon of the New Testament*, trans. W. F. Arndt and F. W. Gingrich (Chicago, 1957), p. 864, for the possible renderings of φθείρω. The AV 'defile' fits in very well with our theme but is not supported in the sources.
31 Robertson and Plummer, *1 Corinthians*, p. 67. Cf. 2 Sam. 6:2-8.
32 Robertson and Plummer, *1 Corinthians*, p. 67.
33 On the punishment due to those who defile the sanctuary see Jub. 30:14ff.; M. San. 9.6. Note that the Mishnah that deals with the severe punishments for the priest who serves in uncleanness and the non-priest who serves in the Temple is followed in M. San. 10.1 by 'All Israelites have a share in the world to come.'
34 See p. 88 on 1 Cor. 5:5.
35 P. Vielhauer, *Oikodome. Das Bild vom Bau in der christlichen Literatur vom Neuen Testament bis Clemens Alexandrinus* (Karlsruhe, 1940), p. 32.
36 Wenschkewitz, *Kultusbegriffe*, pp. 58ff., 82ff.; cf. Klinzing, *Die Umdeutung*, pp. 83ff.
37 R. J. McKelvey, *The New Temple* (Oxford, 1969), p. 104; cf. Gärtner, *The Temple and the Community*, p. 141.
38 Cf. Gärtner, *The Temple and the Community*, p. 141.
39 Cf. L. Cerfaux, *The Church in the Theology of Paul* (New York, 1959), p. 148.
40 *de Somniis* I.146f.; cf. Wenschkewitz, *Kultusbegriffe*, pp. 83f.
41 Gärtner, *The Temple and the Community*, p. 141.
42 R. Kempthorne, 'Incest and the Body of Christ. A Study of I Cor. 6:12-20', *NTS*, 14 (1967/8), 568-74.

43   C. F. D. Moule, *An Idiom Book of New Testament Greek* (Cambridge, 1953), p. 196.
44   Moule, *New Testament Greek*, p. 121; Bauer, *Lexicon* (Arndt and Gingrich, trans.) p. 370; cf. John 1:41; Matt. 22:5.
45   Kempthorne, 'Incest', 573.
46   Ibid.
47   The definite article is lacking here in the Greek as it is in 1 Cor. 3:16 and 2 Cor. 6:16.
48   McKelvey (*The New Temple*, p. 104) notes that, for Paul, 'God the Spirit does not dwell in the individual *qua* individual but as member of the Christian community.' Cf. 1 Cor. 12:13: 'For by one Spirit we were all baptized into one body'; also Cerfaux, *The Church*, p. 148. Note, however, that Paul also emphasized that the individual believer is in possession of the Spirit by virtue of being 'in Christ' (Rom. 8:9ff.).
49   Conzelmann, *I Corinthians*, p. 77; Robertson and Plummer, *1 Corinthians*, p. 66; Cerfaux, *The Church*, pp. 147f.
50   Cf. Gaston, *No Stone Upon Another*, pp. 187f.
51   Levine, *In the Presence of the Lord*, pp. 75f.
52   Cf. Sanders, *Paul*, pp. 467f.
53   Davies, *Land*, p. 191; cf. Gal. 4:25 on the heavenly Jerusalem.
54   Davies, *Land*, p. 193. We may note here that for Paul even circumcision *in and of itself* was acceptable (Gal. 6:15; 1 Cor. 7:19) and *in and of themselves* dietary and sabbath laws were unobjectionable (Rom. 14:1–6). The same can be said of Paul's attitude to the Temple, see p. 67. A far stronger support for Paul's positive attitude to the Temple is found in John T. Townsend, 'The Jerusalem Temple in the First Century' in *God and His Temple*, ed. L. E. Frizzell (South Orange, 1980), pp. 52ff.
55   K. Weiss, 'Paulus – Priester der christlichen Kultgemeinde', *TLZ*, 79 (1954), 359.
56   Weiss, 'Paulus', 357.
57   J. M. Ford ('The First Epistle to the Corinthians or the First Epistle to the Hebrews?', *CBQ*, 28 (1966), 409), maintains that both 'temple' and 'altar' here, which 'are in the singular and have the definite article . . . must refer to the Temple at Jerusalem'.
58   Conzelmann, *I Corinthians*, p. 157.
59   Cf. J. M. Ford ('The First Epistle to the Corinthians', 402ff.), who sees an entirely Jewish audience for the letter and W. D. Davies (*Paul*, p. 50), who states: 'there must have been a considerable Jewish element in the Church at Corinth'. An understanding of the biblical tradition does not, as these two authors suggest, necessitate a Jewish readership but only proselytes and God-fearers familiar with the reading of the Greek Bible in the synagogues. Cf. W. D. Davies, review of H. D. Betz, *Galatians. A Commentary on Paul's Letter to the Churches of Galatia, RSR*, 7 (1981), 311ff.
60   Bauer, *Lexicon* (Arndt and Gingrich trans.), p. 629.
61   It occurs only in Prov. 1:21; 8:3, with a different meaning.

62 Cf. H. G. Liddell and R. Scott, *A Greek-English Lexicon* (Oxford, 1948), p. 812.
63 David Daube, *The New Testament and Rabbinic Judaism* (London, 1956), p. 395; cf. Ford, 'The First Epistle to the Corinthians', 409.
64 Cf. Davies (*Paul*, p. 145), who writes: 'Paul would not find it strange to regard himself as a Christian Rabbi charged to be a steward not only of a κήρυγμα but of a διδαχή.'
65 Daube, *Rabbinic Judaism*, p. 396.
66 See below pp. 68ff.
67 Joshua 1:1; 2 Sam. 13:18; 1 Kings 10:5; 2 Kings 4:43; 6:15; 2 Chron. 9:4; 3 Macc. 5:5.
68 Sir. 10:2.
69 See on Phil. 4:17f. pp. 62ff.
70 Cf. Philo, *Leg. All.* 3.135, λειτουργὸς τῶν ἀγιῶν, Bauer, *Lexicon* (Arndt and Gingrich trans.), p. 472.
71 Cf. W. Sanday and A. C. Headlam, *The Epistle to the Romans* (Edinburgh, 1896), p. 405.
72 Cf. Rom. 12:1.
73 *A hapax legomenon* in the NT.
74 Sixtine edition.
75 Written 'sometime between A.D. 40 and 118'. J. H. Charlesworth, *The Pseudepigrapha and Modern Research with a Supplement* (Chico, 1981), p. 151. Cf. D. Hill, *Greek Words and Hebrew Meanings* (Cambridge, 1967), p. 43.
76 R. H. Charles, ed., *The Apocrypha and Pseudepigrapha of the Old Testament*, vol. 2 (London, 1913), p. 674.
77 Weiss, 'Paulus', 357.
78 F. W. Beare, *The Epistle to the Philippians* (London, 1973), p. 155.
79 Gen. 25:6; 47:2; 1 Sam. 18:25; 1 Kings 13:7.
80 Lev. 23:38: τῶν δομάτων ὑμῶν . . . ἃ ἂν δῶτε τῷ κυρίῳ.
81 Cf. Phil. 4:15.
82 Cf. ἀγίοι, 'saints', in Rom. 1:7; 1 Cor. 1:2; 2 Cor. 1:1.
83 See below.
84 Lev. 21:6.
85 Regarding κάρπωμα George Buchanan Gray (*Sacrifice in the Old Testament* (Oxford, 1925), p. 12) points out that 'etymologically this word should mean a fruit offering'. See also A. Deissmann, *Bible Studies* (Edinburgh, 1901), p. 135.
86 Cf. the same reading in Philo, *Leg. All.* 1.52.
87 N. H. Snaith, *Leviticus and Numbers* (London, 1967), p. 134.
88 Cf. Lev. 23:20; 27:21. See also Phil. 3:3: 'we are the true circumcision'. In alluding to the converts as Levites as well as referring to them as 'fruit' Paul lacks the allegorical consistency of the Qumran covenanters.
89 Cf. also Sir. 35.1.
90 Cf. Phil. 4:19.
91 *TDNT* 4, p. 284.

92   ἀγιάσῃ τῷ κυρίῳ.
93   Cf. Luke 4:18-22. See John Howard Yoder, *The Politics of Jesus* (Grand Rapids, 1972).
94   Cf. 2 Cor. 2:15f.: 'we are the aroma of Christ'.
95   Note, Phil. 4:19, God, in return, supplies every need.
96   Lev. 7:18; 19:7; 22:3, 22, 25, 27; Deut. 33:11.
97   In the English versions *laqaḥ* is usually taken to mean 'to take' but it also has the sense of 'receive' or 'accept', BDB, p. 543. *Codex Alexandrinus* has λήμψῃ with the other versions in verse 26. For λῆμψις or λῆψις see Phil. 4:15. G. W. H. Lampe, *Patristic Greek Lexicon* (Oxford, 1961), p. 801; J. H. Moulton and G. Milligan, *The Vocabulary of the Greek Testament* (London, 1930), p. 374.
98   Cf. Lev. 22:27 where the burnt offering (κάρπωμα) is received (δεχθήσεται) as a gift (δῶρα) and Num. 8:14, 15 LXX where the Levites are cleansed and offered as a gift before God.
99   See Hatch and Redpath, *Concordance*, vol. 2, pp. 1018f.
100   On the use of δουλεύω see p. 68.
101   Cf. here 'fruit' of Phil. 4:17 and Paul's use of ἀπαρχή elsewhere.
102   Exod. 29:24, 26, 27; Lev. 10:15; 14:12; Num. 8:11.
103   Weiss, 'Paulus', 455. Cf. Richardson, *Israel*, p. 116, who believes Weiss overstates his case.
104   Note the cultic λειτουργέω (Rom. 15:27) in a context undoubtedly material.
105   See below the discussion of Rom. 12:1 and the understanding of λογικός as rational, reasonable etc.
106   Beare, *Philippians*, p. 156.
107   Verse 9 has λατρεύω.
108   There is a trace here of a *do ut des* contract.
109   Weiss, 'Paulus', 357.
110   E.g. Deut. 13:14; Judges 2:7; 1 Sam. 7:3, 4 etc.
111   In Psalm 102:22 *'avad* δουλεύω are usually translated 'worship' in the English versions in order to maintain the parallelism with the previous stanza. The *hiphil* of *'avad* is translated by δουλεύω in the LXX *Sinaiticus* and *Alexandrinus* versions of Isa. 43:23.
112   Cf. Phil. 4:18.
113   Note that LXX has εἰς τέλος for the MT *be'arets*.
114   Note that the LXX includes both male and female slaves here.
115   This service is directed also towards the members of the Church, for in 2 Cor. 4:5 he describes himself as a servant to the Corinthians. He is not alone in this service. Timothy is also a servant of Jesus Christ (Phil. 1:1) who serves with Paul in his Gospel. Paul, in referring to himself as 'a servant of Christ' in Gal. 1:10 may well be alluding to the secular relationship of slave-master in which the slave, in this case Paul, can serve only one master, Christ. This secular understanding of δοῦλος-δουλεύω is pursued by Paul in Rom. 6:1ff., where he contrasts the slave of sin with the slave of righteousness.
116   Weiss, 'Paulus', 357.

117 See p. 86, on 1 Thess. 5:23.
118 Cf. 2 Cor. 5:9. Paul seeks to be acceptable (εὐάρεστος) to the Lord. Neither εὐάρεστος or the verb εὐαρεστω have any cultic connotations in the LXX. Εὐαρέστησις however, appears in Aquila, Symmachus, Theodotion at Exod. 29:18 and in Symmachus at Ezek. 20:41 with reference to the acceptability of the sacrifice. Both these verses in the major versions have ὀσμὴ εὐωδίας.
119 Ἐργάζεσθαι τὰ ἔργα κυρίου, cf. 1 Cor. 9:13.
120 The Hebrew *badal*, which is translated by ἀφορίζω in Lev. 20:25, 26, is frequently used to denote the separation of cultic functionaries for their priestly service. This is shown in Num. 16:9. *Badal* is here translated by διαστέλλω which is used in a similar way to ἀφορίζω in the LXX. Cf. Lev. 10:10; 11:47; Num. 8:14.
121 C. E. B. Cranfield, *The Epistle to the Romans*, vol. 1 (Edinburgh, 1975), p. 53.
122 Cf. Cranfield, *Romans*, p. 54. See also Gal. 1:15.
123 Cf. Paul's μάρτυς, Rom. 1:9.
124 See Psalm 16:5 (LXX) where κληρονομία translates *ḥeleq* which appears in Joshua 22:25 as μερίς, 'portion', cf. Isa. 61:7.
125 It is suggested by Roland de Vaux, *Ancient Israel* (New York, 1965), p. 341, that Joshua 22:25, 26 may have served as a justification for the setting up of Temples outside of Jerusalem in Israel's later history, e.g. Leontopolis. Paul has of course set up a Temple apart from Jerusalem in treating the Church as the Temple of God.
126 Weiss, 'Paulus', 357; Sanday and Headlam, *Romans*, p. 20; 'the πνεῦμα is the organ of service; the εὐαγγέλιον (=τὸ κήρυγμα τοῦ εὐαγγελίου) the sphere in which the service is rendered'. See Cranfield, *Romans*, pp. 76f. for the various interpretations of these phrases. Paul's priestly service may also be suggested by his use of διάκονος and διακονία (Weiss, 'Paulus', 358). No such cultic use is to be found in the LXX, while διακονέω is found only twice in reference to priestly service in Josephus (*Ant.* 7.365; 10.72; Beyer, *TDNT*, 1, p. 83). But in Rom. 15:31 Paul hopes that his διακονία may be acceptable, εὐπρόσδεκτος to the saints. Εὐπρόσδεκτος is used cultically elsewhere in Rom. 15:16.
127 Cf. Exod. 29:18, Aquila, Symmachus, Theodotion; Ezek. 20:41, Symmachus.
128 Sanday and Headlam, *Romans*, p. 352. See also Bauer (Arndt and Gingrich, trans.), p. 367. Cf. Josephus, *Ant.* 4.6, 4.
129 Bauer, *Lexicon* (Arndt and Gingrich, trans.), p. 633.
130 On 'acceptable', see above, in note 118.
131 Cf. Exod. 12:16; Lev. 23:2ff.; Num. 28:25 where κλητὴ ἁγία is the liturgical assembly of the Jews gathered together on feast days (cf. 1 Cor.5:8) at God's behest. See Cerfaux, *The Church*, p. 118.
132 Lev. 22:14; cf. Phil. 4:17f.
133 Cf. Num. 6:20.

134 Bauer, *Lexicon* (Arndt and Gingrich, trans.), p. 477: 'a favourite expression of philosophers since Aristotle'.
135 Sanday and Headlam, *Romans*, p. 231.
136 Λατρεία is used in Joshua 22:27 LXX for the service, *'avodah*, which the Transjordanian tribes performed as a witness. See above, 69, on Rom. 1:9.
137 Not in LXX.
138 The acceptable, good and perfect may refer back to the will of God, but there is the connection to the first part of this verse, which calls on the Church not to conform to the present age, that enables these three adjectives to apply to the body of believers. This understanding can be further substantiated by noting the use of τέλειος in a cultic setting in the LXX. Cf. Exod. 12:5; Deut. 18:13; Judg. 20:26; 21:4 (B text); Ezra 2:63 (τέλειος = sacred objects).
139 Cf. 2 Cor. 2:15; Phil. 4:18.
140 Cf. Phil. 2:17.
141 Rom. 15:6; 1 Cor. 6:20; Phil. 2:15.
142 Note the cultic use of this word in 1 Peter 2:5.
143 Moulton and Milligan, *Vocabulary*, p. 264. Cf. Ben Sira 35.6.
144 Cf. Phil. 4:18.
145 Cf. 1 Cor. 6:11.
146 Cf. the Levites as a gift to Aaron and Phil. 4:17f.
147 M. R. Vincent, *The Epistles to the Philippians and to Philemon* (Edinburgh, 1897), p. 71.
148 For possible alternatives see Vincent, *Philippians and Philemon*, p. 71.
149 Klinzing, *Die Umdeutung*, p. 217; 'Weil die Christen selbst ihr Leben darbringen, sind sie nicht nur Opfer, sondern zugleich *Priester.*'
150 Beare, *Philippians*, p. 94, who accepts the hendiadys against Vincent, *Philippians and Philemon*, p. 217.
151 *TDNT*, 4, p. 60.
152 Kempthorne, 'Incest', 573, takes this to mean 'keep God's Temple holy (cf. 3:17) by removing the man who is defiling it'. (Cf. Deut. 28:59.)
153 Also 2 Thess. 2:13.
154 Further use of ἀπαρχή with other terms familiar to us in Paul's use of cultic terminology is found in Ezek. 45:1, 6, 13, 16.
155 This cultic dimension may well be present in 1 Cor. 15:20, 23, where Christ is described as the 'first fruits'.
156 W. G. Kummel, 'Πάρεσις and ἔνδειξις. A Contribution to the Understanding of the Pauline Doctrine of Justification', *Journal for Theology and the Church*, 3 (1967), 6.
157 Sanday and Headlam, *Romans*, p. 87, cite Origen as saying that Christ is 'at once priest and victim and place of sprinkling'. Cf. S. Lyonnet and L. Sabourin, *Sin, Redemption and Sacrifice* (Rome, 1970), p. 159.
158 See Davies, *Paul*, pp. 237ff.; Hill, *Greek Words*, pp. 38ff.; Cran-

field, *Romans*, pp. 214ff.; A Nygren, 'Christus der Gnadenstuhl', in *In Memoriam Ernst Lohmeyer* (Stuttgart, 1951), pp. 89-93; Lyonnet and Sabourin, *Sin*, p. 159. B. F. Meyer, in a forthcoming article, discusses the pre-Pauline nature of these verses. See also P. Stuhlmacher, 'Zur neueren Exegese von Röm 3, 24-26', in *Jesus und Paulus*, eds. E. E. Ellis and E. Grässer (Göttingen, 1975), pp. 315-33.

159 Levine, *Presence*, p. 75.
160 Milgrom, 'Israel's Sanctuary', 393.
161 Ibid.
162 An example of the underestimation of this aspect of the religious life of Judaism is found in Cranfield, *Romans*, p. 215, where the *kapporet* is described as '*only* an inanimate piece of temple furniture' (my italic).
163 Milgrom, 'Israel's Sanctuary', 396: 'The God of Israel will not abide in a polluted sanctuary. The merciful God will tolerate a modicum of pollution. But there is a point of no return. If the pollution continues to accumulate the end is inexorable: "The cherubim lifted their wings" (Ez. 11.22). The divine chariot flies heavenward and the sanctuary is left to its doom.'
164 Cf. Isa. 53:5-12; Rom. 4:25; 8:3; 1 Cor. 15:3. B. Lindars, *New Testament Apologetic* (London, 1961), p. 82.
165 The *kapporet* is also the place where God reveals himself, Exod. 25:22, and in Philo, *Vita Mos.* II (III), 8.95, *De fuga* 19 (100) a symbol of God's benevolent power.
166 On προέθετο as 'set forth publicly' see Lyonnet and Sabourin, *Sin*, pp. 159, 165.
167 This is only one aspect of the significance of Christ's death. Cf. 2 Cor. 5:14f.; 1 Thess. 5:10. See Sanders, *Paul*, pp. 463-8.
168 Paul does not make use of the term ἱλαστήριον again but we note within his letters a reiteration that Christ forms part of a structure which makes up the Church; e.g. 'foundation', 'body', 'in Christ'.
169 See Davies, *Paul*, p. 239, and his answer to Vincent Taylor's objection. Cf. Rom. 12:1 where the believer is seen as both offering and priest (Klinzing, *Die Umdeutung*, p. 217), and Phil. 2:17, 'Even if I am to be poured as a libation upon the sacrificial offering of your faith . . . .'
170 See the connection that is made between grace, cleansing and atonement from sin and uncleanness in 1QS 11.12-15.
171 J. Milgrom, 'Sin Offering or Purification Offering?', *VT*, 21 (1971), 237-9. It has been suggested frequently that ἁμαρτία in Rom. 8:3, and 2 Cor. 5:21 means sin or preferably purification offering: Plummer, *II Corinthians*, p. 187; Sanday and Headlam, *Romans*, p. 193. D. E. H. Whiteley, *The Theology of Saint Paul* (Oxford, 1974), p. 100 comments that: 'II Cor. 5.21 probably does employ sacrificial language in order to illuminate the apostle's thought on redemption'.
172 Milgrom, 'Kipper', p. 1040.

4. Purity and membership of the Church

1 Levine, *Presence*, p. 77.
2 Levine, *Presence*, p. 76; cf. Lev. 16:16.
3 P. Carrington, *The Primitive Christian Catechism* (Cambridge, 1940), pp. 16ff.
4 Davies, *Paul*, p. 130.
5 If not a Pharisee *per se* Paul did at least see himself as being within that tradition, cf. Phil. 3:5f. On the role of purity in the Diaspora see E. R. Goodenough, *The Jurisprudence of the Jewish Courts in Egypt* (New Haven, 1929), p. 144. He writes: 'these laws for purification probably bulked very much larger in Jewish life in the Diaspora than one would infer from their slight emphasis in Philo's discussion'.
6 Neusner, *Idea*, pp. 114f.
7 Morton Smith, 'The Dead Sea Sect', 352.
8 Sanders, *Paul*, p. 468.
9 *Spec. Leg.* III. 209.
10 Douglas, *Purity and Danger*, p. 53; Sorel, 'Dietary Prohibitions', 29.
11 Cf. Jer. 2:22 (LXX).
12 In the tannaitic literature 'immorality as well as idolatry are proved from various biblical passages to cause the withdrawal of God's presence', Büchler, *Studies in Sin and Atonement*, p. 294. Cf. Sifre Deut. 258 (to 23.15); 254 (to 23.10); Mekilta *Baḥodesh* 9 (II 274; Exod. 20:21).
13 I.e. a proselyte baptism. It has even been questioned whether proselyte baptism was, in fact, regarded at this time as a purificatory act performed on Gentiles simply because of their impurity as Gentiles. It was Büchler's view that the idea of the levitical uncleanness of Gentiles was not recognized until the end of the period of the Second Temple; Büchler, 'The Levitical Impurity of the Gentile', p. 2 passim. Alon (*Jews, Judaism and the Classical World*, pp. 147f.) has argued against this view: 'The impurity of the non-Jews is one of the early Halakhot, current among the nation a long time before the destruction of the Temple', and 'the impurity of non-Jews served as the initial reason for the ritual immersion of proselytes'. He argues that the impurity of Gentiles is tied up with the view that the idol and its worshippers were defiled.
14 It is more likely that the majority were Gentile in Paul's churches. For the view that Paul preached exclusively to Gentiles see E. P. Sanders, 'Paul's Attitude Toward the Jewish People', *USQR*, 33 (1978), 175-87, and Stendahl's reply, 'A Response', ibid., 189-91.
15 For Paul, the Jew, Gentiles were sinners by definition, cf. Gal. 2:15.
16 Sanders, *Paul*, p. 468; J. Jeremias, *The Origins of Infant Baptism* (London, 1963), p. 84.

17 Cf. 2 Cor. 6:17: 'therefore come out from among them, says the Lord, and touch nothing unclean'.

18 Sanders, *Paul*, pp. 463, 468.

19 Robertson and Plummer, *1 Corinthians*, p. 119; Sanders, *Paul*, p. 471; Bauer, *Lexicon* (Arndt and Gingrich transl.), p. 197: 'in the context of I Cor. 6:11 ἐδικαιώθητε means *you have become pure*'.

20 Acts 22:16: Paul's speech: 'Rise and be baptized, and wash away [ἀπολούω] your sins'.

21 'If I wash myself [ἀπολούω] with snow, and cleanse my hands with lye.'

22 E.g. Aaron and the priests: Exod. 29:4; 40:12; Lev. 8:6; 16:4, 24, 26, 28. Corpse uncleanness: Lev. 11:40. Leprosy: Lev. 4:8, 9. Bodily discharges: Lev. 15:6.

23 Not found in Paul, but see John 13:10; Heb. 10:22; cf. Rev. 1:5.

24 See, for example, Beasley-Murray, *Baptism in the New Testament*, p. 163: 'the voice of scholarship is unanimous in affirming the association with baptism'.

25 Cf. Beasley-Murray, ibid., p. 164: 'The aorists for the verbs in I Cor. 6.11 point to a once and for all event.'

26 However see Sanders, *Paul*, pp. 463ff. for the inadequacy of seeing Paul's understanding of Christ's death entirely in the light of forgiveness of past transgressions.

27 Cf. G. W. H. Lampe, 'Church Discipline and the Interpretation of the Epistles to the Corinthians', in *Christian History and Interpretation*, ed. W. R. Farmer (Cambridge, 1967), p. 339.

28 The term δίκαιος for believer is lacking in Paul.

29 Sanders, *Paul*, p. 503.

30 Davies, *Paul*, p. 130.

31 Carrington, *Catechism*, pp. 16ff.

32 The Church as such, of course, had no specific 'environment' but existed wherever the 'saints' were located.

33 Levine, *Presence*, p. 75.

34 Cf. εἰλικρινεα in 1 Cor. 5:8 and Wisd. 7:25 where wisdom is described as being 'a pure [εἰλικρινής] emanation of the Glory of God the Almighty; therefore nothing defiled gains entry into her.'

35 Cf. 1 Cor. 10:32; Prov. 11:30; Amos 6:12.

36 Josephus uses ἄμωμος to describe the purity of the priests who serve in the Temple, *Bell.* V. 229; *Ant.* III. 276ff.

37 Cf. 1 Cor. 5:8.

38 Cf. Qumran's 'perfect of way'.

39 Cf. J. C. Hurd, *The Origin of I Corinthians* (London, 1965), pp. 50f.

40 Conzelmann, *I Corinthians*, p. 96: 'The simplest explanation is that after the death of his father he has married the latter's widow, his stepmother.' Cf. Lev. 18:8 LXX, γυνὴ πατρός, where 'stepmother is understood'.

41 Plummer, *II Corinthians*, p. 370; E. de Witt Burton, *The Epistle to the Galatians* (Edinburgh, 1921), p. 305.

42   Note also the specifically impure nature of sexual immorality in the Hebrew Bible.

43   Ford, 'The First Epistle to the Corinthians', 414. Cf. Daube, *The New Testament and Rabbinic Judaism*, p. 113. Ford goes on to suggest, albeit tentatively, 'that the Corinthian correspondence was written to recipients among whom the majority were Jewish Christians, whether pure Jews or former proselytes to the Jewish faith' (p. 415).

44   On the question of Jews and Gentiles at Corinth and in the other Pauline churches see Sanders, 'Paul's Attitude Toward the Jewish People', 175-87. Paul's readers, Jew or Gentile, were in any case familiar with the Bible which Paul gave them. It is clear that he knew that the allusions to, and the quotation of, biblical texts, e.g. in Galatians, and the reference to Passover in this chapter would be accepted and understood even though some, if not all, of his readership was unfamiliar with Judaism itself.

45   Bauer, *Lexicon* (Arndt and Gingrich, trans.), p. 23.

46   Elsewhere αἴρω refers to the carrying of unclean things such as the carcasses of unclean animals, Lev. 11:25, 28, 40; or objects made impure by a bodily discharge, Lev. 15:10.

47   Forkman, *Limits*, p. 146.

48   Ibid., pp. 141ff.

49   E. Käsemann, 'Sentences of Holy Law in the New Testament', in *New Testament Questions of Today* (London, 1969), p. 71: 'the antithesis of baptism'.

50   Forkman, *Religious Community*, p. 146.

51   Some commentators take it to mean just that; death outside the Church at the hands of Satan, e.g. Conzelmann, *I Corinthians*, p. 97, cf. Rom. 5:12f., 17.

52   In spite of the attractiveness of Forkman's proposal.

53   Robertson and Plummer, *I Corinthians*, p. 67; 'all sin is a defiling of the Temple and is destructive of its consecrated state'.

54   The exception is Rom. 8:24 where σῴζω is in the past tense, but the element of hope is still there.

55   Cf. Paul's use of σῶμα in verse 3 of this chapter.

56   Cf. 1 Thess. 5:23: 'may your spirit and soul and body [σῶμα] be kept sound and blameless at the coming of our Lord Jesus Christ'. The greater intensity of the eschatological expectation in 1 Thessalonians allows Paul to write with certainty that the whole man, body and soul, as well as spirit, will be preserved until the end.

57   Forkman, *Religious Community*, p. 144.

58   Sanders' own translation (*Paul*, p. 462).

59   Käsemann, *New Testament Questions*, p. 72: 'the community excommunicates from the body of Christ as from the realm of the grace of God. But it cannot annul the event of baptism, nor place limitations on the right of its Lord over one whom that Lord has claimed as his own in baptism.'

60   It was, of course, the standard Jewish view that a man's death, if preceded by repentance, would atone. M. Yoma 8.8; Sanders, *Paul*, pp. 172f.

61 Relationships which they may have felt were justified by virtue of their new life as a new creation in Christ, cf. Daube, *The New Testament and Rabbinic Judaism*, p. 113. Paul seems to be countering this tendency in 1 Cor. 7:17ff.: 'Everyone should remain in the state in which he was called' (1 Cor. 7:20).

62 J. Jeremias (*The Eucharistic Words of Jesus* (London, 1966), p. 59) sees Paul basing what he writes here 'upon an early Christian passover *haggadah*'. See also Forkman, *Religious Community*, p. 147.

63 Conzelmann, *I Corinthians*, p. 98.

64 *Encyclopedia Judaica*, vol. 7, p. 1237. Sorel, 'The Dietary Prohibitions of the Hebrews', 28. Leaven is a fermented substance and 'a fermented substance is an altered substance, one that has become other. Fermentation is the equivalent of a blemish.'

65 Davies, *Paul*, p. 105: 'the whole Christian life, because of the crucified Christ, can be thought of as a Passover festival of joy'.

66 BDB, p. 129.

67 *Saraph*, however, is the verb that is usually found in this case, but see on 1 Cor. 5:13 p.96; cf. M. Pes. 2:1.

68 E.g. *de Ebrietate* 28.

69 He agrees with Wenschkewitz, *Kultusbegriffe*, p. 116.

70 *TDNT* 2, p. 903.

71 See G. F. Moore, 'The Rise of Normative Judaism', *HTR*, 17 (1924), 321, and Gavin, *The Jewish Antecedents of the Christian Sacraments*, pp. 7ff.

72 Cf. Rom. 12:1 and references to λειτουργός and λειτουργέω.

73 ἀλλ' ἐν. See Forkman, *Religious Community*, p. 149.

74 Ἑορτάζω is a *hapax legomenon* in the New Testament.

75 Jeremias, *Eucharistic Words*, pp. 59f.

76 Cf. Whiteley, *The Theology of Saint Paul*, p. 205; cf. Rom. 12:1f.; 1 Cor. 3:16; 6:19; 2 Cor. 6:14 to 7:1.

77 BDB, p. 290, see Exod. 12:14; 23:14.

78 Elsewhere Paul uses εἰλικρίνεια in 2 Cor. 1:12; 2:17; and εἰλικρινής in Phil. 1:10. In 2 Cor. 1:12 he describes his life in the world and before the Corinthians as being enacted with holiness (ἁγιότης, cf. Heb. 12:10) and εἰλικρίνεια τοῦ Θεοῦ. We should prefer, in place of the RSV rendering of this last phrase as 'godly sincerity' to read 'purity of God'. Paul has behaved as befits one who is in God's service, with both holiness and purity. He has been set apart for this service like the priests who performed their duties in the Temple. He describes himself in terms which reflect his own awareness of being a priest in the Temple of God. The stronger 'purity' for εἰλικρίνεια (cf. *TDNT* 2, p. 397) is, then, to be preferred to the 'sincerity' of the RSV. Cf. 2 Cor. 2:17 and Ps. 15:2.

79 Those who suffered from any impurity were prevented from taking part in the Passover festival, M. Pes. 8.5ff.

80 Cf. 1 Cor. 3:9.

81 Bauer, *Lexicon* (Arndt and Gingrich (transl.), p. 792.

82 Lev. 2:4 etc.

83 Paul's choice of συναναμείγνυμι may be based on this link through the Hebrew *balal* to φύραμα.
84 I.e. in idolatry.
85 The LXX omits the reference to idolatry which appears in the MT.
86 Cf. 2 Thess. 3:14 where συναναμείγνυμι is used in a similar way.
87 Gen. 43:32; Exod. 18:12; 2 Sam. 12:17; Ps. 101:5.
88 It was recognized that Jethro was a priest.
89 Lampe, 'Church discipline . . .', p. 343.
90 Cf. Num. 12:1f. and the tradition arising from this episode that understood leprosy as coming as the result of slander. See also Lev. 18:4; Jer. 16:8; Sifre Deut. (to 23.15) 258, 121a; Mekilta (to 20.21) 72a, II p. 274.
91 Hurd, p. 153.
92 Hoph. *yakol*, to endure.
93 Κατάλαλος cf. Rom. 1:30.
94 Cf. 1 Thess. 2:15.
95 Μηδὲ συνεσθίειν.
96 See on 2 Cor. 6:14 to 7:1 below, a passage which is considered to give rise to some of the concerns expressed in this chapter.
97 BDB, pp. 128f.
98 BDB, p. 129.
99 B. Pes. 6a; Jastrow, *Dictionary*, p. 182.
100 For an understanding of 1 Cor. 5 which comes close to that presented here, see A. Y. Collins, 'The Function of "Excommunication" in Paul', *HTR*, 73 (1980), 251–63.

5. Purity and the continuing life of the Church

1 J. M. Ford, ' "Hast Thou Tithed thy Meal?" and "Is thy Child Kosher?" ', *JTS*, n.s. 17 (1966), 75.
2 She does, however, make a valuable contribution to some other points regarding Paul and purity in this same article.
3 Kempthorne, 'Incest', 573.
4 Neusner, *Idea*, p. 13.
5 Ibid., p. 25.
6 Paul uses the same argument against idolatry as he does against immorality. Both the worship of idols and fornication invalidate, for the believer, the union he has with Christ and the Church. On idolatry see 1 Cor. 10:14ff.; on sexual immorality see 1 Cor. 6:15ff.
7 See Robertson and Plummer, *I Corinthians*, p. 221, against the view of Conzelmann, *I Corinthians*, p. 177.
8 Cf. Daube, *The New Testament and Rabbinic Judaism*, p. 127 and 1 Cor. 7:15.
9 Neusner, *Idea*, p. 59: 'a highly rabbinic conception'.
10 Paul may have been influenced here by the traditions, maintained in some churches, of Jesus' teaching on the subject. Cf. Mark 7:15; Matt. 15:11; Davies, *Paul*, p. 138; but see Sanday and Headlam, *Romans*, p. 390.

11   Cf. 1 Macc. 1:62.
12   Regarding the heavenly Jerusalem, Rev. 21:27 reads: 'nothing
     unclean shall enter it', cf. Mark 7:2; Heb. 10:29.
13   Cf. Matt. 5:8; 23:26; 27:59; Luke 11:41.
14   Cf. Isa. 59:3; Sir. 13.1; 21.28.
15   Neusner, *Idea*, p. 60.
16   Ibid., p. 59.
17   For the link between these two sins see Wisd. 14:12: 'For the
     idea of making idols was the beginning of fornication (πορνεία)';
     cf. Cranfield, *Romans*, p. 122.
18   Cf. Lev. 15:24; 20:21 where MT has *niddah*.
19   Cf. Wisd. 14:26 where ἀσέλγεια appears as a member of a list of
     sexual sins.
20   Cf. Cranfield, *Romans*, p. 327.
21   See the use of 'sanctification' (ἁγιασμός) in Heb. 12:14.
22   Carrington, *Catechism*, p. 16.
23   I leave aside here the vexed problems of chronology and the
     relationship between Acts 15 and Gal. 2:1-10.
24   Lev. 18:6ff.
25   Cf. 1 Cor. 5:1ff.
26   J. Jeremias, *Infant Baptism in the First Four Centuries* (Phila-
     delphia, 1962), p. 46.
27   Conzelmann, *I Corinthians*, p. 121.
28   Cf. M. Kidd. 3.13: 'Bastard stock can be rendered clean (*ṭahar*).
     Thus if a bastard married a bondwoman, the offspring is a bond-
     man. If he is set free the son thereby becomes a freeman.'
29   Plummer, *II Corinthians*, p. 144.
30   Conzelmann, *I Corinthians*, p. 122.
31   On the offspring of the marriage of Jew and non-Jew see T.
     Kidd. 4.16. The offspring of a non-Jew or slave and a Jewish
     woman is a Jew albeit of low estate. In contrast, in Paul ('There
     is neither . . . male nor female', Gal. 3:28) it does not matter
     what the sex of the believer is.
32   Among the more recent works on this topic are: M. Hooker,
     'Authority on Her Head: An Examination of I Cor. XI.10', *NTS*,
     10 (1963/4), 410-16; M. Boucher, 'Some Unexplained Parallels
     to I Cor. 11.11-12 and Gal. 3.28: The NT on the Role of Women',
     CBQ, 31 (1969), 50-8; A. Jaubert, 'Le voile des femmes (I Cor.
     XI.2-16)', *NTS*, 18 (1971/2), 419-30; J. B. Hurley, 'Did Paul
     Require Veils or the Silence of Women? A Consideration of I
     Cor. 11.2-16 and I Cor. 14.33b-36', *WTJ*, 35 (1973), 216-18;
     W. O. Walker, 'I Corinthians 11.2-16 and Paul's Views Regarding
     Women', *JBL*, 94 (1975), 94-110; J. Murphy-O'Connor, 'The
     Non-Pauline Character of I Corinthians 11.2-16?', *JBL*, 95
     (1976), 615-21; J. P. Meier, 'On the Veiling of Hermeneutics (I
     Cor. 11.2-16)', *CBQ*, 40 (1978), 212-26.
33   See J. A. Fitzmyer, 'A Feature of Qumran Angelology and the
     Angels of I Cor. 11.10', *Essays on the Semitic Background of the
     New Testament* (London, 1971), pp. 187ff.

34 Ibid., p. 199.
35 Cf. Levine, *Presence*, pp. 75f.
36 Robertson and Plummer (*I Corinthians*, p. 233) think this to be the case. Cf. Isa. 6:ff; Ps. 138:1 (LXX); Jaubert, 'Le voile des femmes', 427, Meier, 'Hermeneutics', 220.
37 It is often argued that Paul only refers to angels in the bad sense, having seen Christians pass from under their influence. Reference is often made to the angels of Gen. 6:4, but Plummer (*II Corinthians*, p. 233) is correct in dismissing the view that women without head covering may be a temptation to angels (Gen. 6:1, 2) as 'somewhat childish'. The angels of 1 Cor. 11:10 are a device to indicate the divine presence and not a power to which man might owe allegiance, 'οἱ ἄγγελοι always means good angels, I Cor. 13.1, Mt. 13.49; 25.31, Lk. 16.22; Heb. 1.4,5', Plummer, *II Corinthians*, p. 233.
38 Walker ('I Corinthians 11:2-16', 97) sees all of 1 Cor. 11: 2-10 as an interpolation, partly on the basis that 'except in matters of sexual purity, Paul appears to have had little concern for such differences between Jews and Greeks'. But, as we shall see, the covering of the heads of women did relate, for Paul, to sexual purity.
39 Loose hair for women was probably the Greek custom but it was for the Jew, among other things, a sign of idolatry, and, in Paul's terms, allegiance to another lord. A. Isaksson, *Marriage and Ministry in the New Temple* (Lund, 1965), p. 168, suggests that some women at Corinth may have seen themselves as pure brides of Christ (cf. 2 Cor. 11:2) and as such wore their hair loose in the style of the Jewish virgin on her wedding day, cf. M. Ket. 2.1.
40 Hurley ('Did Paul Require Veils. . . .?', 216) believes, as a result of a study of the LXX terms, that Paul was not asking for women to wear veils so much as insisting that they wear their hair tied up and not loose. See also Hurd, *I Corinthians*, p. 184.
41 See Fitzmyer, 'Qumran Angelology', p. 193, for bibliographical details concerning Kittel's argument and Meier, 'Hermeneutics', 220, for a cautionary note on this play on words.
42 Hooker, 'Authority on her head', 414.
43 Ibid., 415.
44 Jaubert, 'Le voile des femmes', 427ff.
45 Cf. Hurley, 'Did Paul Require Veils . . . ?', 216f.
46 Commenting on Num. 5:18; 'And the priest shall . . . unbind the hair of the woman's head', Sifre Num. 11 reads: 'This suggests that daughters of Israel should cover their heads and although there is no direct proof from Scripture for it, yet there is an allusion: "And Tamar put a *covering* on her head" (II Sam. 12.12).' See P. P. Levertoff, *Midrash Sifre on Numbers* (London, 1926), p. 17.
47 W. C. van Unnik, 'Les cheveux défaits des femmes baptisées', *VigChr*, 1 (1947), 95; 'La définition, donnée dans le Talmud au sujet des préceptes dans Num. 5.18 nous le montre clairement ainsi que le contraste: une tête couverte = une tête dont les

cheveux étaient relevés (cf. Sota 8b-9a). Les cheveux flottants indiquaient donc que la femme était impure.' Note the caution expressed by R. J. Werblowsky, 'On the Baptismal Rite According to St Hippolytus', *Studia Patristica*, 7 (1957), 99, regarding van Unnik's suggestion that menstruous women wore their hair loose and dishevelled.

48 Plummer (*II Corinthians*, p. 233) believes that in the use of this phrase Paul 'assumes as obvious to his readers, a connection no longer obvious to us'. Jaubert ('Le voile des femmes', 428) comments; 'C'est une sorte de citation, une opinion courante que rappelle Paul.'

49 Cf. Conzelmann, *I Corinthians*, p. 188.

50 The relatively late Midrash Rabbah Numbers 19:20 on 20:29 reads: 'You find that when Aaron died, the clouds of glory departed, and Israel appeared like a woman whose hair had been uncovered.'

51 J. M. Ford, 'Rabbinic Humour Behind Baptism for the Dead (I Cor. XV, 29)', *Studia Evangelica*, 4 (1968), 400-3, *TU* 102.

52 Ibid., 400.

53 Cf. 2 Kings 5:14 LXX.

54 Bauer, *Lexicon*, (Arndt and Gingrich, trans.), p. 846.

55 A decomposed body with worms in it or a cremated body is declared by the sages to be clean, M. Oholoth 2.2.

56 Cf. Daube, *Rabbinic Judaism*, pp. 307f.

57 Ford, 'Rabbinic Humour', 403.

58 It can, of course, be argued that both sacred books and corpses are looked upon as making one unclean as a means of offering them protection from misuse.

59 R. Bultmann, *The Theology of the New Testament*, vol. 1 (New York, 1951), p. 205. G. Bornkamm, 'The History of the . . . so-called Second Letter to the Corinthians', *NTS*, 8 (1961-2), 258-64; J. A. Fitzmyer, 'Qumran and the Interpolated Paragraph in II Cor.VI.14-VII.1', *CBQ*, 23 (1961), 271-80; J. Gnilka, '2 Cor. 6.14-7.1 in the Light of the Qumran Texts and the Testaments of the Twelve Patriarchs', *Paul and Qumran*, ed. J. Murphy-O'Connor (London, 1968), pp. 48-68; H. Koester, 'GNOMAI DIAPHORAI', in *Trajectories Through Early Christianity*, eds. J. M. Robinson and H. Koester (Philadelphia, 1971), p. 154; M. E. Thrall, 'The Problem of II Cor. vi.16-vii.1 in some recent discussions', *NTS*, 24 (1977), 132-48.

60 Fitzmyer, 'The Interpolated Paragraph'; on the Testaments of the Twelve Patriarchs, see Gnilka, '2 Cor. 6.14-7.1'.

61 Hurd, *I Corinthians*, pp. 213-39. E. B. Allo (*Saint Paul: Deuxième Epître aux Corinthiens* (Paris, 1937), pp. 189-93) gives a history of the scholarship on this question and a bibliography.

62 G. D. Fee, 'II Corinthians VI.14-VII.1 and Food Offered to Idols, *NTS*, 23 (1977), 143. He believes this passage refers to the question of food offered to idols.

63 Ibid., 144.

64   Ibid.
65   P. C. Craigie, *The Book of Deuteronomy* (Grand Rapids, 1976), p. 290.
66   Sorel, 'Dietary Prohibitions', 29; Douglas, *Purity and Danger*, p. 53: 'holiness requires that different classes of things shall not be confused'.
67   Gnilka, '2 Cor. 6:14-7.1', p. 50.
68   Fitzmyer, 'The Interpolated Paragraph', 273ff.
69   Cf. Fee, 'II Corinthians VI.14-VII.1', 153ff., 156.
70   Note that Paul's only other use of ἅπτομαι, 'touch', is in 1 Cor. 7:1: 'It is well for a man not to touch a woman', a statement in reply to a question posed by the Corinthians in a letter they had written to Paul. We would ask whether the Corinthians' query was brought about by what Paul says in 2 Cor. 6:17. Did the Corinthians understand 'unclean' (ἀκάθαρτος), to refer to, among other things, menstruants and request some clarification on this point? The verb, in the form of ἅπτεσθαι (*naga‘*) is used throughout the purity regulations of Leviticus and Numbers and in particular with regard to the menstruant, e.g. Lev. 15:19ff.
71   Those banned from the Pharisaic community were considered like lepers and mourners, Forkman, *Religious Community*, pp. 100f. Forkman also argues that up to AD 70 and for a short period thereafter the ban was mainly directed against scribes who deviated on the question of the interpretation of the rules of purity (p. 103).
72   Neusner, *Idea*, p. 118.
73   Douglas, *Purity and Danger*, p. 113.
74   Ibid., p. 2.

6. Conclusion

1   See K. Stendahl, 'The Apostle Paul and the Introspective Conscience of the West', *HTR*, 56 (1963), 199-215.
2   See Sanders, *Paul*, p. 544, and his references to such purity terms as 'blameless', 'innocent', 'sound', and 'guiltless'.

BIBLIOGRAPHY

1. Texts and tools

Aland, K., *et al. Novum Testamentum Graece*. Stuttgart: United Bible
    Societies, 1966.
Barthélemy, D. and J. T. Milik. *Discoveries in the Judaean Desert 1: Qum-*
    ran Cave 1. Oxford: Clarendon Press, 1955.
Bauer, W. *A Greek-English Lexicon of the New Testament*. Trans. W. F.
    Arndt and F. W. Gingrich. Chicago: University of Chicago Press,
    1957.
Blackman, Philip. *Mishnayoth*. 6 vols. 3rd ed. New York: Judaica Press,
    1965.
Botterweck, G. Johannes, *et al.*, eds. *Theological Dictionary of the Old*
    Testament. Trans. John T. Willis. Grand Rapids: Wm. B. Eerdmans,
    1974.
Brown, F., S. R. Driver and C. A. Briggs. *A Hebrew and English Lexicon of*
    the Old Testament. Oxford: Clarendon Press, 1903.
Burrows, Millar. *The Dead Sea Scrolls of St Mark's Monastery. Vol. 1: The*
    Isaiah Manuscript and the Habukkuk Commentary. New Haven:
    American Schools of Oriental Research, 1950.
Charles, R. H. *The Apocrypha and Pseudepigrapha of the Old Testament*.
    2 vols. London: Oxford University Press, 1913.
Danby, Herbert. *The Mishnah*. London: Oxford University Press, 1967.
Epstein, I., ed. *The Babylonian Talmud*. London: Soncino Press, 1935-48.
Goldin, J., ed. *The Fathers According to Rabbi Nathan*. New York:
    Schocken, 1974.
Habermann, A. M., ed. *The Scrolls from the Judaean Desert* (in Hebrew).
    Jerusalem: Machbaroth Lesifruth Publishing House, 1959.
Hatch, E. and H. A. Redpath. *A Concordance to the Septuagint*. 3 vols.
    Oxford: Clarendon Press, 1897-1906.
Herford, R. Travers. *The Ethics of the Talmud: Sayings of the Fathers*.
    New York: Schocken, 1962.
Jastrow, M. *A Dictionary of the Targumim, the Talmud Babli and Yeru-*
    shalmi and the Midrashic Literature. Berlin: Choreb, 1926.
Kittel, Gerhard, ed. *Theological Dictionary of the New Testament*. 10 vols.
    Trans. G. W. Bromiley. Grand Rapids: Wm. B. Eerdmans. 1964-76.
Kuhn, K. G. *Konkordanz zu den Qumrantexten*. Göttingen: Vandenhoeck
    and Ruprecht, 1960.
Lampe, G. W. H. *Patristic Greek Lexicon*. Oxford: Clarendon Press, 1961.

Lauterbach, Jacob Z., ed. *Mekilta de-Rabbi Ishmael.* 3 vols. Philadelphia: Jewish Publications Society of America, 1933-5.

Levertoff, Paul P., ed. *Midrash Sifre on Numbers.* Translations of Early Documents, Series III, Rabbinic Texts. London: SPCK, 1926.

Liddell, H. G. and R. Scott. *A Greek-English Lexicon.* Revised H. S. Jones. Oxford: Clarendon Press, 1948.

Lisowsky, Gerhard. *Konkordanz zum Hebräischen Alten Testament.* Stuttgart: Privileg. Württ. Bibelanstalt, 1958.

Lohse, E., ed. *Die Texte aus Qumran.* 2nd rev. ed. Darmstadt: Wissenschaftliche Buchgesellschaft, 1971.

Maier, Johann. *Die Texte vom Toten Meer.* 2 vols. München: Ernst Reinhardt Verlag, 1960.

Mandelkern, S. *Veteris Testamenti Concordantiae.* Graz: Akademische Druck, 1955.

Moulton, W. F. and A. S. Geden. *A Concordance to the Greek Testament.* Edinburgh: T. and T. Clark, 1897.

Rahlfs, A., ed. *Septuaginta.* 2 vols. Stuttgart: Privileg. Württ. Bibelanstalt. 1935.

Schechter, S. *Aboth de Rabbi Nathan.* New York: Jewish Theological Seminary, 1967.

Vermes, Geza., ed. *The Dead Sea Scrolls in English.* Harmondsworth: Penguin, 1962.

2. Books and articles

Abelson, J. *The Immanence of God in Rabbinical Literature.* London: Macmillan, 1912.

Allegro, John. *The Dead Sea Scrolls.* Harmondsworth: Penguin, 1956.

Allo, E. B. *Saint Paul: Première Epître aux Corinthiens.* Paris: J. Gabalda, 1934.
Saint Paul: Deuxième Epître aux Corinthiens. Paris: J. Gabalda, 1937.

Alon, G. 'The Bounds of Levitical Cleanness' (in Hebrew), *Tarbiz*, 9 (1937-8), 1-10, 179-95. ET in *Jews, Judaism and the Classical World.* Jerusalem: Magnes Press, 1977.

Asting, R. *Die Heiligkeit im Urchristentum.* Göttingen: Vandenhoeck and Ruprecht, 1930.

Bamberger, B. J. *Proselytism in the Talmudic Period.* New York: Ktav, 1968. First published 1939.

Baumgarten, Joseph M. 'Sacrifice and Worship Among the Jewish Sectarians of the Dead Sea (Qumran) Scrolls', *HTR*, 46 (1953), 141-59.
'The Essene Avoidance of Oil and the Laws of Purity', *RQ*, 6 (1967-9), 183-92.
Studies in Qumran Law. Leiden: Brill, 1977.
Review of *Megillat ha-Miqdaš, The Temple Scroll* (Hebrew Edition). Edited by Yigael Yadin in *JBL*, 97 (1978), 584-9.

Beare, F. W. *The Epistle to the Philippians.* London: A. and C. Black, 1973.

Beasley-Murray, G. R. *Baptism in the New Testament.* London: Macmillan, 1962.

Beidelman, T. O. W. *Robertson Smith and the Sociological Study of Religion.* Chicago: University of Chicago Press, 1974.

Betz, Hans-Dieter. '2 Cor. 6.14–7.1: an anti Pauline fragment?', *JBL*, 92 (1973), 88–108.

Betz, Otto. 'Felsenmann und Felsengemeinde. (Eine Parallele zu Mt. 16.17–19 in dem Qumranspsalmen)', *ZNTW*, 48 (1957), 49–77.

'Die Proselytentaufe der Qumransekte und die Taufe im Neuen Testament', *RQ*, 1 (1958), 213–34.

'Le ministère cultuel dans la secte de Qumran et dans le Christianisme primitif', in *La secte de Qumran et les origines du christianisme.* Ed. J. van der Ploeg. Bruges: Desclée de Brouwer, 1959.

Black, Matthew. *The Essene Problem.* London: Dr. Williams' Trust, 1961.

Bornkamm, G. 'The History of the Origin of the So-called Second Letter to the Corinthians', *NTS*, 8 (1961–2), 258–64.

Boucher, M. 'Some Unexplained Parallels to I Cor. 11.11–12 and Gal. 3.28: The NT on the Role of Women', *CBQ*, 31 (1969), 50–8.

Bousset, W. *Die Religion des Judentums im späthellenistischen Zeitalter.* Ed. H. Gressmann. HNT 21. Tübingen: Mohr, 1926.

Bowman, J. 'Did the Qumran Sect Burn the Red Heifer?', *RQ*, 1 (1958), 73–84.

Braun, H. *Qumran und das Neue Testament.* 2 vols. Tübingen: Mohr, 1966.

Brownlee, W. H. 'The Dead Sea Manual of Discipline', *BASOR Supplemental Studies.* New Haven: American Schools of Oriental Research, 1951.

'John the Baptist in the Light of the Dead Sea Scrolls', in *The Scrolls and the New Testament.* Ed. Krister Stendahl. New York: Harper and Row, 1957.

Buchanan, George Wesley. 'The Role of Purity in the Structure of the Essene Sect', *RQ*, 3 (1960), 397–406.

The Consequences of the Covenant. Leiden: Brill, 1970.

Büchler, Adolf. 'The Levitical Impurity of the Gentile in Palestine before the Year 70', *JQR*, n.s. 17 (1926–7), 1–82.

Studies in Sin and Atonement in the Rabbinic Literature of the First Century. London: Oxford University Press, 1928.

Bultmann, Rudolf, *The Theology of the New Testament.* New York: Scribner's, 1951.

Primitive Christianity in its Contemporary Setting. ET. Cleveland: World, 1956.

Burrows, Millar. *The Dead Sea Scrolls.* London: Secker and Warburg, 1956.

Burton, E. de Witt. *The Epistle to the Galatians.* Edinburgh: T. and T. Clark, 1921.

Carrington, P. *The Primitive Christian Catechism.* Cambridge: Cambridge University Press, 1940.

Cerfaux, L. *The Church in the Theology of Paul.* New York: Herder and Herder, 1959.

Charlesworth, James H. *The Pseudepigrapha and Modern Research with a Supplement.* Chico: Scholars Press, 1981.

Clements, R. E. *God and Temple. The Idea of the Divine Presence in Ancient Israel.* Oxford: Basil Blackwell, 1965.
Collins, A. Y. 'The Function of "Excommunication" in Paul', *HTR*, 73 (1980), 251-63.
Conzelmann, Hans. *I Corinthians.* Philadelphia: Fortress, 1975.
Coppens, J. C. 'The Spiritual Temple in the Pauline Letters and its Background', *TU*, 112 (1973), 53-66.
Craigie, Peter C. *The Book of Deuteronomy.* Grand Rapids: Wm. B. Eerdmans, 1976.
Cranfield, C. E. B. *The Epistle to the Romans.* Vol. 1. Edinburgh: T. and T. Clark, 1975.
Cross, Frank Moore, Jr. *The Ancient Library of Qumran and Modern Biblical Studies.* Garden City: Doubleday, 1958.
Dahl, N. A. 'The Origin of Baptism', in *Interpretationes ad Vetus Testamentum pertinentes Sigmundo Mowinckel.* Ed. A. S. Kapelrud. Oslo: Forlaget Land og Kirke, 1955.
'A Fragment and its Context: 2 Corinthians 6.14-7.1', in *Studies in Paul.* Minneapolis: Augsburg, 1977.
Daube, David. *The New Testament and Rabbinic Judaism.* London: Athlone, 1956.
Davies, W. D. *Paul and Rabbinic Judaism.* London: SPCK, 1970. 3rd edition.
The Gospel and the Land. Berkeley: University of California Press, 1974.
Review of Hans Dieter Betz, *Galatians: A Commentary on Paul's Letter to the Churches of Galatia, RSR*, 7 (1981), 311f.
Deissmann, Adolf. *Bible Studies.* Edinburgh: T. and T. Clark, 1901.
Delcor, M. *Les Hymnes de Qumran (Hodayot).* Paris: Letouzey et Ané, 1962.
'Le vocabulaire juridique, cultuel et mystique de l' "initiation" dans la secte de Qumran", in *Qumran-Probleme.* Ed. H. Bardtke. Berlin: Akademie Verlag, 1963.
'Repas cultuels esséniens et thérapeutes Thiases et Haburoth', *RQ*, 6 (1967-9), 401-25.
Dodd, C. H. *The Bible and the Greeks.* London: Hodder and Stoughton, 1955.
Douglas, Mary. *Purity and Danger. An Analysis of Concepts of Pollution and Taboo.* London: Routledge and Kegan Paul, 1966.
'Pollution', *International Encyclopedia of the Social Sciences.* 12. New York: Macmillan, 1968, pp. 333-42.
Natural Symbols. Explorations of Cosmology. New York: Random House, 1973.
Implicit Meanings. Essays in Anthropology. London: Routledge and Kegan Paul, 1975.
Dupont-Sommer, A. 'Culpabilité et rites de purification dans la secte juive de Qoumran', *Semitica*, 15 (1965), 61-70.
Durkheim, E. *The Elementary Forms of the Religious Life.* New York: Free Press, 1967. First published 1912.

Eliade, Mircea. *The Sacred and the Profane.* New York: Harcourt, Brace and World, 1959.
Ellis, E. E. *Paul's Use of the Old Testament.* Edinburgh: Oliver and Boyd, 1957.
Epstein, I. *Judaism.* Harmondsworth: Penguin, 1959.
Fee, Gordon D. 'II Corinthians VI.14–VII.1 and Food Offered to Idols', *NTS*, 23 (1977), 140–61.
Fiorenza, Elizabeth Schüssler. 'Cultic Language in Qumran and in the New Testament', *CBQ*, 38 (1976), 159–79.
Fitzmyer, J. A. 'Qumran and the Interpolated Paragraph in II Cor. VI.14–VII.1', *CBQ*, 23 (1961), 271–80.
'A Feature of Qumran Angelology and the Angels of I Cor. 11:10', in *Essays on the Semitic Background of the New Testament.* London: Chapman, 1971.
Flusser, David. 'The Dead Sea Sect and pre-Pauline Christianity', in *Scripta Hierosolymitana.* Vol. IV. *Aspects of the Dead Sea Scrolls.* Ed. Chaim Rabin and Yigael Yadin. Jerusalem: Magnes Press, 1965.
Ford, J. Massingberd. ' "Hast thou tithed thy meal?" and "Is thy child kosher?" ', *JTS*, n.s. 17 (1966), 71–9.
'The First Epistle to the Corinthians or the First Epistle to the Hebrews?', *CBQ*, 28 (1966), 402–16.
'Rabbinic Humour behind Baptism for the Dead (I Cor.15.29)', *TU*, 102 (1968), 400–3.
Forkman, G. *The Limits of the Religious Community.* Lund: Gleerup, 1972.
Fraeyman, M. 'La Spiritualisation de l'Idée du Temple dans les Epîtres pauliniennes', *ETL*, 23 (1947), 378–412.
Gärtner, B. *The Temple and the Community in Qumran and the New Testament.* Cambridge: Cambridge University Press, 1965.
Gaston, L. *No Stone Upon Another.* Supplements to Novum Testamentum. Vol. 23. Leiden: Brill, 1970.
Gavin, F. *The Jewish Antecedents of the Christian Sacraments.* London: SPCK, 1928.
Gnilka, J. 'Die essenischen Tauchbäder und die Johannestaufe', *RQ*, 3 (1961), 185–207.
'Das Gemeinschaftsmahl der Essener', *BZ*, n.f. 5 (1961), 39–55.
'2 Cor. 6.14–7.1 in the Light of the Qumran Texts and the Testaments of the Twelve Patriarchs', in *Paul and Qumran.* Ed. J. Murphy-O'Connor. London: Chapman, 1968.
Goldberg, Arnold M. *Untersuchungen über die Vorstellung von der Shekinah in der frühen rabbinischen Literatur.* Berlin: de Gruyter, 1969.
Goodenough, E. R. *The Jurisprudence of the Jewish Courts in Egypt.* New Haven: Yale University Press, 1929.
Gray, George Buchanan. *Sacrifice in the Old Testament.* Oxford: Clarendon Press, 1925.
Haag, H. 'Das liturgische Leben der Qumrangemeinde', *ArchLit*, 10 (1967), 78–109.
Haenchen, E. *The Acts of the Apostles.* ET, Oxford: Blackwell, 1971.

Hengel, Martin. *Judaism and Hellenism*. London: SCM, 1974.
Hermisson, Hans-Jürgen. *Sprache und Ritus im altisraelitischen Kult*. Neukirchen: Neukirchen Verlag, 1965.
Hill, D. *Greek Words and Hebrew Meanings*. Cambridge: Cambridge University Press, 1967.
Hoenig, S. B. 'Qumran Rules of Impurities', *RQ*, 6 (1967-9), 559-68.
Honeyman, A. M. 'Isaiah 1.16 *hizaku*', *VT*, 1 (1951), 63-5.
Hooker, Morna. 'Authority on Her Head: an Examination of 1 Cor. XI. 10', *NTS*, 10 (1963-4), 410-16.
Hunzinger, C. H. 'Beobachtung zur Entwicklung der Disziplinarordnung der Gemeinde von Qumran', in *Qumran-Probleme*. Ed. H. Bardtke. Berlin: Akademie Verlag, 1963.
Huppenbauer, H. W. '*Tahar* und *taharah* in der Sektenregel von Qumran', *TZ*, 13 (1957), 350-1.
Hurd, J. C., Jr. *The Origin of I Corinthians*. London: SPCK, 1965.
Hurley, J. B. 'Did Paul Require Veils or the Silence of Women? A Consideration of 1 Cor. 11.2-16. and 1 Cor. 14.33b-36', *WTJ*, 35 (1973), 216-18.
Isaksson, A. *Marriage and Ministry in the New Temple*. Lund: Gleerup, 1965.
Isenberg, S. R. and D. E. Owen. 'Bodies, Natural and Contrived: The Work of Mary Douglas'. *RSR*, 3 (1977), 1-17.
Jacob, F. *La Logique du Vivant*. Paris: Editions Gallimard, 1970.
Jaubert, Annie, *La notion d'alliance dans le judaisme de l'ère chrétienne*. Paris: Editions de Seuil, 1963.
'Le voile des femmes (1 Cor. XI.2-16)', *NTS*, 18 (1971-2), 419-30.
Jeremias, Joachim. *Infant Baptism in the First Four Centuries*. Philadelphia: Westminster, 1962.
The Origins of Infant Baptism. London: SCM, 1963.
The Eucharistic Words of Jesus. London: SCM, 1966.
Jerusalem in the Time of Jesus. London: SCM, 1969.
Käsemann, Ernst. *New Testament Questions of Today*. London: SCM, 1969.
Kempthorne, R. 'Incest and the Body of Christ. A Study of I Cor. VI.12-20', *NTS*, 14 (1967-68), 568-74.
Klinzing, Georg. *Die Umdeutung des Kultus in der Qumrangemeinde und im Neuen Testament*. Göttingen: Vandenhoeck and Ruprecht, 1971.
Knox, John. *Chapters in the Life of Paul*. New York: Abingdon, 1950.
Koester, H. 'GNOMAI DIAPHORAI', in *Trajectories Through Early Christianity*. Ed. J. M. Robinson and H. Koester. Philadelphia: Fortress, 1971.
Kuhn, H. W. *Enderwartung und gegenwärtiges Heil. Untersuchungen zu den Gemeindeliedern von Qumran*. SUNT 4. Göttingen: Vandenhoeck und Ruprecht, 1966.
Kuhn, K. G. 'The Lord's Supper and the Communal Meal at Qumran', in *The Scrolls and the New Testament*. Ed. Krister Stendahl. New York: Harper and Row, 1957.
Kümmel, W. G. 'Πάρεσις and ἔνδειξις. A Contribution to the Understand-

ing of the Pauline Doctrine of Justification', *Journal for Theology and the Church*, 3 (1967), 1–13.
Introduction to the New Testament. London: SCM, 1975.
Lampe, G. W. H. 'Church Discipline and the Interpretation of the Epistles to the Corinthians', in *Christian History and Interpretation.* Ed. W. R. Farmer. Cambridge: Cambridge University Press, 1967.
Leaney, A. R. C. *The Rule of Qumran and its Meaning.* London: SCM, 1966.
Levine, Baruch A. *In the Presence of the Lord.* Leiden: Brill, 1974.
Lieberman, Saul. 'The Discipline in the So-called Dead Sea Manual of Discipline', *JBL*, 71 (1952), 199–206.
Greek in Jewish Palestine. New York: Feldheim, 1965.
Lindars, Barnabas. *New Testament Apologetic.* London: SCM, 1961.
Lohse, E. *Märtyrer und Gottesknecht. Untersuchungen zur urchristlichen Verkündigung vom Sühntod Jesu Christi.* FRLANT 64. Göttingen: Vandenhoeck and Ruprecht, 1963.
Lyonnet, S. and L. Sabourin. *Sin, Redemption and Sacrifice.* Rome: Biblical Institute Press, 1970.
McKelvey, R. J. *The New Temple.* London: Oxford University Press, 1969.
Maier, J. *Die Tempelrolle vom Toten Meer.* München: Reinhardt, 1978.
Mansoor, M. *The Thanksgiving Hymns.* Grand Rapids: Wm. B. Eerdmans, 1961.
Mealand, D. L. 'Community of Goods at Qumran', *TZ*, 31 (1975), 129–39.
Meier, John P. 'On the Veiling of Hermeneutics (I Cor. 11.2–16)', *CBQ*, 40 (1978), 212–26.
Michel, Otto. *Paulus und seine Bibel.* Gütersloh: Bertelsmann, 1929.
Milgrom, Jacob. 'Sin Offering or Purification Offering?', *VT*, 21 (1971), 237–8.
'Kipper', *Encyclopedia Judaica.* Vol. 10. Jerusalem: Keter, 1973.
'Purity and Impurity', *Encyclopedia Judaica.* Vol. 13. Jerusalem: Keter, 1973.
Review of *In the Presence of the Lord*, by Baruch Levine, *JBL*, 95 (1976), 291–3.
'Two Kinds of ḥaṭṭā't', *VT*, 26 (1976), 333–7.
'Israel's Sanctuary: The Priestly Picture of Dorian Gray', *RB*, 83 (1976), 390–9.
'Studies in the Temple Scroll', *JBL*, 97 (1978), 501–23.
'The Temple Scroll', *BA*, 41 (1978), 105–20.
Milik, J. T. *Ten Years of Discovery in the Wilderness of Judaea.* London: SCM, 1959.
Moore, George Foot. *The History of Religion.* Vol. 2. New York: Scribner's, 1919.
'Intermediaries in Jewish Theology', *HTR*, 15 (1922), 41–85.
'The Rise of Normative Judaism', *HTR*, 17 (1924), 307–73.
Judaism in the First Centuries of the Christian Era. 3 vols. Cambridge: Harvard University Press, 1927–30.
Morris, L. 'The Meaning of ἱλαστήριον in Romans 3.25', *NTS*, 2 (1955–6), 33–43.
Moule, C. F. D. 'Sanctuary and Sacrifice in the Church of the New Testament', *JTS*, n.s. 1 (1950), 29–41.

An Idiom Book of New Testament Greek. Cambridge: Cambridge University Press, 1953.
Moulton, J. H. and G. Milligan. *The Vocabulary of the Greek Testament.* London: Hodder and Stoughton, 1930.
Murphy-O'Connor, J. 'The Non-Pauline Character of I Corinthians 11.2-16?', *JBL*, 95 (1976), 615-21.
Neusner, Jacob. 'The Fellowship (*havurah*) in the Second Jewish Commonwealth', *HTR*, 53 (1960), 125-42.
The Idea of Purity in Ancient Judaism. Leiden: Brill, 1973.
A History of the Mishnaic Law of Purities. 22 vols. Leiden: Brill, 1974-7.
'Method and Structure in the History of Judaic Ideas: An Exercise', in *Jews, Greeks and Christians.* Edited by R. Hamerton-Kelly and Robin Scroggs. Leiden: Brill, 1976.
'History and Structure: The Case of Mishnah', *JAAR*, 45 (1977), 161-92.
Newton, Michael. *The Concept of Secrecy in the Hodayot.* Unpublished M.A. Thesis. McMaster University, 1975.
Nikiprowetzy, V. 'Temple et communauté. A propos d'un ouvrage récent', *REJ*, 126 (1967), 8-25.
Nötscher, F. 'Heiligkeit in den Qumranschriften', *RQ*, 1 (1958/59), 163-81, and 2 (1959/60), 315-44.
Nygren, A. 'Christus der Gnadenstuhl', in *In Memoriam Ernst Lohmeyer.* Ed. W. Schmauch. Stuttgart: Evangelisches Verlagswerk, 1951.
Paschen, Wilfried. *Rein und Unrein. Untersuchungen zur biblischen Wortgeschichte.* München: Kösel, 1970.
Ploeg, J. van der. 'The Meals of the Essenes', *JSS*, 2 (1957), 163-75.
Plummer, A. *Second Epistle of St. Paul to the Corinthians.* Edinburgh: T. and T. Clark, 1915.
Priest, J. F. 'The Messiah and the Meal in 1QSa', *JBL*, 82 (1963), 95-100.
Pryke, J. 'The Sacraments of Holy Baptism and Holy Communion in the Light of the Ritual Washings and Sacred Meals at Qumran', *RQ*, 5 (1964-66), 543-52.
Przybylski, Benno. *Righteousness in Matthew and his World of Thought.* Cambridge: Cambridge University Press, 1980.
Rabin, Chaim. *Qumran Studies.* Oxford: Oxford University Press, 1957.
The Zadokite Documents. Oxford: Clarendon Press, 1958.
Richardson, Peter. *Israel in the Apostolic Church.* Cambridge: Cambridge University Press, 1969.
Ringgren, H. *The Faith of Qumran.* Philadelphia: Fortress, 1963.
Robertson, A. and A. Plummer. *The First Epistle of St Paul to the Corinthians.* Edinburgh: T. and T. Clark, 1911.
Rowley, H. H. 'Jewish Proselyte Baptism', *HUCA*, 15 (1940), 313-34.
'The Baptism of John and the Qumran Sect', in *New Testament Essays.* Edited by A. J. B. Higgins. Manchester: Manchester University Press, 1959.
The Zadokite Fragments and the Dead Sea Scrolls. Oxford: Blackwell, 1962.

Sanday, W. and A. C. Headlam. *The Epistle to the Romans*. Edinburgh: T. and T. Clark, 1896.

Sanders, E. P. *Paul and Palestinian Judaism*. Philadelphia: Fortress, 1977.

'Paul's Attitude Toward the Jewish People', *USQR*, 33 (1978), 175–87.

Schäfer, Peter. *Die Vorstellung vom Heiligen Geist in der rabbinischen Literatur*. München: Kösel, 1972.

Schiffman, Lawrence H. *The Halakhah at Qumran*. Leiden: Brill, 1975.

Skehan, P. W. 'A Fragment of the Song of Moses from Qumran', *BASOR*, 136 (1954), 12–15.

Smith, Morton. 'The Dead Sea Sect in Relation to Ancient Judaism', *NTS*, 7 (1960), 347–60.

Smith, W. Robertson. *The Religion of the Semites*. 3rd edition. London: A. and C. Black, 1927.

Snaith, N. H. *The Distinctive Ideas of the Old Testament*. London: Epworth, 1947.

Leviticus and Numbers. London: Nelson, 1967.

Sorel, J. 'Sémiotique de la nourriture dans la Bible', *Annales: Economies, Sociétés, Civilisations*, 28 (1973), 943–55. ET: 'The Dietary Prohibitions of the Hebrews', in *The New York Review of Books*, 26 (June, 1979), 24–30.

Stendahl, K. 'The Apostle Paul and the Introspective Conscience of the West', *HTR*, 56 (1963), 199–215.

'A Response', *USQR*, 33 (1978), 189–91.

Strugnell, J. 'The Angelic Liturgy at Qumran, 4Q Serek Širot 'Olat Haššabat', *Supplements to VT*, 7. Congress Volume, Oxford, 1959. Leiden: Brill, 1960.

Stuhlmacher, P. 'Zur neueren Exegese von Röm 3, 24–26', in *Jesus und Paulus*. Edited by E. E. Ellis and E. Grässer. Göttingen: Vandenhoeck and Ruprecht, 1975.

Sutcliffe, E. F. 'Sacred Meals at Qumran?', *The Heythrop Journal*, 1 (1960), 48–65.

'Baptism and Baptismal Rites at Qumran', *The Heythrop Journal*, 1 (1960), 179–88.

Talbert, C. H. 'A non-Pauline Fragment at Romans 3.24–26?', *JBL*, 85 (1966), 287–96.

Terrien, S. L. *The Elusive Presence*. San Francisco: Harper and Row, 1978.

Thackeray, H. St J. *Josephus, the Man and the Historian*. London, 1929.

Thackeray, H. St J., *et al. Josephus*. 9 vols. London: Heinemann, 1926–65.

Thomas, J. *Le mouvement baptiste en Palestine et Syrie*. Paris: Gembloux, 1965.

Thrall, M. E. 'The Problem of II Cor. vi. 16–vii.1 in some recent discussions', *NTS*, 24 (1977), 132–48.

Townsend, J. T. 'The Jerusalem Temple in the First Century', in *God and His Temple*. Ed. L. E. Frizzell. South Orange: Institute of Judaeo-Christian Studies, 1980.

Unnik, W. C. van. 'Les cheveux défaits des femmes baptisées', *Vigiliae Christianae*, 1 (1947), 77–100.

Urbach, E. E. *The Sages, Their Concepts and Beliefs.* 2 vols. Jerusalem: Magnes, 1975.

Vaux, Roland de. *The Bible and the Ancient Near East.* London: Darton, Longman and Todd, 1972.

'Fouilles de Khirbet Qumran; rapport préliminaire sur les 3ᵉ, 4ᵉ et 5ᵉ campagnes', *RB*, 63 (1956), 533-77.

Ancient Israel. New York: McGraw-Hill, 1965.

Vermes, G. *Scripture and Tradition.* Leiden: Brill, 1961.

The Dead Sea Scrolls. Qumran in Perspective. London: Collins, 1977.

Vielhauer, P. *Oikodome. Das Bild vom Bau in der christichen Literatur vom Neuen Testament bis Clemens Alexandrinus.* Karlsruhe: Gebr. Tron, 1940.

Vincent, M. R. *The Epistles to the Philippians and to Philemon.* Edinburgh: T. and T. Clark, 1897.

Walker, W. O. 'I Corinthians 11. 2-16 and Paul's Views Regarding Women', *JBL*, 94 (1975), 94-110.

Weiss, K. 'Paulus – Priester der christlichen Kultgemeinde', *TLZ*, 79 (1954), 355-64.

Wenham, G. J. *The Book of Leviticus.* Grand Rapids: Wm. B. Eerdmans, 1979.

Wenschkewitz, H. *Die Spiritualisierung der Kultusbegriffe. Tempel, Priester und Opfer im Neuen Testament.* Leipzig: Pfeiffer, 1932.

Werblowsky, R. J. Zwi. 'On the Baptismal Rite According to St. Hippolytus', *Studia Patristica*, 7 (1957), 93-105.

'A Note on Purification and Proselyte Baptism', in *Christianity, Judaism and Other Greco-Roman Cults.* Edited by Jacob Neusner. Leiden: Brill, 1975.

Wernberg-Møller, P. *The Manual of Discipline.* Leiden: Brill, 1957.

Whiteley, D. E. H. *The Theology of Saint Paul.* 2nd edn. Oxford: Blackwell, 1974.

Yadin, Yigael. *Megillat ham-Miqdas. The Temple Scroll* (Hebrew Edition). Vols. I-IIIa. Jerusalem: Israel Exploration Society, Hebrew University Institute of Archaeology, 1977.

Yoder, John Howard. *The Politics of Jesus.* Grand Rapids: Wm. B. Eerdmans, 1972.

INDEX OF PASSAGES CITED

GENERAL INDEX

adultery, 6
angels, 49f., 106ff.; as a sign of the divine presence, 107ff.
anthropology, 1, 2, 115
Apostolic Decree, 103f.
atonement, 1, 47; Day of Atonement, 3, 7, 54, 76f.

baptism, 27ff., 83, 87, 89f., 105, 109, 141n., 142nn.
bath, 23, 26, 27, 29, 31, 32, 33f., 42; initiation bath, 30
blameless, 73f., 83, 84f., 86, 89f., 106, 129n., 142n., 148n.
bones, 35f.
burnt offering, 64, 70, 74, 136n.

circumcision, 28, 59, 74, 134n.; true circumcision, 135n.
clean and unclean animals, 4f.
community of goods, 22f.
contagion, 2
corpses, 20, 147n.
corpse uncleanness, 2, 27f., 31, 46, 83, 109f., 130n., 141n.
covenant, 14, 18, 30; covenant renewal ceremony, 27; rejection of covenant, 32; new covenant, 37

dietary rules, 4f.
divine presence, 43, 46, 48, 49f., 52, 55f., 58f., 64, 69, 71, 73f., 76f., 79, 83, 88f., 90, 94f., 97, 104, 106, 108f., 112; divine presence and purity, 36, 84, 107, 111, 113, 115f., 118n.
drink, 10ff., 21, 25, 27, 45, 125n.; drink of the Many, 21, 26, 35

Epaphroditus, 61, 65f., 68, 74
ethics, 2, 3

eucharist, 36
excreta, 6

first fruits, 63, 66, 75, 138n.
food, 11, 26, 94, 98ff., food laws, 80f.
fornication, 18, 90, 92

Gentiles, 29, 28, 60, 64, 72f., 74, 77, 81f., 93ff., 97, 101, 102, 115, 125n., 140n., 142n.
gift, 63, 65, 67, 69, 71, 73f., 75

ḥavurot, 32, 36, 41
Hillelites, 27; Hillelite–Shammaite dispute, 28
Holy of Holies, 14, 15, 37, 43, 46, 49, 54, 76f.
Holy Place, 14, 37, 46, 49, 54, 123n.

idolatry, 3, 18, 82, 94, 100f., 102, 140n., 144nn., 146n; idols, 22, 69; food offered to idols, 100; idolaters, 93f., 112
immorality, 98, 94, 112; immorality and pollution, 3
impurity: ritual impurity, 28; moral impurity, 28, 31; levitical impurity, 28, 31; waters of impurity, 31, 87; sexual impurity, 31, 87; menstrual impurity, 31, 32; biblical impurity, 76; impurity of idols, 31
incest, 6

John the Baptist, 26
Josephus, 11, 20, 22, 35, 83, 91, 121n., 141n.

kapporet, 7, 43, 75ff., 120n., 139nn.
kosher, 102

leaven, 87, 89, 91ff., 128n., 143n.

170

For EU product safety concerns, contact us at Calle de José Abascal, 56–1°, 28003 Madrid, Spain or eugpsr@cambridge.org.

www.ingramcontent.com/pod-product-compliance
Ingram Content Group UK Ltd.
Pitfield, Milton Keynes, MK11 3LW, UK
UKHW012342130625
459647UK00009B/477